SEER OF THE FIFTH VEDA

Kṛṣṇa Dvaipāyana Vyāsa in the Mahābhārata

Seer of the Fifth Veda

Kṛṣṇa Dvaipāyana Vyāsa in the Mahābhārata

BRUCE M. SULLIVAN

MOTILAL BANARSIDASS PUBLISHERS
PRIVATE LIMITED • DELHI

First Indian Edition: Delhi, 1999

First Published in Leiden in 1990 Under The Title "Kṛṣṇa Dvaipāyana Vyāsa and the Mahābhārata: A New Interpretation"

ISBN: 81-208-1676-5

Also available at:

MOTILAL BANARSIDASS

41 U.A. Bungalow Road, Jawahar Nagar, Delhi 110 007
8 Mahalaxmi Chamber, Warden Road, Mumbai 400 026
120 Royapettah High Road, Mylapore, Chennai 600 004
Sanas Plaza, 1302, Baji Rao Road, Pune 411 002
16 St. Mark's Road, Bangalore 560 001
8 Camac Street, Calcutta 700 017
Ashok Rajpath, Patna 800 004
Chowk, Varanasi 221 001

PRINTED IN INDIA
BY JAINENDRA PRAKASH JAIN AT SHRI JAINENDRA PRESS,
A-45 NARAINA, PHASE I, NEW DELHI 110 028
AND PUBLISHED BY NARENDRA PRAKASH JAIN FOR
MOTILAL BANARSIDASS PUBLISHERS PRIVATE LIMITED,
BUNGALOW ROAD, DELHI 110 007

TABLE OF CONTENTS

PREFACE TO THE SECOND EDITION

It is with pleasure that I thank those who have encouraged me to reprint this book, originally published as *Kṛṣṇa Dvaipāyana Vyāsa and the Mahābhārata: A New Interpretation* (Leiden, The Netherlands: E.J. Brill, 1990). The title for this second edition is the one I originally proposed to Brill, but their suggestion prevailed. I would especially like to take note of the persistence over several years of Mr. N.P. Jain of Motilal Banarsidass, who repeatedly asked to publish this work. I considered extensively revising it for publication, as so much excellent work has been done on the *Mahābhārata* in the past decade since this work went to press originally, but decided instead to reprint the book with only a few corrections. I am hopeful that this reprinted edition of my work will be of use to others interested in the *Mahābhārata*.

Flagstaff, Arizona, BRUCE M. SULLIVAN
September, 1998

LIST OF ABBREVIATIONS

ABORI	*Annals of the Bhandarkar Oriental Research Institute*
BEFEO	*Bulletin de l'École Française d'Extrême-Orient*
BhG	*Bhagavad-Gītā*
EPHE	École pratique des hautes études, V[e] section: Sciences religieuses
HR	*History of Religions*
IIJ	*Indo-Iranian Journal*
JAAR	*Journal of the American Academy of Religion*
JAOS	*Journal of the American Oriental Society*
JBBRAS	*Journal of the Bombay Branch of the Royal Asiatic Society*
JSAL	*Journal of South Asian Literature*
MBh	*Mahābhārata*
UNESCO	United Nations Educational, Scientific, and Cultural Organization
WZKM	*Wiener Zeitschrift für die Kunde Morgenlandes*
WZKSO	*Wiener Zeitschrift für die Kunde Süd- und Ostasiens*
ZDMG	*Zeitschrift der Deutschen Morgenländischen Gesellschaft*

CHAPTER ONE

AUTHOR AND AUTHORITY

In the religious traditions of the Hindus, the most important author of sacred texts is Kṛṣṇa Dvaipāyana Vyāsa. He is traditionally credited with the arrangement of the *Veda* into four texts, as well as the composition of the epic *Mahābhārata* (MBh), many *Purāṇas*, and other works. Vyāsa, however, has often been described as mythical,[1] because his existence is impossible to prove except in myths and legends such as are preserved in the epic. The texts attributed to Vyāsa are considered by modern scholars as certainly the products of many contributors over the course of centuries, and Vyāsa's authorship has accordingly been described as "symbolic."[2] Obviously, the texts have their own power and appeal, whoever composed them. Yet in saying that Vyāsa is the editor or author of these many and various texts, Hindus have said something profoundly meaningful about both the texts and their composer Vyāsa, namely, that their status and authority as religious texts are to some extent dependent on the status and authority of Vyāsa.

Vyāsa is thus in a crucial position in the transmission of knowledge for his culture. Since the congeries of religious traditions we call Hinduism has no single founder, the most authoritative spokesman for Hinduism is the original teacher of its sacred literature, Vyāsa. He is credited not only with arranging the collection of the *śruti* ("Revelation") into the four texts of the *Ṛg*, *Yajur*, *Sāma*, and *Atharva Vedas*, but also with composing much of the *smṛti* ("Tradition"). The sage Kṛṣṇa Dvaipāyana has the title of Vyāsa, which is used as his name, because of his division of the *Veda* into four texts.[3] He was born into the brahmin family of Vasiṣṭha; his father was Parāśara, whose father was Śakti, whose father was Vasiṣṭha, all three famous seers to whom portions of the *Veda* are

---

[1] For example, see V. S. Sukthankar's "Prolegomena," in *The Mahābhārata*, ed. V. S. Sukthankar et al., 19 vols. (Poona: B.O.R.I., 1933-59), 1:ciii. All citations to the text will be to this critical edition unless otherwise stated, and roman numerals will be used to refer to the text's *parvans*, its eighteen major sections. The conventional abbreviation for the text, MBh, will be used.

[2] J. A. B. van Buitenen, *The Mahābhārata*, 3 vols. (Chicago: University of Chicago Press, 1973-78), 1:xxiii; hereafter cited as *MBh*.

[3] See I.54.3-6. and I.57.72-75. *Vyāsa* is a noun derived from the preverb *vi-* ("apart") + $\sqrt{}$*as* ("throw"); *vyāsa* means "division" or "divider."

attributed.[4] Thus, while the *Veda* does not attribute any hymns to Vyāsa, he is depicted by the MBh as heir to the Vedic tradition, having been born in a line of eminent Vedic *ṛṣis*.

The epic MBh, said to be his composition, is the best source of information on Vyāsa. Unlike the *Purāṇas* and other texts in which he appears as a static expositor or interlocutor, Vyāsa in the MBh is an important and active participant in the story. This unusual situation of the author appearing in his own composition points to the nature of Vyāsa's authorship of the epic. Vyāsa is doubly the creator of the MBh, its author, for not only is he the reputed composer of the text, but is also the creator of the Bhārata family on which the story is centered. The epic's view of itself is as the "fifth *Veda*,"[5] a new *Veda* for a new era, with Vyāsa as its *ṛṣi*, the seer who revealed the composition to humanity. Certain differences between the four *Vedas* and the MBh are noteworthy, however. While the four *Vedas* could be heard only by men of the three "twice-born" classes, the MBh was intended for all people.[6] While the four *Vedas* were regarded as divinely created and eternal truths, and the *ṛṣis* of the *Veda* not as the creators of their text, the fifth *Veda* was regarded as created by Vyāsa at a particular, though unspecified, time and place. The roles of the gods who created, and the *ṛṣis* who promulgated, the four *Vedas* are performed by Vyāsa for the fifth *Veda*, the MBh. This study will show how the depiction of Vyāsa in the MBh serves to validate its claim to be the fifth *Veda*, and how Vyāsa thus augments the epic's status and authority. In view of the importance of the MBh to the interpretation of Vyāsa, detailed consideration of the origin of this unique text will follow.

The poem attributed to Vyāsa, the MBh, is the national epic of India, and has been widely known and very popular for over 2,000 years. The text's critical edition, produced at the Bhandarkar Oriental Research Institute in Poona between 1919 and 1959, contains over 73,000 verses, most in the simple *śloka* meter, but includes also the longer *triṣṭubh* meter and even some prose. The Vulgate edition of the seventeenth century commentator Nīlakaṇṭha is approximately 84,000 verses, and some South Indian manuscripts are even longer. The length of 100,000 verses which tradition claims for the MBh[7] should probably be considered an

---

[4] Book 7 of the *Ṛg Veda* is the Vasiṣṭha family's book; see *Ṛgveda Saṃhitā*, 5 vols. (Poona: Vaidika Saṃśodhana Maṇḍala, 1972-78).

[5] See I.57.74. and XII.327.18., where the MBh describes itself as the fifth *Veda*, and the discussion below. One may also consult James Fitzgerald, "India's Fifth Veda: The *Mahābhārata*'s Presentation of Itself," *JSAL* 20 (1985); 125-40.

[6] The MBh describes itself as a text for all four social classes (*varṇa*) at XII.314.45.

[7] See I.56.12-13., as well as the inscription cited below. Some MBh texts, primarily of the Northern recension, refer to this 100,000 verse MBh as an abridgement. Vyāsa is said to have composed a version having sixty hundred thousand verses, of which the

approximation. The appendix (*khila*) of the MBh, the *Harivaṃśa*, which has some 16,000 verses in its vulgate version, may have been considered part of the MBh, which would bring the total of verses up to the traditional 100,000. However, in view of the fact that the *Harivaṃśa* is not part of the MBh proper, it would be best to regard the 100,000 verses as a "round figure." As Sylvain Lévi observed,[8] the designation of the MBh as a *śatasāhasrī-saṃhitā* inevitably recalls the Buddhist work *Śatasahasrikā Prajñāpāramitā*, "The Perfection of Wisdom in 100,000 Lines." In secular literature, the *Bṛhatkathā* of Guṇāḍhya presents an analogous case which, lacking the pious zeal of the copyists of the Buddhist and epic traditions, has survived only in shorter adaptations. The Buddhist collection of 100,000 lines may even have inspired the Hindus to claim 100,000 verses (200,000 lines!) for their epic MBh. In any case, the two texts are roughly contemporaneous, and may be regarded as reflecting the same desire to conserve and preserve for everyone the wisdom enunciated by a dharma-knowing sage.

The age of the MBh must be determined from references to it in other literature. Apparently the earliest reference to the story and its characters is in the work of the grammarian Pāṇini, dated in the fourth century B.C.[9] Pāṇini's commentator Patañjali, dated in the second century B.C., provides further evidence of the MBh's existence in some form at that date,[10] as do the Buddhist *Jātaka* tales, which are from the same period.[11] The MBh as known today certainly seems to reflect a period in Indian history posterior to the invasion by Alexander the Great and also after the Mauryan Empire, i.e., the third century B.C. and afterwards.[12] Various inscriptions refer to the MBh as the composition of Vyāsa the *Veda*-divider, the son of Parāśara, and as containing 100,000 verses; one such is by King Śarvanātha of Uchchakalpa in central India, dated by

gods knew thirty hundred thousand, the *pitṛs* fifteen hundred thousand, the *gandharvas* fourteen hundred thousand, and mankind only 100,000; see passage *29 below I.1.63.

[8] Sylvain Lévi, "Tato Jayam Udīrayet," in *Commemorative Essays Presented to Sir R. G. Bhandarkar* (Poona: B.O.R.I., 1917), pp. 104-5.

[9] Pāṇini refers to various major characters of the epic, including Yudhiṣṭhira (8.3.95.) and the pair Vāsudeva and Arjuna (4.3.98.), and to the MBh itself (6.2.38.). On dating Pāṇini, see M. Winternitz, *History of Indian Literature*, 3 vols. S. Ketkar and H. Kohn, trans. of vols. 1 and 2 (Calcutta: University of Calcutta, 1927-33); Subhadra Jha, trans. of vol 3 in 2 parts (Delhi: Motilal Banarsidass, 1963-67), 3:423. It is cited hereafter as *History*.

[10] Patañjali's commentary on Pāṇini's grammar refers to Yudhiṣṭhira and Arjuna (2.2.34. and 8.1.15.), and to the fact that the Kauravas had fought fairly (3.2.122.); see the discussion of these and other references in R. G. Bhandarkar, "Consideration of the Date of the Mahābhārata," *JBBRAS* 10 (1871-72): 81-91.

[11] See Chapter 5 for discussion of Vyāsa's appearances in the *Jātaka* tales.

[12] As maintained by E. W. Hopkins in his *Great Epic of India* (New York: Scribner's & Sons, 1901), pp. 391-96; hereafter cited as *Great Epic*.

Bühler A.D. 532-33.[13] Other inscriptions from the fifth century A.D. recording land-grants include verses attributed to Vyāsa or to the MBh threatening retribution upon one who rescinds the grant; the conclusion Bühler drew is that the MBh was regarded as an authoritative text on matters of dharma throughout much of India in the fifth century A.D.[14] He summarized his survey of the data bearing upon the age and character of the MBh with the following statement.

> It is evident that those who quoted the Mahābhārata as an authority teaching the rewards of pious donors and the punishments for impious despoilers of the donnees must have considered it as a Smṛiti or Dharmaśāstra, proceeding from a Ṛishi. And, as the quotations occur in grants from various parts of India, it is not less evident that the Mahābhārata cannot have been endowed with this sacred character merely just about A.D. 450, but that it must have held the same position for at least a century earlier. ... The results of the preceding enquiry are sufficient to warrant the assertion that the Mahābhārata certainly was a Smṛiti or Dharmaśāstra from A.D. 300, and that about A.D. 500 it certainly did not differ essentially in size and in character from the present text.[15]

Hopkins cited evidence indicating that virtually the whole of the MBh was in existence by A.D. 200.[16] Archeological evidence from north-central India, though meager, suggested to van Buitenen that an historical event may have been the basis of the epic tale; "... it seems more likely than not that the origins of *The Mahābhārata* fall somewhere in the eighth or ninth century" B.C.[17] In summary, the evidence indicates that the story of the MBh was known in some form as early as the fourth century B.C., if not earlier, and that the composition, largely as known to us today, probably existed by the third century A.D., and perhaps considerably earlier.

Although the MBh is the text having the most information about Vyāsa, there are a few references to him in Sanskrit literature that predates the MBh, or is at least contemporaneous with the early phase

---

[13] Georg Bühler and J. Kirste, "Indian Studies No. II: Contributions to the History of the Mahābhārata," *Sitzungsberichte der philosophisch-historischen Classe der kaiserlichen Akademie der Wissenschaften*, 127, no. 12 (1892): 26.

[14] Ibid., pp. 25-26.

[15] Ibid., pp. 26-27.

[16] Hopkins, *Great Epic*, pp. 387-89, discusses such evidence as Roman coins and the practice of inscribing land-grants on copper plates.

[17] Van Buitenen, *MBh*, 1:xxiv, refers to an article by B. B. Lal, "Excavation at Hāstinapura and other explorations in the Upper Gaṅgā and Sutlej basins, 1950-52," *Ancient India*, vols. 10-11 (1954-55). But Alf Hiltebeitel cautions: "One cannot, in my opinion, deduce from such information the historicity of the *Mahābhārata* war. If the splendid palaces of the epic are works of the imagination, it is rather arbitrary to decide that the story isn't." See "Kṛṣṇa and the *Mahābhārata*," *ABORI* 60 (1979): 99-100.

of the epic's composition. The *Sāmavidhāna Brāhmaṇa*, from the *Sāma Veda* tradition, includes Vyāsa Pārāśarya in its *guru-paramparā*, the list of the text's teachers.[18] The *Gopatha Brāhmaṇa*, from the *Atharva Veda* tradition, quotes Vyāsa as saying that whoever knows the *Atharva Veda* knows all.[19] The *Taittirīyāraṇyaka*, from the *Yajur Veda* tradition, briefly and enigmatically quotes Vyāsa Pārāśarya to the effect that one without desire does not die.[20] Thus, although the *Vedas* do not refer to Vyāsa, he was depicted as an authoritative teacher in certain late Vedic texts, including texts from three of the four branches of the *Veda*. Patañjali's commentary on Pāṇini's *sūtras*, which probably dates from the second century B.C., as observed above, makes reference to Śuka Vaiyāsāki in the commentary on *sūtra* 4.1.97. Vaiyāsāki is a patronymic formed from Vyāsa, confirming that at this time Śuka was known as Vyāsa's son. Another early text which refers to Vyāsa is the *Buddhacarita* of Aśvaghoṣa. This biography of the Buddha written by a brahmin convert to Buddhism is dated by its translator E. H. Johnston as having been written between 50 B.C. and A.D. 100, "with a preference for the first half of the first century A.D."[21] *Buddhacarita* 1.42. refers to Vyāsa's arrangement of the *Vedas* in many sections. *Buddhacarita* 4.16. refers to "the great *ṛṣi* Vyāsa, with whom even the gods could hardly contend," and alludes to an incident in his life which does not appear in the MBh; at least, it is not in the written tradition in the way depicted here.[22] Thus, Vyāsa is depicted as the brahmin sage who divided the *Vedas* in this Buddhist work of the first century A.D., and is depicted as an authoritative teacher in certain late Vedic texts.

While Vyāsa is rarely mentioned in the whole of the Vedic literature, he is prominent in the epic. Vyāsa's introduction to the audience of the MBh occurs immediately in the first chapter. Brahmins assembled at Śaunaka's twelve year long sacrificial session in the Naimiṣa forest asked for a recitation from the wandering bard Sauti, saying, "We want to hear the Collection of Vyāsa the wonder-worker, a dharmic collection that removes the danger of evil and is equal to the four *Vedas*."[23] The

---

[18] *Sāmavidhāna Brāhmaṇa* (Tirupati: Kendrīya Saṃskṛta Vidyā Pīṭham, 1964), 3.9.8. gives the following list of its gurus: Prajāpati; Bṛhaspati; Nārada; Viṣvaksena; Vyāsa Pārāśarya; Jaimini; Pauṣpiñjya; Pārāśaryāyaṇa; Bādarāyaṇa; Tāṇḍi and Śāṭyāyanin.

[19] *Gopatha Brāhmaṇa*, Rajendralal Mitra, ed. (Delhi: Indological Book House, 1972), 1.1.29.

[20] *Taittirīyāraṇyaka*, B. Ś. Phaḍke, ed. (Poona: Ānandāśrama, 1897), 1.9.2.

[21] *Buddhacarita, or Acts of the Buddha*, ed. and trans. by E. H. Johnston (Lahore: Motilal Banarsidass, 1936), p. xvii.

[22] See also a very similar scene in another poem by Aśvaghoṣa entitled *Saundarananda*, verses 7.29-30, and the discussion of these in Chapter 2.

[23] I.1.19.; the word *sa-mita* ("equal to") might also be read as *sam-ita* ("joined with").

bard responded, "I shall relate the entire thought of that great-spirited *ṛṣi* who is worshiped in the whole world, Vyāsa of unlimited energy" (I.1.23.). Sauti the bard also described the composition of the epic by Vyāsa.

> The son of Satyavatī, having arranged the eternal *Veda* by the power of his asceticism and celibacy, composed this holy history. Kṛṣṇa Dvaipāyana, son of Parāśara, the wise brahmin *ṛṣi* who was faithful to his vows ... recited the *Bhārata* in the world of men. Asked to do so by Janamejaya and thousands of brahmins, he taught it to his pupil Vaiśaṃpāyana, who sat before him. He (Vaiśaṃpāyana), seated with the priests, made known the *Bhārata* in the intermissions of the sacrifice, having been asked to again and again. ... He (Vyāsa) composed the *Bhārata* collection in 24,000 verses, without the minor stories; this is called by the wise the *Bhārata*.[24]

Sauti gave a brief summary of Vyāsa's MBh, and an account of the deeds of the Bhārgava brahmins, after which Śaunaka again asked to hear "the tale composed by Vyāsa" (I.53.28.). The bard replied, "In the intervals between the rites, the brahmins told tales based on the *Vedas*, but Vyāsa told his own tale, the great *Bhārata*" (I.53.31.). Śaunaka insisted upon hearing Kṛṣṇa Dvaipāyana's MBh, "born from the oceanic mind of that great seer" (I.53.32-34.). The bard agreed to recite for the king the MBh, which had been "conceived by Kṛṣṇa Dvaipāyana" (I.53.35.).

Sauti the bard then recounted how he had heard the MBh. Vyāsa had appeared at the site of Janamejaya's sacrifice and was asked to tell of the war between the Pāṇḍavas and Kauravas, Janamejaya's forebears. Vyāsa instructed his pupil Vaiśaṃpāyana to tell the king how the breach in the family had occurred, just as he had heard it from Vyāsa himself (I.54.21-22.). Vaiśaṃpāyana gave a brief summary of the epic's events, centered on the rivalry between the Pāṇḍavas and Kauravas in which the Pāṇḍavas had triumphed (I.55.). Janamejaya wanted to hear the full epic, of course, not a mere précis, and Vaiśaṃpāyana agreed to relate Vyāsa's whole epic; all 100,000 verses (I.56.12-13.). He praised the MBh and its composer, and said that "Kṛṣṇa Dvaipāyana, desiring to do good, composed this to give wealth, fame, long life, merit, and heaven, while he spread throughout the world the fame of the great-spirited Pāṇḍavas and the other warriors ..." (I.56.25-26.). He further informs the epic's audience that "the sage Kṛṣṇa Dvaipāyana rose daily for three years and created this marvelous tale of the *Mahābhārata*."[25] At this point, Vyāsa's epic about the Pāṇḍavas and their struggle for sovereignty over the Bhārata kingdom actually begins.

---

[24] I.1.52-61.; *itihāsa* ("history") is a genre of which the MBh is the foremost example.
[25] I.56.32.; and similarly, XVIII.5.41.

Vyāsa taught five brahmins who were his pupils, and who appear throughout the epic as his only brahmin pupils.

> A great lord and foremost granter of boons, he taught the *Vedas* and the MBh as the fifth *Veda* to Sumantu, Jaimini, Paila, and his own son Śuka, **as well as to Vaiśaṃpāyana. In their separate ways, they promulgated the Collections of *Bhārata*.**[26]

The extant MBh depicts itself as the recitation of Vaiśaṃpyāna. No versions of the MBh by the other pupils of Vyāsa have survived, but one text entitled *Jaimini-Aśvamedha* is extant. It parallels the account of the MBh's *Āśvamedhika Parvan*, though with significant differences, as R. D. Karmarkar has observed.

> Tradition also says that Jaimini wrote a Mahābhārata (all the five pupils of Vyāsa, Paila, etc. are also credited with having written the Mahābhārata independently) but as the Pāṇḍavas were there shown in an unfavorable light, it was never published; only the Aśvamedha portion of it has survived ...[27]

His detailed comparison of the two texts led him to comment that the text attributed to Jaimini "appears to be conceived in a different spirit altogether. It is composed to glorify Kṛṣṇa ..." whom he describes as the text's "central figure."[28] This text attributed to Jaimini which treats a portion of the epic story from a different perspective, while by no means proving that each pupil promulgated a version of the MBh, does show how the Hindu tradition could attribute different versions of the epic to Vyāsa's various pupils, hence giving to each version the authority of the composer Vyāsa himself.

Texts other than the MBh also refer to the same pupils of Vyāsa. A ritual manual which is roughly contemporaneous with the MBh refers to Sumantu, Jaimini, Vaiśaṃpāyana, and Paila as commentators on the *sūtras* and teachers of the *Bhārata*, the *Mahābhārata*, and the dharma.[29] This text has omitted from the list of students Vyāsa's son Śuka, whom the epic always includes as the fifth. He is different from the others in that he is depicted as a *saṃnyāsin* who renounces the world and attains spiritual release (*mokṣa*) in the MBh, while Vyāsa and the other students do not (XII.310-20.). In view of the fact that *mokṣa* transcends the con-

---

[26] I.57.74-75.; see also XII.314-15., where these five asked to be his only brahmin pupils and Vyāsa agreed. They also appear as a group at XII.327.15-16. and XII.337.11.

[27] R. D. Karmarkar, "Introduction" in *Āśvamedhika Parvan*, p. xxiv; he compares the two texts, pp. xxiv-xliv.

[28] Ibid., p. xliii.

[29] *Āśvalāyana Gṛhyasūtra*, N. N. Sharma, trans. (Delhi: Eastern Book Linkers, 1976).

cerns of such texts, which advocate the this-worldly performance of all the sacrifices that support the dharma, the omission of Śuka the ascetic pupil is understandable. A text with a completely different set of values, the *Yatidharmaprakāśa*, also omits Śuka from the group of pupils associated with Vyāsa. This manual for ascetics, composed by Vāsudevāśrama in the seventeenth century A.D.,[30] advocates that the worship of Viṣṇu be performed by *saṃnyāsins* in the following manner. They should worship the god Kṛṣṇa, the sage Vyāsa, the commentary writer Śaṃkara, and certain gods. Kṛṣṇa, Vyāsa, and Śaṃkara each have four attendants in this manual, Vyāsa's being listed as Sumantu, Jaimini, Vaiśaṃpāyana, and Paila.[31] In this text, it is likely that Śuka has been omitted from the list of Vyāsa's pupils so that they would form, with Vyāsa, a pentad which corresponds to Kṛṣṇa's and the other pentads in Vaiṣṇava worship. Śuka is also omitted from the list of Vyāsa's pupils in the *Purāṇas*. In naming Vyāsa's students, the *Purāṇas* substitute Romaharṣaṇa Sūta for the epic's Śuka.[32] He is the father of Ugraśravas Sauti who recites portions of the MBh, and, according to the *Purāṇas*, he taught his son the *itihāsapurāṇa* material he had learned from Vyāsa. The *Purāṇas* also say that each pupil learned one *Veda* from Vyāsa; Paila the *Ṛg Veda*, Vaiśaṃpāyana the *Yajur Veda*, Jaimini the *Sāma Veda*, and Sumantu the *Atharva Veda*, while Romaharṣaṇa Sūta learned *itihāsapurāṇa*. Jaimini is certainly associated very strongly with the *Sāma Veda* tradition, many texts in that tradition bearing his name. Paila is associated with the *Ṛg Veda* in the MBh, having performed the role of *hotar*, the priest who recites *Ṛg Veda*, at the Rājasūya sacrifice (II.30.33-35.). The association of Sumantu and Vaiśaṃpāyana with the *Vedas* mentioned above in connection with their names is not pronounced, however. The MBh, in any case, does not say that each pupil learned one *Veda* from Vyāsa, but that each pupil learned all five *Vedas*, and that each in his own way "promulgated the Collections of the *Bhārata*."

That Vyāsa has five "spiritual sons" seems to echo a frequent theme in the MBh's mythology about warriors: groups of five brothers abound. Of course, the epic's heroes, the five Pāṇḍavas, are an obvious example. Each one had a son by Draupadī, giving rise to the five Draupadeya brothers (I.213.70-72.), and the Pāṇḍavas may have been the model for some other epic groups of five brothers. The Kekayas (V.56.) and the Trigartas (VII.16.) are groups of five *kṣatriya* brothers; the demon

---

30 *Vāsudevāśrama Yatidharmaprakāśa*, ed. and trans. by Patrick Olivelle, 2 vols. (Vienna: Universität Wien, 1976-77), 1:17-18.

31 Ibid., 1:97-98 for the text's chapter 64, which is translated in 2:183-84.

32 See, e.g., *Agni Purāṇa* (Bombay: Veṅkaṭeśvara Press, 1900), chap. 150; *Kūrma Purāṇa* (Bombay: Veṅkaṭeśvara Press, 1908), chap. 1.4.

Rāvaṇa and his four brothers (III.259.) and the martial brahmin Paraśurāma and his four brothers (III.116.) are other examples of this phenomenon in the epic. Among the five sons of a king, necessarily only one could inherit the kingdom. Thus, Yayāti gave the inheritance to the youngest of his five sons, and the others were exiled to the periphery of the realm (I.70-80.). Similarly, Vasu Uparicara had five sons, of which one became king of Magadha and the others went elsewhere. In a comparative study of Irish, Iranian, and Indian mythology, Georges Dumézil has shown that this pattern of a king giving the inheritance to one of his five sons and sending the other four away to the periphery recurs in these cultures, and does so in conjunction with other correspondences, suggesting that these are versions of the same Indo-European myth.[33] He analyzes the Yayāti and Vasu stories, comparing them with the Iranian Yima and Irish Eochaid as "first kings" who populate the earth. The story of Vyāsa is analogous to this pattern in the royal mythology, in that only Vaiśaṃpāyana among the five spiritual sons of Vyāsa is in possession of the MBh as the inheritance from Vyāsa, an inheritance he then transmits to all mankind.

For most of the epic, Vaiśaṃpāyana is the reciter of a text he repeatedly says he heard from Vyāsa, who is not ever depicted reciting his text to an audience. As indicated above, however, Vaiśaṃpāyana is not the epic's only reciter; Sauti recites the first quarter of Book I, the *Ādi Parvan*. He is also occasionally the reciter for a brief portion of the text, e.g., two chapters of the *Putradarśana* section of the *Āśramavāsika Parvan* (XV.42-43.), where he describes a dialogue between Vaiśaṃpāyana and Janamejaya and the revelation by Vyāsa of a vision of Janamejaya's deceased father. Sauti also is the reciter of the end of the epic, where he says that he has now told everything Vaiśaṃpāyana said, but then he recites another twenty-four verses (XVIII.5.30.ff.). The sections narrated by Sauti seem to be self-consciously later than the parts in which Vaiśaṃpāyana is the reciter. They usually do not directly concern the Bhārata war, but present myths or teachings such as Sauti's *Ādi Parvan* discourse relating the deeds of the Bhārgava brahmins, which is not at all part of the epic's main story. The MBh as it now exists seems to incorporate within it two later stages of the text's transmission. Vaiśaṃpāyana's recitation of what he had heard from Vyāsa, and then Sauti's recitation of what he had heard from Vaiśaṃpāyana. In fact, the epic incorporates two other very long discourses as well, one by Saṃjaya, the

---

[33] See Georges Dumézil, *The Destiny of a King*, trans. by Alf Hiltebeitel (Chicago: University of Chicago, 1973); trans. from *Mythe et épopée*, 3 vols. (Paris: Éditions Gallimard, 1968-73), vol. 2.

other by Bhīṣma. Saṃjaya was the bard of the blind king Dhṛtarāṣṭra, and described to him the fighting between the massed warriors in Books VI through IX. Bhīṣma delivers the world's longest deathbed soliloquy, Books XII and XIII, teaching Yudhiṣṭhira about dharma while lying on the battlefield mortally wounded. Both these long discourses, which are often interrupted by questions from the speakers' audiences, are presented as integral parts of Vyāsa's composition, being events that occurred during the struggle for sovereignty over the Bhārata kingdom.

Such, at least, is the epic's account of its own transmission. Vyāsa composed the story, taught it to his pupils, and they recited it from memory, each in his own way. Hence, reciters know versions of Vyāsa's composition that vary; "There are brahmins who learn the *Bhārata* from Manu onward, others from the tale of Āstīka onward, others again from the tale of Uparicara onward" (I.1.50.). The MBh of 100,000 verses, a length approximately equal to that of the text known today, is mentioned within the text itself (I.56.12-13.). But the text recognizes that versions of the epic differing in length and contents are known and recited. Some attempt is made to attribute all the variation in the MBh's versions to Vyāsa himself: "He composed the *Bhārata* collection in 24,000 verses, without the minor stories ..." (I.1.61.), and refers elsewhere to much longer versions which he composed, as detailed above. Efforts to recover Vyāsa's text of 24,000 verses from the extant MBh have not been successful, and are exercises in subjective judgment.[34] Whatever character may be reciting the epic in any given chapter, its composition is always attributed to the revered sage Vyāsa who, nevertheless, is not the reciter of his own composition as we have it, and hence does not speak of himself in the first person in the text.

The MBh depicts its composition by a brahmin and its transmission by brahmins. The Brahmin Vaiśaṃpāyana[35] recited it for a king and brahmins at a sacrifice. Later, the *sūta* Ugraśravas recited the MBh for brahmins at another sacrifice. Most of the characters in the epic are *kṣatriyas* but there are substantial numbers of characters from other social groups as well. The epic thus does not depict itself as the exclusive property of any one class; its reciters and transmitters may well have been

---

[34] Two examples of this futile attempt are Sri Aurobindo, *Vyasa and Valmiki* (Pondicherry: Sri Aurobindo Ashram, 1964), and Keshavram K. Shastree, *Jaya-Saṃhitā, i.e., the Ur-Mahābhārata* (Ahmedabad: Gujarat Research Society, 1977). Mary Carroll Smith believes that *triṣṭubh* verses are the oldest part of the MBh; see her "The *Mahābhārata*'s Core," in *JAOS* 95.3 (1975):479-82.

[35] The name Vaiśaṃpāyana, however, suggests *kṣatriya* or *sūta* status; presumably it would be derived from *viśaṃpa* ("protector of people" or king), and mean "king's descendant."

as varied as the characters in the story, and its audience included people of all classes.

All these references in the MBh to its composition and transmission have been to an oral, rather than to a written, text. Despite Karmarkar's comment above concerning Vyāsa's pupils "having written" the MBh, the epic itself does not say that the text was written and read, rather that it was recited and heard. Yet today there are many manuscripts of the MBh, some of them hundreds of years old.[36] Clearly, at some point in the history of the MBh it was committed to writing but precisely when this happened is not known. The epic, at least some versions of it, includes a wonderful myth describing how Vyāsa's poem was first written down.[37] Brahmā, the Guru of the World, appeared before Vyāsa, who was pondering the problem of transmitting his poetic composition. Vyāsa said, "O Lord, I have created this highly venerated poem in which I have proclaimed the profundity of the *Veda* and other topics, O Brahmā." Vyāsa went on to describe his poem at length as containing almost everything, but he confessed that no writer could be found on earth for his composition. Brahmā told him to think of Gaṇeśa for the role of scribe. Vyasa thought of Gaṇeśa, and when the god appeared, asked him to write down the composition Vyāsa had in his mind as he recited it. Gaṇeśa agreed to do so, as long as he never had to stop writing, a condition to which Vyāsa agreed as long as Gaṇeśa would not write anything that he did not understand. They agreed to their mutual conditions, and the recitation and writing began. But Vyāsa, "for the sake of diversion, mysteriously wove knots into the composition." Sauti the bard commented that because of these knotty verses, "even the omniscient Gaṇeśa would ponder for a moment, and all the while Vyāsa created

---

[36] Some 235 manuscripts of the *Ādi Parvan* were known and accessible to the staff preparing the critical edition. They examined many of these and, after rejecting duplicates, used some sixty manuscripts in preparing their critical edition; see *Ādi Parvan*, "Prolegomena," p.v.

[37] Sec the Appendix for a translation of a passage from Nīlakaṇṭha's vulgate text which contains this myth. Another translation can be found in *The Mahabharata*, K. M. Ganguli, trans., 12 vols., 3d ed. (New Delhi: Munshiram Manoharlal, 1972-75), 1:3-5. This work is often called the Roy edition of the MBh because the original 1887-96 edition was published by P. C. Roy, with the translator anonymous, and will be so cited hereafter. See also the *Ādi Parvan*, Appendix I, No. 1, and the twenty line passage in the Notes below it, for details on the occurrence of this passage in various manuscripts. The passage containing this myth is found in manuscripts from South India and some from Kashmir. In a review of the critical edition's first few pages, Heinrich Lüders maintained that this passage is an interpolation from South India, basing his argument on the fact that it occurs in almost every southern manuscript and that it makes reference to the Pāśupata philosophy; see *Deutsche Literaturzeitung* 24 (1929):1138-46. It was excluded from the critical edition because it was considered to occur in only a small portion of the manuscript tradition.

many more verses." As a result, he said, "even today, no one is able to penetrate that closely woven mass of verses because of the profundity of their hidden meaning."

The myth of the MBh's debut as a written text, although it came into the epic's textual tradition fairly late, has been quite popular, and not only in South India, the area from which it probably originated. Vyāsa is strongly associated with Gaṇeśa as a result of this myth. In the one temple dedicated to Vyāsa which is known to me, the Vedo-Vyās Maṇḍir across the river from Banaras, between Rāmnagar and Mughal Serai, there is an image of Vyāsa expounding his teachings while Gaṇeśa, seated beside him, busily writes.

The myth of Vyāsa's oral composition becoming a written text depicts Vyāsa as an authoritative teacher without peer. He describes his poem as embodying the full range of his culture's knowledge. Vyāsa's formulation of this epitome of all learning was so valuable that Brahmā came to encourage the sage to promulgate his composition, and suggested Gaṇeśa as his assistant in the creation of the written text. Vyāsa's repeated references to the Vedic texts in his description of his own composition emphasize the epic's claim to be another *Veda*, the fifth *Veda*, and an all-inclusive text in which all topics are presented. It is remarkable, however, that in the creation of the MBh's written text, Vyāsa and Gaṇeśa invert the Vedic paradigm. Whereas the *Vedas* were regarded as divinely created, with the Vedic seers merely transmitting the divinely created verses, the seer Vyāsa created the MBh and the god Gaṇeśa helped to transmit the text more effectively by committing it to writing. In another departure from the Vedic paradigm, the *Vedas* were always transmitted orally, while the MBh was in written form as well as being transmitted orally. Thus, Vyāsa's role as the seer of the fifth *Veda* reveals certain differences from the relationship between the Vedic seers and the four *Vedas*.

Brahmā, the Guru of the World, was always associated with the creation and dissemination of knowledge, and is depicted performing a similar task in many texts. In the MBh, Brahmā is credited with creating the *Vedas*,[38] and many texts depict him as their author and first teacher.[39] Similar to the scene of Brahmā appearing before Vyāsa to encourage the sage to disseminate the MBh is Brahmā's appearance before Valmīkī in the *Rāmāyaṇa*'s second chapter. The sage Valmīkī knew the story of

---

[38] See Chapter 4 for references and discussion.

[39] See, e.g., *Bṛhadāraṇyaka Upaniṣad* 4.6.3. and 6.5.4.; *Chāndogya Upaniṣad* 3.11.5., both in *The Principal Upaniṣads*, ed. and trans. by S. Radhakrishnan (London: George Allen & Unwin, Ltd., 1953); *Mānava Dharmaśāstra*, ed. J. Jolly (London: Trübner & Co., 1887), chapter 1.

Rāma, and had conceived the metrical pattern of the *śloka*, when Brahmā came to him and encouraged him to promulgate the tale of Rāma's deeds for the world's benefit. Also quite similar to this myth is Brahmā's appearance before the Buddha after his attainment of *nirvāṇa* under the *bodhi* tree.[40] Brahmā encouraged the Buddha to preach his dharma among men, to overcome their ignorance with the knowledge he alone possessed. In each case, Brahmā appeared to a sage who had knowledge about dharma and encouraged him to promulgate that knowledge for the benefit of all humanity. Thus, Brahmā has the same role in relation to the dissemination of the dharma in these myths, which are so similar that they may be regarded as versions of the same myth.

The creation of a written text of the MBh did not eliminate the oral epic tradition which had been its genesis; the oral and written texts of the MBh flourished symbiotically, and continue to do so today. The many oral poets who recited versions of the epic story, whether brief or extensive, elaborated upon the received tradition and introduced new elements into that tradition at times. The written texts served to hold the epic tradition together, providing order and continuity to a story so vast and complex that, without those written texts, the epic might have degenerated into unconnected episodes and abridgements. It is possible that the activity of the Buddhists in committing their canonical texts to writing influenced the Hindus to write down the MBh, though no such influence is admitted, or even hinted at, in the epic. Beyond the myth of its origin, in which Gaṇeśa was the scribe for Vyāsa's dictation, the MBh has nothing more to say about its written text.

Scholars, however, have written extensively on the origin and development of the MBh, and have expressed sometimes radically divergent views on the subject. A brief survey of the history of European and American scholarship concerning the origin and development of the MBh will help to clarify the approach taken in this study.[41]

Most Western scholars of the MBh have regarded the text as having evolved over the course of some centuries, its heterogeneity being the

[40] See *Dīgha Nikāya*, eds. T. W. Rhys Davids and J. Estlin Carpenter, 3 vols. (London: H. Frowde, 1890-1911), 2.36.ff.; *Majjhima Nikāya*, ed. V. Trenckner et al., 4 vols. (London: H. Frowde, 1888-1925), 1.136.ff. For additional references, see André Bareau, *Recherches sur la Biographie du Buddha*, 2 vols. (Paris: E.F.E.O., 1963), 1:135-43.

[41] For lengthy treatments of MBh criticism, see Adolf Holtzmann, *Das Mahābhārata und seine Theile*, 4 vols. (Kiel: C. F. Haesler, 1892-95), especially vol. 1. More recently, see G. J. Held, *The Mahābhārata: An Ethnological Study* (London: Kegan Paul, 1935), pp. 1-26; and V. S. Sukthankar, *The Meaning of the Mahābhārata* (Bombay: Asiatic Society of Bombay, 1957), pp. 1-31. Most recently, see J. W. de Jong, "Recent Russian Publications on the Mahābhārata," *Adyar Library Bulletin* 39 (1975):1-42; Wendy O'Flaherty, Review article of recent publications on the *Mahābhārata*, *Religious Studies Review* 4.1 (January 1978): 19-28; and Alf Hiltebeitel, "Kṛṣṇa and the *Mahābhārata*."

result of many authors contributing to it diverse and even conflicting points of view. The historian of Indian literature, Moriz Winternitz, for example, interpreted the MBh's heterogeneity as the result of the competition of various social groups and cultural traditions; the warrior caste's epic had been appropriated by brahmins, who made it the vehicle for their particular interests and doctrines.[42] The text produced by this wholesale addition of brahmin lore to the epic of the warriors was harshly indicted by Winternitz, for whom the MBh was

> ...a literary monster. Never has the hand of an artist attempted the well-nigh impossible task of combining the conflicting elements into one unified poem. It is only unpoetical theologians and commentators and clumsy copyists who have succeeded in conglomerating into a heterogeneous mass parts which are actually incompatible, and which date from different centuries.[43]

Winternitz and most other nineteenth and early twentieth century Western scholars of the MBh saw the text as an epic poem transformed by the addition of other material, primarily didactic in nature, by "priestly interests."[44] Winternitz attempted to categorize the contents of the MBh as either belonging to or not belonging to the principal storyline, the tale of the Bhārata dynasty, and decided that fully half of the material in the epic, as now constituted, did not pertain to the principal story.[45] Although he was certain that the MBh developed from an epic poem which was transformed by added material,[46] Winternitz did not think that his efforts were restoring the original heroic epic from which the MBh had grown; any such attempt would be arbitrary and subjective in his view.[47]

One of the most influential of the early Western scholars of the MBh was the American E. W. Hopkins. His view of the MBh's origin and evolution largely coincided with those of the Europeans discussed above, and he expressed himself trenchantly on the subject. "It appears to be a heterogeneous collection of strings wound about a nucleus almost lost sight of. The nucleus, however, is a story."[48] He sharply distinguished

---

[42] Winternitz, *History*, 1:316-17.

[43] Ibid., 1:326.

[44] Ibid., 1:466-67; Holtzmann, *Das Mahābhārata und seine Theile*, 1:153 and 194. See also Hopkins, *Great Epic*, pp. 368-69, where he argues that the school of priests responsible for transforming the epic "was probably that of the Yajurvedins." On p.385 he comments, "That the priests developed the epic for their own interests goes without saying; hence the long chapters of priestly origin on the duty of charity—to priests."

[45] Winternitz, *History*, 1:375.

[46] Ibid., 1:317 and 459 ff.

[47] Ibid., 1:328.

[48] Hopkins, *Great Epic*, p. 363; see his chapter "The Origin and Development of the Epic," pp. 363-85.

between the narrative of the epic story and the didactic elements, most of which were added later in his view, and which he called "pseudo-epic." Indeed, the priestly additions to the epic were "its tumors,"[49] with all the connotations of cancerous, uncontrolled, unnatural growth that the word conveys. Elsewhere he described the pseudo-epic additions as a "fungus" on the epic.[50]

For most early Western scholars of the MBh, Hopkins, Winternitz, Oldenberg,[51] et al., Vyāsa was a mythical sage, irrelevant to their concern, which was the text's actual historical development. Hopkins dismissed the traditional attribution to Vyāsa of MBh authorship, describing him as merely the editor and distributor of "the huge and motley pile" of the MBh:

> ... there was no one author of the great epic, though with a not uncommon confusion of editor with author, an author was recognized, called Vyāsa. Modern scholarship calls him The Unknown, or Vyāsa for convenience.[52]

Thus, for Hopkins, the MBh "lacks an author with a real name," and the text suffers from "disputed authorship."[53] Although a vast compendium had been brought together under Vyāsa's name, he was not its true author; the MBh "is really, as it is designated, a collection, Saṃhitā, the reputed author of which, corresponding generally to the parallel figure in Greece, yet out-Homers Homer; ..."[54] As Hopkins observed with annoyance and even contempt, the MBh had not one author but a myriad.

> In what shape has epic poetry come down to us? A text that is no text, enlarged and altered in every recension, chapter after chapter recognized even by native commentaries as prakṣipta (interpolated), in a land without historical sense or care for the preservation of popular monuments, where no check was put on any reciter or copyist who might add what beauties or polish what parts he would, where it was a merit to add a glory to the pet god, where every popular poem was handled freely and is so to this day.[55]

In the eyes of most early Western scholars of the MBh, the text developed in haphazard fashion.

Hopkins believed that the first task of the epic scholar was to

---

[49] Ibid., p. 385.

[50] Hopkins, "The Bhārata and the Great Bhārata," *American Journal of Philology* 19.1 (1898):1-24; p. 10.

[51] Hermann Oldenberg, *Das Mahābhārata: Seine Entstehung, sein Inhalt, seine Form* (Göttingen: Vandenhoeck & Ruprecht, 1922).

[52] Hopkins, *Great Epic*, p. 58.

[53] Ibid.

[54] Ibid.

[55] Hopkins, *Great Epic*, p. 400.

distinguish more recent passages from older ones so as to get a clearer idea of the original form of the MBh, and thereby to "reconstruct the past."[56] He referred to his approach to the MBh as "an examination of constituents."[57] His method of analysis reached its limit in his other major work on the MBh, *Epic Mythology*,[58] in which he made no attempt to interpret the text as a whole. Instead, he extracted from the text a great many pieces of data which he grouped into categories; in the process, however, he reduced the MBh to piles of rubble.

One reason these scholars expressed their views with such vehemence is that another scholar was simultaneously approaching the MBh with a diametrically opposed method, and was interpreting the text's origin and development in a strikingly different way. Joseph Dahlmann wrote two studies in which he interpreted the MBh as a unitary text redacted by one person, a single diaskeuast.[59] He argued that there is no evidence of the MBh developing from a simple epic into a complex text of epic and didactic material, that it has, in fact, always incorporated both elements.[60] Dahlmann attempted to interpret the MBh's apparent heterogeneity as the product of conscious and purposeful structuring of the epic by a poet whose intention was to communicate the dharma by means of the story. He termed his approach the synthetic method and denigrated the analytic method employed by others.[61] Despite his insistence on the MBh being the work of a single redactor, Dahlmann did not argue that Vyāsa was this single epic diaskeuast, and was not particularly interested in the depiction of Vyāsa in the MBh.[62] Dahlmann maintained that the MBh was given its present form in the fifth century B.C.,[63] despite evidence that portions of it could be dated with confidence to A.D. 200. His insistence on faulty historical arguments made his approach easy prey for the "analytical" critics, and it was discredited as a result. This is unfortunate because Dahlmann treated the MBh as a meaningful whole, while Hopkins and most others of the "analytical"

---

[56] Ibid., p. vii.

[57] Ibid.

[58] E. W. Hopkins, *Epic Mythology* (Strassburg: Verlag Trübner, 1915).

[59] Joseph Dahlmann, *Das Mahābhārata als Epos und Rechtsbuch* (Berlin: Verlag F. L. Dames, 1895), hereafter cited as *Rechtsbuch*; and *Genesis des Mahābhārata* (Berlin: Verlag F. L. Dames, 1899), hereafter cited as *Genesis*.

[60] Dahlmann, *Rechtsbuch*, pp. 123-65, and *Genesis*, pp. 114-15.

[61] Dahlmann, *Genesis*, pp. 7-115.

[62] And this despite Julius Eggeling's observation a decade earlier that Vyāsa was "the personification of Indian diaskeuasis" in the 1886 edition of the *Encyclopedia Britannica*, 21:281. As close as Dahlmann came to naming Vyāsa as the diaskeuast is in *Rechtsbuch*, pp. 301-2.

[63] Dahlmann, *Rechtsbuch*, p. 165, and *Genesis*, p. 81.

school did not regard the text as a meaningful whole and made little effort to interpret it as a whole.

Both these early approaches to the MBh were somewhat immature, or premature. The philologists of the "analytical" school sought to reveal the epic poem contained within the MBh by cutting away whatever in their view did not organically cohere with the narrative of the Bhārata dynasty.[64] Even Winternitz had recognized the arbitrariness and subjectivity in the effort to restore the epic kernel around which he saw the MBh growing; after all, who was to say what was organic to the text and what was not? At that time, a detailed examination had yet to be made of the whole textual tradition for the purpose of determining what exactly the various manuscripts of the MBh had in common. Winternitz urged that this be done, and in 1919 the production of a critical edition of the MBh was undertaken at the Bhandarkar Oriental Research Institute in Poona, India, under the direction of a German-trained philologist, Vishnu S. Sukthankar.[65]

The editors examined manuscripts from all over India, and developed their critical principles on the model of classical philology.[66] After examining many manuscripts, they decided that the extent of agreement between the various written versions of the MBh was so great that the only explanation was the existence at some time of a written text from which the variant versions evolved, an Archetype text. Their objective, accordingly, was to compare the various manuscripts, and adopt as correct the reading that seemed to be closest to the Archetype; "... to reconstruct the oldest form of the text which it is possible to reach on the basis of the manuscript material available."[67] They believed that this was possible because, though additions were made to the versions of the MBh, virtually nothing was ever lost: "... our manuscripts contain all that was there originally to hand down, and more."[68] Franklin Edgerton, the only non-Indian editor, was skeptical of this when he began to examine manuscripts, but became convinced.

> It is only long and careful study which has finally forced me to this conclusion... that probably not one of the some fifty MSS I have studied for Book

---

[64] Winternitz, Review of *Genesis des Mahābhārata* by Joseph Dahlmann, *WZKM* 14 (1900):51-77. The approach has appropriately been termed "surgical criticism" by Vittore Pisani, "The Rise of the Mahābhārata," in *A Volume of Eastern and Indian Studies*, eds. S. M. Katre and P. K. Gode (Bombay: Karnatak Publishers, 1939), pp. 166-76.

[65] Sukthankar, "Prolegomena," in *Ādi Parvan*, pp. i-ii.

[66] See "Prolegomena," in *Ādi Parvan*, by Sukthankar, and the "Introduction" to the *Sabhā Parvan* by F. Edgerton.

[67] Sukthankar, "Prolegomena," in *Ādi Parvan*, p. lxxxvi.

[68] Ibid., p. xcv.

> 2, nor any of their genealogical ancestors, ever *deliberately* or *intentionally* omitted a single line of the text...[69]

The editors worked to produce a text which was more reliable than any one manuscript because it had been purified of scribal errors and some additions; it was an earlier form of the text than any one manuscript presented.

The editors knew that they were not restoring Vyāsa's original text.

> The editor is firmly convinced that the text presented in this edition is *not* anything like the autograph copy of the work of its mythical author, Maharṣi Vyāsa. It is *not*, in any sense, a reconstruction of the Ur-Mahābhārata or of the Ur-Bhārata, that ideal but impossible desideratum. It is also *not* an exact replica of the poem recited by Vaiśaṃpāyana before Janamejaya. It is further wholly uncertain how close it approaches the text of the poem said to be recited by the Sūta (or Sauti) before Śaunaka and the other dwellers of the Naimiṣa forest.
>
> It is but a modest attempt to present *a version of the epic as old as the extant manuscript material will permit us to reach*... It only claims to be *the most ancient one according to the direct line of transmission*, purer than the others in so far as it is free from the obvious errors of copying and spurious additions. It may be regarded, if the editor has done his work properly, the ancestor of all extant manuscripts, or, to be precise, of the manuscripts examined and collated for this edition.[70]

Because variant readings are listed in the notes for each verse, and episodes which appear in only a small proportion of the textual tradition have been put in Appendices, the critical edition is, in a sense, the most complete edition of the text, and certainly the most convenient one to use.

Sukthankar thought that the MBh had been given its final redaction by brahmins of the Bhṛgu family, which accounts for the presence and character of myths about Bhārgava brahmins throughout the epic. As Sukthankar observed, the MBh is "the richest mine for the exploration of the Bhārgava material, a veritable thesaurus of Bhārgava legends..."[71]

> ... we cannot avoid the conclusion that the Bhārgava heroes occupy a surprisingly large portion of the canvas—which is said to depict the Bhārata War—filling up as they do much of the background... The figures of the Bhārgavas have also been magnified to colossal proportions, painted with a thick brush and in vivid colours.[72]

---

[69] Edgerton, "Introduction," in *Sabhā Parvan*, p. xxxiv.

[70] Sukthankar, "Prolegomena," in *Ādi Parvan*, pp. cii-ciii. See also the acceptance of the editorial principles used, and the suggestions for slight modifications, in Mahesh Mehta, "A Study of the Critical Edition—Part II," *Bhāratīya Vidyā* 32 (1972):1-74.

[71] Sukthankar, "The Bhṛgus and the *Bhārata*: A Text-Historical Study," *ABORI* 18 (1936-37):1-76; p. 3.

[72] Ibid., p. 67.

Sukthankar concluded that "...in our version of the *Mahābhārata* there is a conscious—nay deliberate—weaving together of the *Bhārata* legends with the Bhārgava stories."[73] In a study of the Bhārgava myths of the MBh, Robert Goldman has stated that "Although the Bhṛgus appear in many texts, it is only the *Mahābhārata* that they may be said to dominate. The *Bhārata* is the definitive Bhārgava text."[74] This overstates the impact on the epic of the material about Bhārgavas, material which constitutes about five percent of the text.[75] Moreover, it is questionable whether only a Bhārgava brahmin could add to the epic a myth about Bhārgava brahmins; if the myth were known and deemed appropriate in some way, any reciter or redactor of the epic could include it. Goldman's analysis of Bhārgava myths revealed several recurrent themes, among them the violent conflict between brahmins and *kṣatriyas*, culminating in the annihilation of the warriors by Paraśurāma, and frequent resurrection from death by Bhārgavas. Such myths would perhaps be seen as appropriate for inclusion in the MBh because of their resonance with epic themes. The Bhārata war involved the near-annihilation of the warrior class, and the prominent roles in the war of fighting brahmins such as Aśvatthāman, Droṇa, and Kṛpa would bring to mind the Bhārgava myths, particularly that of Paraśurāma. The resurrection from death of Parikṣit in the epic, and perhaps also Vyāsa's summoning from heaven all the deceased warriors for one night with their families, would recall the restoration to life of various Bhārgavas. Given the thematic similarities between the epic and the Bhārgava myths, it is not so suprising that the epic includes these brahmins "filling up as they do much of the available space of the background." Sukthankar may be correct in maintaining that the MBh received its final redaction from Bhārgava brahmins, but the epic must have been composed long before it came to them.

Sukthankar's work of creating this first critical edition of the MBh has been hailed as a success widely, but not universally. Most insistent in opposition to the effort has been Madeleine Biardeau, who regards the MBh as largely the product of the oral tradition. She believes that there never was a single written text of the MBh, "the Archetype," from which all the manuscripts have evolved, but instead that the various manuscripts are simply written versions of the story.[76] While the editors

---

[73] Ibid., p. 70.

[74] Robert P. Goldman, *Gods, Priests, and Warriors: The Bhṛgus of the Mahābhārata* (New York: Columbia University Press, 1977), p. 3.

[75] The largest single piece of text about the Bhārgavas is in the *Ādi Parvan*, I.3-53 , which is less than two percent of the whole MBh.

[76] See Madeleine Biardeau, "Some More Considerations About Textual Criticism," *Purāṇa* 10.2 (July 1968):115-23.

admitted that the text exhibited some considerable degree of "fluidity,"[77] they were convinced that the procedure they had developed for representing the MBh was appropriate and helpful. Biardeau, however, regards their method as inappropriate for the material, and their purpose as religious rather than scientific.

> In using a seemingly Western scientific method, which was not meant for that kind of literature, they had in mind a purpose which could only superficially be stated in scientific terms; in fact it remained purely religious. The question whether Vyasa was a mythic or an historical author could not even be clearly raised, since he was primarily the symbol of the authoritativeness of the epic and purāṇic texts. What was to be reached was not so much the original text as the most authoritative one, and it was hoped that the oldest possible version would come closer to the truthful version, having less intermediary transmitting agents to alter it.[78]

Biardeau sees the MBh not as one text in variant versions, but as many variant versions which together constitute an epic tradition, and it is precisely the variants which are of the greatest interest to her. Biardeau consequently prefers the inclusive approach of Nīlakaṇṭha's vulgate text over the exclusive approach of the critical edition because she is concerned that none of the tradition be lost.[79] She feels that interpreting the epic requires taking all versions of a story into account.

> The regional variants are all authentic as long as the overall significance of the epic remains. There may be mistakes, nonsensical verses or obviously corrupt readings, owing to some defects in the transmission, but the major variations in the text are likely each to have its own significance fitting into the whole. That is why it would be more fruitful to search out the meaning of each and every part of all versions rather than to try to reconstruct one text out of the existing many.[80]

For Biardeau, the history of any part of the MBh tradition, such as knowing that one version of a myth is from seventeenth century Bengal rather than fifth century Mathurā, is largely irrelevant; what is crucial is the comparison and combination of them into a whole, by which the myth's meaning is elucidated.[81] She illustrated her method of myth analysis in

---

[77] See especially Sukthankar's "Prolegomena," in *Ādi Parvan*, pp. lxxxii and lxxxvi, and his comments on "textual dynamics," that the MBh is "the whole of the epic tradition: the *entire* Critical Apparatus" on p. ciii.

[78] Biardeau, "Some More Considerations..." p. 119.

[79] In her view, the critical edition, in placing some portions of the tradition in Notes and Appendices, has lost some of the text; it "has suffered a loss of meaning, which is equal to a loss of authenticity." See "The Story of Arjuna Kārtavīrya Without Reconstruction," *Purāṇa* 12.2 (July 1970):286-302; p. 301.

[80] Ibid., pp. 301-2.

[81] She explicitly advocates resisting any hypotheses of historic order in analyzing myths in *EPHE Annuaire* 77 (1969-70):170.

an article,[82] and regards the whole of the MBh as myth to be so analyzed.

Biardeau's approach to the MBh prompted a rebuttal from the MBh's translator, J. A. B. van Buitenen. He refers to her "method of homogenization"[83] in which all versions of a myth are considered simultaneous and to be interpreted in concert, and he argues that "those who from the outset decline to accept the historical dimension of the *Mahābhārata* impoverish their text.'[84] Van Buitenen wrote that "the verities of time and place are inescapable for me,"[85] and that

> ... every scholar who regards Hinduism not as a changeless simultaneity of elements significant only "dans les structures idéologiques d'ensemble," but as a civilization that has known change over more than two millennia, is quite properly interested in the history of a text like the *Mahābhārata*, which laid the groundwork for Hinduism. The text of the critical edition takes us back to a text of about the sixth century A.D., fluid no doubt but, considering its size, of remarkable consistency; ... The sixth-century text and the ensuing versions permit the study of changing, or reaffirmed, interests, concerns, and emphases over a period of time and expanse of space.[86]

Van Buitenen defended the method of the critical edition's editors, noting that textual criticism is concerned only with written manuscripts, not the oral literature which existed simultaneously and influenced the written versions.[87] He also demonstrated the difference between his method of interpreting myth and Biardeau's by adding a third version of the Arjuna Kārtavīrya myth which Biardeau had analyzed, but suggesting a way of accounting for the variations between the versions as the result of historical change.[88] His general attitude toward MBh criticism is summarized in the following statement:

> I wish to submit that the most satisfactory explanation of the *Mahābhārata* and the elements thereof is from within the text itself, its present. That it is a forbiddingly long present, five historically fateful centuries, must not deter us; nor should its extension into a still lengthier past or an indefinite future seduce us too soon. A present protracted so long will be fluid: we must accept that stories and incidents in the *Mahābhārata* have sequels in the text itself. We must also expect that the text is not oblivious of its times, and that actual history may brush it.[89]

---

[82] Biardeau, "The Story of Arjuna Kārtavīrya Without Reconstruction."
[83] van Buitenen, *MBh*, 3:146.
[84] Ibid., 3:144.
[85] Ibid., 3:143.
[85] Ibid., 3:151; van Buitenen is quoting Biardeau from her "Brāhmaṇes et potiers," *EPHE Annuaire* 79 (1971-72):55.
[87] van Buitenen, *MBh*, 3:151.
[88] Ibid., 3:142-54.
[89] Ibid., 3:153.

Van Buitenen took seriously the Indian description of the MBh as *itihāsa*, "history."

Recent studies have interpreted parts or the whole of the MBh through comparison of the epic narrative with themes and structures from ritual and myth. Van Buitenen demonstrated that the narrative structure of the MBh's second book, the *Sabhā Parvan*, closely follows and clearly is based on the structure of the Rājasūya ritual, a performance of which is the major event of this section of the epic.[90] Heino Gehrts has attempted to show that the Rājasūya ritual has provided the structure for the whole epic, but his thesis has not been widely accepted.[91] It is noteworthy that neither van Buitenen nor Gehrts has made any significant observations about Vyāsa as the priest who supervised the sacrifice which they discussed.

Comparisons of the epic with themes and structures of mythology have been very fruitful. Stig Wikander and after him Georges Dumézil have presented a view of the Bhārata war as an eschatological myth of Indo-European heritage transposed into the epic.[92] Wikander has revealed structural parallels between the MBh and the Norse saga of Ragnarök, the battle of Bravellir, suggesting the possibility that both stories have preserved elements from their Indo-European inheritance. Dumézil has drawn attention to the "transposition" of Vedic, para-Vedic, and even pre-Vedic mythic themes into the epic.[93] His studies have emphasized the continuities between the various deities and the epic characters said to be their incarnations, e.g., the Vedic Viṣṇu and epic Kṛṣṇa, and hence have deepened our understanding of the interrelations between the epic characters, e.g., Kṛṣṇa and Śiśupāla's relationship reveals meaningful correspondences with Viṣṇu and Śiva's relationship.[94] Madeleine Biardeau has approached the MBh from a very different perspective, maintaining that the eschatological myth which has been transposed into the epic narrative and which structures the story is the myth of cosmic dissolution

---

[90] van Buitenen, *MBh*, 2:3-30; see also his "On the Structure of the Sabhāparvan of the Mahābhārata," in *India Maior*, eds. J. Ensink and P. Gaeffke (Leiden: E. J. Brill, 1972), pp. 68-84.

[91] Heino Gehrts, *Mahābhārata: Das Geschehen und Seine Bedeutung* (Bonn: H. Grundmann, 1975); reviewed critically by Alf Hiltebeitel in *Erasmus* 29 (1977):86-91, and more positively by M. Biardeau in *Indo-Iranian Journal* 18 (1976):124-27.

[92] See Stig Wikander, "Pāṇḍava-sagan och Mahābhāratas mytiska förutsättningar," *Religion och Bibel* 6 (1947): 27-39; translated into French by G. Dumézil, *Jupiter Mars Quirinus IV* (Paris: Presses Universitaires de France, 1948), pp. 37-53. See also his other works cited below.

[93] See especially Dumézil's *Mythe et épopée*.

[94] See chaps. 2 and 3 of Georges Dumézil, *Stakes of the Warrior* (Berkeley: University of California Press, 1983), which is a translation of part of *Mythe et épopée*, 2, and is hereafter cited as *Stakes*.

(*pralaya*) which is so prominent in the *Purāṇas.*[95] Biardeau interprets the epic as a narrative expression of the Hindu myth of *pralaya*, in which the destructive role of Śiva and the recreative role of Viṣṇu Nārāyaṇa are transposed to the epic characters Aśvatthāman and Kṛṣṇa. Dumézil and Biardeau have also for the most part ignored Vyāsa, concentrating instead on Kṛṣṇa and other epic figures.

Alf Hiltebeitel's book *The Ritual of Battle* discusses the recent interpretations of the MBh by Wikander, Dumézil, and Biardeau while focusing on the role of Kṛṣṇa.[96] He shows how themes and structures of both the mythic and ritual heritage of ancient India have been utilized in the epic, and suggests how this must have taken place.

> ... a long process seems likely in which an epic story of ancient contours, probably at no point completely free of mythic elements, was continually compared and integrated with mythic themes—in fact, with myths and structures of different periods. The process would have to have been conservative to explain certain longstanding para-Vedic, Indo-Iranian, and even Indo-European myths whose influences, as Dumézil has demonstrated, show through. But the way in which they took their footing in the *Mahābhārata* would seem to have been not so much through a process of "transposition" as through a process of correlation between two levels of continually changing and growing tradition: myth and epic. The epic poets would thus emerge not so much as programmers, transposing one set of information into another form, but as ṛṣis, in this case the ṛṣis of the "Fifth Veda" whose "school" is covered by the name of the elusive but ever-available ṛṣi Vyāsa.[97]

As Hiltebeitel comments, the *ṛṣi* is a "seer" who "sees" correspondences, homologies, continuities. The word *ṛṣi* is explained by an ancient Indian dictionary, Yāska's *Nirukta*, in terms of the *ṛṣi*'s capability of seeing *brahman.*[98] The *ṛṣi*, by means of his supernormal faculty of vision, perceived *brahman* and expressed *brahman* poetically. As Jan Gonda has written in *The Vision of the Vedic Poets*, the ancient Indians thought that *ṛṣis* had "such a spiritual power and faculty of vision as to possess omniscience and that through them the sacred texts were revealed to man."[99] The ancient *ṛṣis* "saw" and revealed the *Vedas* to mankind.

---

[95] See Madeleine Biardeau's "Études de mythologie hindoue," *BEFEO* 54 (1968):19-54; *BEFEO* 55 (1969):59-105; *BEFEO* 58 (1971):17-89; *BEFEO* 63 (1976):111-262; and *BEFEO* 65 (1978):87-238. These articles will be cited hereafter as "Études" and differentiated by year.

[96] Hiltebeitel, *The Ritual of Battle: Krishna in the Mahābhārata* (Ithaca: Cornell University Press, 1976); cited hereafter as *Ritual.*

[97] Ibid., p. 359.

[98] *Nirukta* 2.11.: ... *ṛṣir darśanāt /stomān dadarśa* ... which may be translated as follows: "(He was) a *ṛṣi* because of (his) seeing. He saw the Vedic verses...". *Yāska Niruktam* (Delhi: Mehercandra Lakṣmaṇdās, 1963), p. 85.

[99] Jan Gonda, *The Vision of the Vedic Poets* (The Hague: Mouton & Co., 1963), p. 42.

The MBh repeatedly insists that Vyāsa is a *ṛṣi*, the epic's foremost *ṛṣi*, the only *ṛṣi* of the MBh, and in so saying, is making an implicit comparison of Vyāsa with the ancient Vedic seers. Van Buitenen and others have described Vyāsa's authorship of the MBh as "symbolic," but have not said of what it is symbolic, until Hiltebeitel's statement quoted above. Vyāsa is the symbolic representation of all the epic poets, the *ṛṣis* of the fifth *Veda*, who perceived correspondences between the epic they were composing and the myths and rituals of their heritage.

Recent research by Alf Hiltebeitel and Madeleine Biardeau has focused on the influence of goddess myths and rituals on the MBh and on religious practice in south India.[100] In volume 1 of *The Cult of Draupadī*, Hiltebeitel compares south Indian versions of the MBh, as revealed in Tamil texts, mythology, ritual enactments, and dramatic performances, with the classical Sanskrit text of the MBh. In this south Indian tradition, Draupadī is a goddess who purifies her devotees of sin and brings salvation. As Hiltebeitel observes,

> ... despite the fact that the classical *Mahābhārata* makes little direct reference to the goddess, the epic narrative would seem to be informed by the goddess's mythology... If this is so, it means that a folk interpretation of the *Mahābhārata* that places the goddess at its center has every chance of revealing much to us about the classical epic itself.[101]

Hiltebeitel has approached the MBh as a living tradition, existing in several different modes of expression, all of which contribute to his interpretation of the cult of Draupadī.

Dramas based on the MBh have received a great deal of attention recently. Two classical Sanskrit dramas attributed to Bhāsa have been translated.[102] David Gitomer has written a study of Bhīma as depicted in Sanskrit dramas and the MBh.[103] Most strikingly, a nine-hour play

---

[100] See Hiltebeitel, Alf, *The Cult of Draupadī, vol. 1: Mythologies: From Gingee to Kurukṣetra* (Chicago and London: The University of Chicago Press, 1988). This work is the culmination of research which has already yielded a series of important articles (see the Bibliography) and promises two more volumes on the Draupadī cult. In this work he refers to some similar findings by Madeleine Biardeau, to be published as *Histoire de poteaux: Variations védiques autour de la Déesse*. See the Bibliography for citations of recent articles by Biardeau. The most recent statement of Biardeau's interpretation of the MBh as a whole, and of Vyāsa in particular, may be found in her commentary on the translation of selected epic passages in Péterfalvi, Jean-Michel, and Madeleine Biardeau, *Le Mahābhārata*, 2 vols. (Paris: Flammarion, 1985-86); hereafter cited as Péterfalvi, *MBh*.

[101] Hiltebeitel, *Draupadī*, p. 135.

[102] Both translations appear in *JSAL*, 20.1 (1985): Miller, Barbara Stoler, trans., "*Karṇabhāra*: The Trial of Karṇa," pp. 47-56; and Gerow, Edwin, trans., "*Ūrubhaṅga*: The Breaking of the Thighs," pp. 57-70.

[103] Gitomer, David, "*Rākṣasa* Bhīma," in *Essays on the* Mahābhārata, edited by Arvind Sharma (Leiden, The Netherlands: E. J. Brill, in press). A preliminary version

which portrays the entire epic story has been performed in French and English versions before large, enthusiastic audiences and to critical acclaim in Europe, America, and Australia.[104] In this play, the role of Vyāsa as author, narrator, and sage is quite prominent; he begins and ends the play, and appears repeatedly throughout it. Scholarly reaction to this dramatic version of the epic is just beginning.

The MBh "is a story that India has never ceased to rethink and retell,"[105] and as recent studies have shown, much can be learned through consideration of various versions of the epic story. The interpretation of Vyāsa in this study will be drawn primarily from the classical Sanskrit text, but any part of the epic tradition that bears upon Vyāsa will be used. The Poona critical edition will be the text cited because, aside from the fact that it is the most widely available text, it also comes the closest to representing the whole classical tradition. Through its text, notes, and appendices, the critical edition can be used to determine how widespread in the tradition any particular alternate reading or version of a story may be. Whenever possible, the classical text will be supplemented by oral traditions and the seventeenth century text of the MBh with Nīlakaṇṭha's commentary. Variant readings and interpolations found in only a few manuscripts are of interest and deserve to be taken into account as well. The approach to the MBh employed here treats the text as a meaningful whole without ignoring the fact that some parts of the tradition are not known to the whole tradition. Hence, not every variant version of an epic story or myth is treated as equally important; a version known only from one manuscript, however interesting it may be, is not equal in importance within the tradition to a version known in all manuscripts. The difference between them should be part of the interpretation of the story's meaning and its significance for the tradition as a whole.

The remainder of this study will focus on Vyāsa's actions in the epic story, and an interpretation of his significance for Hindu civilization. As will be seen in succeeding chapters, the depiction of Vyāsa and his actions often call to mind the mythology of the god Brahmā, creator of

---

of this paper was presented at the Conference on South Asia in Madison, Wisconsin, in 1985.

[104] Carrière, Jean-Claude, *The Mahabharata: A Play Based Upon the Indian Classic Epic* (New York: Harper & Row, 1987), a translation by Peter Brook of the original French edition (1985). References to this play will be to this English translation, hereafter cited as Carrière, *The MBh*, and to a performance of the play seen in Los Angeles on October 3, 1987. The play is directed by Peter Brook, formerly director of the Royal Shakespeare Company and now director of the Centre International de Créations Théâtrales in Paris.

[105] Hiltebeitel, *Ritual*, p. 14.

the universe for Hindus. The epic poets, for whom Vyāsa is the symbolic representation, perceived certain correspondences between Vyāsa and Brahmā, correspondences which they wove into the epic they were composing. It will be one purpose of this study to demonstrate how those poets evoke Brahmā through their depiction of Vyāsa.

CHAPER TWO

THE AUTHOR IN HIS OWN COMPOSITION

Kṛṣṇa Dvaipāyana Vyāsa is depicted in the epic attributed to him as the brahmin who most closely approaches the orthodox ideal of brahminhood. The dharma literature and the MBh itself advocate that a brahmin should learn and then teach the *Veda* to qualified pupils, sacrifice both for himself and others according to Vedic injunctions, and also accept gifts from, and give gifts to, good people.[1] Vyāsa is depicted in the MBh as the foremost master of the Vedic tradition, both in its textual and ritual aspects; he is the most authoritative teacher of Vedic texts and is the expert priest who supervises the other priests at rites. He is the master, too, of certain less orthodox/orthoprax traditions which are not based on the *Veda*, namely, the ascetic practices of yoga and *tapas*, and the devotional religion of *bhakti*. Thus, Vyāsa both embodies the ancient traditions of Vedic Brahmanism and certain of the newer traditions which were finding their place in emergent Hinduism. Among all the brahmins in the MBh, Vyāsa is the one whose way of life most corresponds to the orthodox ideal which was then being formulated; he is the epic's most dharmic brahmin.

The MBh's data on Vyāsa are scattered throughout the text, and for the sake of convenient presentation, have been grouped into four categories: seer, priest, ascetic, and spiritual preceptor. Each of these categories is based on an Indian conception, and each is a function Vyāsa performs in the epic. Since these functions are not mutually exclusive, some of the data assembled here will be found in more than one category. Taken together, the data present a comprehensive picture of Vyāsa's activities as the epic's most dharmic brahmin.

The accounts of Vyāsa's birth in the MBh prefigure the greatness of his career, and just as they introduce him to the audience of the epic, they will serve to introduce him to the readers of this work on Vyāsa. Immediately before Vyāsa was summoned to perform his first great deed, fathering princes for the Bhārata dynasty, Satyavatī told the patriarch Bhīṣma how she had given birth to this sage.

---

[1] The classic statement of the ideal for a brahmin is found in the *Mānava Dharmaśāstra*, 1.88 and 10.74-76., hereafter cited as *Manu*. See the conclusion of this chapter for details and similar statements from other texts.

> My father, who was yoked to the dharma, had a ferry, O dharma-spirited sir, and one day when I was in my youth I went on it. Then that greatest of the supporters of the dharma, the great *ṛṣi* Parāśara the wise, came to the ferry because he wanted to cross the Yamunā River. While we were crossing over the Yamunā, that greatest of ascetics approached me and, possessed by love, coaxingly said to me many sweet things. Fearful of both his curse and of my father, but promised desirable boons, I was unable to reject him, O Bhārata. After covering the area with darkness, with his virility he overcame me, a young maiden, and did with me as he desired right in the boat, O Bhārata. Formerly I had had a strong, repellent odor of fish; the ascetic took it away and gave me this pleasant fragrance. Then the ascetic said to me that upon delivering my child on an island in the river, "you will still be a virgin." Thus, Pārāśarya, the great yogi and great *ṛṣi*, the son I had as a virgin, was born at that time, the one who is known as Dvaipāyana—the blessed lord and *ṛṣi* who, by the power of his asceticism, divided the *Vedas* into four, and hence became in the world Vyāsa, and because of his darkness, Kṛṣṇa. He is a speaker of the truth, an ascetic devoted to tranquility, all of whose sins are burned away. Surely when enjoined by me and by you, O brilliant sir, he will father fine children in the fields of your brother, for he has said to me, "Think of me when in need." I shall now think of him if you wish, O strong-armed Bhīṣma, for with your permission, Bhīṣma, that great ascetic will father children in the fields of Vicitravīrya.[2]

The bard Vaiśaṃpāyana tells a very similar story about the birth of Vyāsa (I.57.55.). A brahmin *ṛṣi* named Parāśara, struck by the beauty of the young woman ferrying him across the Yamunā River, made advances toward her. When she protested that holy men on either bank could see them, he created a fog that hid them, and when she said that losing her virginity would make going back home unendurable, the sage had an answer for that as well. He promised her that after their love-making, she would still be a virgin, and that she could choose another boon in addition. She chose as her boon that her body would always smell delightful, and never again smell of fish. The bard continued,

> The blessed lord Parāśara went to his own abode, and Satyavatī, pleased at having obtained her unsurpassed boon, gave birth the very day that she had united with Parāśara. The powerful Pārāśarya was born on an island in the Yamunā River, and as he stood before his mother, he fixed his mind on asceticism. He said, "Think of me when in need, and I will appear." This is how Dvaipāyana was born from Satyavatī by Parāśara, and since he was laid down on an island when he was a child, he became Dvaipāyana. Recognizing that in each successive age the dharma loses one foot, and that mankind's life and power correspond to the age, and wanting to show his

---

[2] I.99.6-17. Pārāśarya is a patronymic of Parāśara. Vyāsa means "divider." Kṛṣṇa means "black" or "dark," especially the blue-black color of a full raincloud.

grace to the *brahman* and brahmins, he divided the *Vedas*, and is therefore remembered as Vyāsa.[3]

The reciter Sauti also gives an account of Vyāsa's birth, in which he describes the *ṛṣi* Kṛṣṇa Dvaipāyana as follows.

> ... he whom Kālī bore from Parāśara, the son of Śakti, even as a virgin, on an island in the Yamunā, and who became the grandfather of the Pāṇḍavas. As soon as he was born, he forced his body to mature that very day by willpower. The famous sage learned the *Vedas* with their ancillary texts, as well as the histories. No one surpassed him in asceticism, in the study of the *Veda*, in vows, in fasts, in offspring, or in wrath. He was the greatest of the scholars of the *Veda*, and divided the one *Veda* into four, a brahmin *ṛṣi* who knew the high and the low, a poet truthful and pure. He, of great fame and meritorious renown, fathered Pāṇḍu, Dhṛtarāṣṭra, and Vidura, thereby perpetuating the lineage of Śaṃtanu.[4]

Each of these birth stories tells how the island-born Kṛṣṇa's mastery of the *Veda* led to his acquisition of the title Vyāsa, and emphasizes his ascetic power.

(1) *Ṛṣi*: Vyāsa the Seer

One of the words used most frequently in the MBh to describe Vyāsa is *ṛṣi*, defined by Yāska as "seer," as noted at the end of Chapter 1. Epithets such as the ones applied to Vyāsa which are presented below, while not definitive because of their wide application in Sanskrit literature, are at least indicative of the perception of Vyāsa in Hindu civilization. Vyāsa is often called a "great seer"[5] or "the best of seers."[6] Lists of the foremost seers sometimes feature Vyāsa as the first of those named.[7] Thus, Vyāsa is quite appropriately described as a "wise brahmin seer."[8]

Vyāsa's act of dividing the one *Veda* into four texts is the deed which brought him the title of Vyāsa, or Vedavyāsa, "the *Veda*-Divider," a title which is used as his name. Vyāsa is "the great repository of *Veda*" and "the great repository of *brahman*."[9] This "greatest of the scholars of the *Veda*"[10] is regarded as "the very abode of Sarasvatī."[11] All the MBh's

---

[3] I.57.68-73. Dvaipāyana means "island-born."

[4] I.54.2-6. Kālī ("the Dark Woman") is another name for Satyavatī.

[5] In a three verse paean (XII.337.3-5), his pupil calls Vyāsa "great seer" twice; see also XII.327.15. and XV.36.3. The terms are *maharṣi* or *mahānṛṣi*.

[6] e.g., III.46.2.

[7] e.g., XII.1.3-4 and XIII.151.4.

[8] vidvān brahmarṣiḥ / I.1.53 and I.54.1.

[9] vedamahānidhānam / XII.337.4; brahmamahānidhānam / XII.337.5.

[10] vedavidāṃ varaḥ / I.54.5 and VI.2.1.

[11] VII.172.43; Sarasvatī is the goddess of eloquence and learning.

references to Vyāsa's re-arrangement of the Vedic texts are quite positive in tone. His alteration of the *Veda*, which seems such a revolutionary act, is presented as perfectly appropriate for its time. The imminent age, *Kaliyuga*, was to be an era of degeneration in which humanity's declining mental capacity necessitated Vyāsa's division of the unitary *Veda* into four texts. The MBh maintains consistently that only the people who learn the *Veda* have degenerated, not the *Veda* itself. Hence, there is no hint of impropriety in Vyāsa's act of dividing the *Veda* into four texts which could be more easily learned; in fact, quite the opposite. For the MBh and all later Hindu civilization, the Vedic heritage is the collection of texts Vyāsa altered and transmitted for the benefit of benighted humanity in *Kaliyuga*. The title Vyāsa reminds the epic's audience of his great deed, and of his unique relationship to the *Vedas*.

In the MBh, Vyāsa is depicted not only as the *ṛṣi* who divided the *Veda*, but as the *ṛṣi* of the fifth *Veda*, as the MBh calls itself.[12] The epic is "the *Veda* of Kṛṣṇa,"[13] namely, the island-born Kṛṣṇa, Vyāsa, who is repeatedly said to be the seer and revealer of this *Veda*. The epic's second chapter contains a table of contents in which the MBh's sections are described in terms emphasizing the role of "Kṛṣṇa the *ṛṣi*" as the one who "saw" the epic and revealed it to humanity.[14] He is depicted in one chapter of the epic as a *ṛṣi* ordained by Nārāyaṇa to divide the *Vedas* in every *manvantara*; Nārāyaṇa says,

> All uncertainty about the meaning of past, present, and future removed, you, being endowed with asceticism, will see thousands of cycles of ages which have elapsed earlier, and all those things will be explained by me. And you will see again (in the future) many thousands of cycles of ages and me, birthless and deathless, O sage, in the world, discus in hand, because of your meditation on me. My speech will not be false, O sage. And in that period of Manu ... you will be superior to the group of seven seers by my grace...[15]

Even in this chapter, which reveals an eternal dimension to Vyāsa's division of the *Veda*, interest remains focused on his involvement with the Bhārata dynasty and the struggle of his kinsmen for sovereignty, and on

---

[12] I.57.74; XII.327.18; see also I.1.19.

[13] I.1.205; I.56.17; see also the Notes to XVIII.5.52.

[14] I.2.215. In the same chapter, Vyāsa is described as "he who sees the truth" (I.2.211. and 219. and 231.); "Vyāsa the ascetic, who sees the truth" (I.2.168); see also I.2.95-96.

[15] XII.337.49-52. This chapter, from the *Nārāyaṇīya* section of the *Śānti Parvan*, is generally considered to be perhaps the most recently interpolated part of the MBh. In saying that Vyāsa is a son of and a portion (*aṃśa*) of Nārāyaṇa, it presents an idea not found elsewhere in the epic, but which is in accord with the *Purāṇas*; see Chapter 3 for discussion.

his division of the *Veda* for the imminent *Kaliyuga*. He transmitted his fifth *Veda* through the same five brahmin pupils who also learned from him the four *Vedas* as he had rearranged them.[16] Vyāsa's composition was regarded as the product of the special vision of the *ṛṣi*: "The seer saw the manifold sciences of dharma, *artha*, and *kāma*, and the rule that arose for the conduct of worldly affairs."[17]

Vyāsa's depiction in the MBh as a *ṛṣi* who possessed a special faculty of vision called "the divine eye" (*divya-cakṣuḥ*)[18] is at times a factor in the epic's plot. With his divine eye, Vyāsa "saw" some events outside his immediate presence that involved the Bhārata dynasty. When the Kaurava warriors resolved to attack the Pāṇḍavas, who were exiled to the forest, "Kṛṣṇa Dvaipāyana perceived with his divine eye that they had set out and the pure-spirited sage appeared. The blessed lord, who is worshiped by all the world, stopped them" and went to persuade Dhṛtarāṣṭra to discipline his sons (III.8.21.-III.11.). Vyāsa also saw omens portending disastrous results for the Bhārata dynasty, which led him to counsel the Bhāratas to make peace (VI.2-4.). With his divine eye, Vyāsa saw Gāndhārī's desire to curse the Pāṇḍavas after they had killed all her sons, and "that superior seer who moves like thought came there" to dissuade her (XI.13.). Vyāsa's omniscience was the result of his divine eye (XVIII.5.31-33.); he saw the past, present, and future as if they were before his very eyes (VI.2.2).

Like the Vedic *ṛṣi* who saw the *stomas* and transmitted them to humanity, Vyāsa saw the Bhāratas' struggle for sovereignty and revealed it as the fifth *Veda*.

(2) Ṛtvij: Vyāsa the Priest

Vyāsa performed the role of priest in several major Vedic rituals for the Pāṇḍavas. Their brahmin chaplain (*purohita*) Dhaumya, who lived with the Pāṇḍavas, performed their ordinary daily and periodic rites, and even presided at the sacraments (*saṃskāras*) for the birth, tonsure, and initiation of the children of the Pāṇḍavas.[19] For the rituals of imperial

---

[16] See Chapter 1 for citations.

[17] I.1.47. These are the three pursuits of mankind, Law, Profit, and Pleasure, to which is sometimes added a fourth, *mokṣa*, Emancipation (from transmigration).

[18] Not only did Vyāsa see with the divine eye, but he gave others that capability as well, including Drupada (I.189.35-40), Gāndhārī (XI.13), Dhṛtarāṣṭra (XV.39), and Saṃjaya (VI.-IX). See S. K. Belvalkar's "Introduction" in *Bhīṣma Parvan* on Saṃjaya's divine eye; his conclusion that Saṃjaya's vision did not extend beyond the normal range of vision does not apply to Vyāsa's vision.

[19] I.213.79-82. Dhaumya is also depicted performing a rite on behalf of the Pāṇḍavas for a good journey (IV.4.47-49). Though with the Pāṇḍavas constantly, Dhaumya is usually silent and is a minor figure in the MBh.

significance, however, Vyāsa was the chief priest of the Pāṇḍavas. He led the Pāṇḍavas in a ritual sanctifying the site on which they then built their capital city of Indraprastha (I.199.28-50.). At Yudhiṣṭhira's Royal Consecration (*rājasūya*) and at the Horse Sacrifice (*aśvamedha*) after the war, Vyāsa was the most important priest.

At Yudhiṣṭhira's Rājasūya rite, Vyāsa introduced the other priests.

> Then, Dvaipāyana led in the priests, worthy brahmins who seemed to be the very embodiment of the *Vedas*, O king. Satyavatī's son himself performed the role of *brahman* priest, while Susāman, the bull of the Dhanaṃjayas, became the chanter of *sāmans*. Yājñavalkya, devoted to the *brahman*, became the chief *adhvaryu*, and Paila, son of Vasu, was the *hotar*, assisted by Dhaumya.[20]

The fact that Vyāsa led in the sacrificial priests and was the first one named among the priests are indications of his prominence in this rite. Even more significant, however, is the ritual role he performed as the *brahman*, the priest who oversees the others in the sacrifice. The *brahman* was required to know all four *Vedas* and the roles of all the other priests and, should any part of the sacrifice be done incorrectly, he would utter the appropriate *mantras* to avert disaster.[21] The MBh does not give a detailed description of the Rājasūya rite which Vyāsa supervised, following instead the actions of the assembled *kṣatriyas* rather than the priests they employed for the sacrifice. The rite began after Dhaumya and Vyāsa anointed the sacrificial paraphernalia (II.49.10.). With Vyāsa as the *brahman* priest, he had the responsibility of overseeing the entire ritual performance, and had the most prominent priestly role in the sacrifice.

At the Aśvamedha which followed the Bhārata war, Vyāsa was the chief priest, although no particular priestly role is specified in the text. Yudhiṣṭhira felt that he had committed a sin in fighting his kinsmen, and Vyāsa encouraged him to offer sacrifice to expiate the sin, telling him to prepare for the Royal Consecration, the Horse Sacrifice, the Sacrifice of All, and the Human Sacrifice (XIV.3.8.). Afterwards, only the Horse Sacrifice engaged the attention of Yudhiṣṭhira, and there was no more discussion of the other rituals. Yudhiṣṭhira told Vyāsa that, with his treasury depleted by the war, there was no gold for such a sacrifice, but Vyāsa knew where gold was to be found. He told Yudhiṣṭhira to go to

---

[20] II.30.33-35.

[21] The *brahman* priest was to correct ritual error through meditation and silent recitation, particularly of *Atharva Veda mantras*; see Book 5 of *Śatapatha Brāhmaṇa*, and the "Introduction" to the translation by Julius Eggeling, 5 vols. (Oxford: Oxford University Press, 1882-1900). See also H. W. Bodewitz, "The Fourth Priest (The *Brahmán*) in Vedic Ritual", in *Selected Studies on Ritual in the Indian Religions* (Leiden: E. J. Brill, 1983), pp. 33-68.

the Himālayas for the gold left over from Marutta's sacrifice long before (XIV.3.20.).

With this done and the treasury replenished, preparations for the Aśvamedha were begun under the direction of Vyāsa. Yudhiṣṭhira asked Vyāsa to consecrate him for the rite at a time known by the seer to be auspicious, saying to Vyāsa, "My sacrifice depends upon you," to which Vyāsa responded that he, with Paila and Yājñavalkya, would conduct the entire ritual performance properly (XIV.71.2-3.). Vyāsa commanded that sacrificial implements be made of gold, and that *sūtas* and brahmins who were knowledgeable about horses select the sacrificial horse. Once a worthy horse had been chosen, Vyāsa decreed that it be set free on the day he had chosen, and that Arjuna follow and protect the horse from any rival kings, while Bhīma and Nakula protected the capital city, and Sahadeva cared for the invited guests. To all these directives from his appointed priest, the king acceded (XIV.71.), and was then consecrated for the rite (XIV.72.).

Vyāsa urged Yudhiṣṭhira to triple the *dakṣiṇā* (gifts to priests), so that the merit from the sacrifice might also be tripled, and the king thereby freed from the sin of killing his kinsmen (XIV.90.14-15.). On the return of the horse after a year of wandering, accompanied by Arjuna, the completion of the sacrifice was at hand. The ritual activity culminated in the sacrifice of the horse, the gift of gold to the priests, and the king's gift to Vyāsa of the whole earth (XIV.90.17.-XIV.91.7). Vyāsa responded that instead of the earth which the king had relinquished, he wanted the purchase price of it, "for brahmins have need of wealth" (XIV.91.9.). Yudhiṣṭhira, however, newly cleansed of the sin of killing kinsmen, wanted to renounce the world and go to the forest for a life of asceticism, as he had so often said in the previous two *parvans* of the epic. Prevailed upon by Kṛṣṇa to do as Vyāsa asked (XIV.91.18.), the king agreed to accept governorship of the earth, and gave Vyāsa gold as his *dakṣiṇā*. Vyāsa divided this gold into four parts and distributed it among the brahmin priests who assisted him in the ritual (XIV.91.21.). His own share of the wealth he gave to Kuntī Pṛthā, mother of Karṇa and the elder Pāṇḍavas (XIV.91.27.), and so ended his role as priest of the Horse Sacrifice. Vyāsa was the only priest with a speaking part in the narrative of the Aśvamedha, and once the rite was reaching its climax after the horse's return, Vyāsa was the only priest even mentioned by name.

The choice by the Pāṇḍavas of Vyāsa as priest for their major rituals was due to their conviction that he was the best priest available. They were certainly not alone among the epic characters in regarding Vyāsa as an outstanding priest. The brahmin Āstīka praised Janamejaya's sacrifice by comparing it with a rite at which Vyāsa was the priest, and concluded that

> There is not a priest the equal of Dvaipāyana in all the worlds, of that I am sure, for his students wander over the earth, all priests who are adept in their ritual roles.[22]

At the Rājasūya of Yudhiṣṭhira, his gift to Kṛṣṇa of the *arghya* was challenged by a rival warrior.[23] Śiśupāla objected to Kṛṣṇa receiving the *arghya* gift since there were more deserving persons present, and he cited Dvaipāyana as more qualified since he was the best priest at the gathering (II.34.9.). Later, both Vyāsa and Kṛṣṇa urged Yudhiṣṭhira to perform the Horse Sacrifice, and Kṛṣṇa reiterated his support for the performance of the rite with Vyāsa as the chief priest.[24]

At their request, Vyāsa performed the role of sacrificial priest for the Pāṇḍavas in rituals of imperial significance: the foundation of the capital city, the installation of the king, and the ritual enactment and renewal of the king's sovereignty through the Horse Sacrifice. The Rājasūya and Aśvamedha rites, at which Vyāsa was the supervising priest, were the major royal rituals of the ancient Hindu tradition.[25] These two rites bracket the war among the claimants to the Bhārata throne in the MBh, the Rājasūya precipitating the exile of the Pāṇḍavas and the Aśvamedha restoring the sovereignty of Yudhiṣṭhira afterwards. As the supervisory *brahman* priest at the Rājasūya and the chief priest at the Aśvamedha, Vyāsa is clearly the epic's most important priest.

(3) *Tapasvin* and *Yogin*: Vyāsa the Ascetic

The MBh depicts Vyāsa as a paragon of asceticism. He displays many powers that are said to be the result of his ascetic practices, including preternatural knowledge of past, present, and future, the ability to appear and disappear mysteriously, and the ability to dispense boons and curses. Epithets applied to Vyāsa in the MBh often emphasize his asceticism; to reiterate, they cannot be regarded as definitive or taken at face value, but are indicative of how Vyāsa is depicted in the epic. Vyāsa is *tapodhana* (XIV.3.18.), "rich in asceticism," and *sumahātapas* (II.49.10.; XIII.153.43.), "a very great ascetic." He is a *mahāyogin* (I.99.13.), *munisattama* (XIV.3.15.), "the very best of ascetics." "Kṛṣṇa

---

[22] I.50.7 and 9.

[23] *Arghya* is a gift of water for a guest; in this rite, it was to be given to a recipient deserving of the highest respect, usually the heir apparent. See van Buitenen's comments on *arghya* in *MBh*, 2:22-24.

[24] XIV.2-3. and XIV.70.15-25.

[25] On these rites, see Jan Heesterman, *The Ancient Indian Royal Consecration* (The Hague: Mouton & Co., 1957), and Paul-Émile Dumont, *L'aśvamedha* (Paris: Geuthner, 1927).

Dvaipāyana the ascetic (*muni*), the great yogi ..." (XIII.18.1.) was regarded as such an authority on yoga that the commentary on Patañjali's *Yogasūtras* is attributed to Vedavyāsa.[26] He is depicted in the MBh in a way strongly suggestive of the forest-dwelling *vānaprastha* who follows the dharmic path of *pravṛtti*, rather than as a *saṃnyāsin* who renounces the dharma and seeks emancipation (*mokṣa*) from rebirth by following the path of *nivṛtti*. Thus, Vyāsa embodies certain ideals of asceticism, and is one of the major spokesmen for asceticism in the epic.

Tapas and *yoga* are the terms used in Sanskrit for the practices of the ascetics. *Tapas* literally means "heat," and is the term for "any specific act of self-deprivation aimed at an increase in spiritual power."[27] As van Buitenen observed, *tapas* in the MBh "is quite often represented as sexual abstinence (thus powerful ascetics can be made to lose their power by seduction), but may proceed to extreme forms of self-torture."[28] The term *yoga* also describes a strenuous effort toward a goal, often a spiritual goal.[29] The classical exposition of *yoga* as a spiritual discipline is the *Yogasūtras* of Patañjali, in which *yoga* is said to result in the acquisition of certain powers, including those attributed to Vyāsa in the MBh, though these powers are not the purpose of doing *yoga*.[30] The terms *tapas* and *yoga* overlap to some extent, and the epic uses them interchangeably at times.[31]

Omniscience is one of the powers said to result from *yoga*, and accord-

---

[26] Winternitz, *History*, 3:518, says that the *Yoga Bhāṣya* attributed to Vyāsa was written sometime between A.D. 350 and 650, probably in the sixth century. James Haughton Woods, in the introduction to his translation, *The Yoga-System of Patañjali* (Cambridge: Harvard University Press, 1914), pp. xx-xxi, discusses the evidence and suggests A.D. 650 to 850. The consensus of opinion is that this text was composed several centuries after the final recension of the MBh.

[27] van Buitenen, *MBh*, 1:436. See also the important study on *tapas* by Chauncey J. Blair, *Heat in the Rig Veda and Atharva Veda* (New Haven: American Oriental Society, 1961).

[28] van Buitenen, *MBh*, 1:436.

[29] Ibid., 1:438. Van Buitenen translated *yoga* as "yoke" quite often, a word which is etymologically related and conveys well the idea of exertion. Because *yoga* means an effort, any effort, the term is used very widely, often without intending any reference to the *yoga* system of Patañjali, which is what Westerners would know as yoga. Often, however, and particularly in the passages about Vyāsa, the word *yoga* does seem to refer to a spiritual discipline based on the *sāṃkhya* philosophy and similar to Patañjali's *yoga* system, as will be seen below.

[30] The third chapter of Patañjali's *Yogasūtra* concerns the powers (*vibhūti* or *siddhi*) the yogi attains, among which are superior capabilities of sight and movement.

[31] See the many references in E. W. Hopkins, "Yoga-Technique in the Great Epic," *JAOS* 22 (1901):333-79. In the account of Vyāsa's ascetic practices to gain the boon of a son (XII.310), the epic uses *tapas* and *yoga* interchangeably. See also XII.337.56, where Vyāsa says that his *tapas* resulted in his attainment of *samādhi*, which is an important technical term in *yoga*.

ing to the MBh Vyāsa was omniscient because of his ascetic practices.[32] Vyāsa's omniscience is often depicted as a special faculty of vision, as was indicated above, but his knowledge went far beyond his senses. The omniscience Vyāsa gained from asceticism often affects the development of the plot in the epic, as the examples below of his many interventions indicate.

Vyāsa's omniscience allowed him to predict the future, reveal the past, and affect the present conflict in the Bhārata dynasty. He predicted that the princes he had fathered would be flawed in particular ways due to the defects of their mothers (I.100.). Vyāsa intervened in the birth of the 100 Kaurava princes, having become aware that their mother was going to abort the monstrous fetus which had been his boon to her (I.107.). He predicted difficult times ahead for the Bhāratas (I.119.), and predicted the exile of the Pāṇḍavas (I.144.7.), as well as their eventual recovery of the kingdom (III.247.46.). Vyāsa perceived the thoughts of Yudhiṣṭhira (III.37.20-24.), and of Dhṛtarāṣṭra and Saṃjaya (V.65.8-9.). He predicted also the outcome of the war between the Pāṇḍavas and Kauravas, and the survival of Saṃjaya (VI.2-4.). He predicted the marriage of Draupadī to the five Pāṇḍavas,[33] and with his knowledge of their previous lives, convinced her father that it was proper for her to marry them. Vyāsa knew that in a former life Draupadī had been a female ascetic whose asceticism had pleased Śiva, who had granted her the boon of five husbands in response to her repeated request for one (I.157.). He also revealed that in this life, she was Śrī incarnate and the five Pāṇḍavas were five former Indras (I.189.). Vyāsa revealed that Aśvatthāman had pleased Śiva with his asceticism in previous lives and had received boons from the god; he further revealed that in this life Aśvatthāman had been born from Śiva, and that Kṛṣṇa and Arjuna were the eternal Nārāyaṇa and Nara on earth.[34] Vyāsa revealed the eternal identities of many of the participants in the Bhārata war, and on several occasions.[35] In fact, the whole of the MBh, with its disclosures about the gods, the ways of attaining emancipation and complying with the dharma, etc., as Vyāsa's composition may be seen as a revelation of Vyāsa's knowledge. Vyāsa's omniscience, certainly one of the most fundamental aspects of his nature in the MBh, was the result of his ascetic practices.

---

[32] XII.327.21.ff; XII.337. See also the discussion, on pp. 505-08 of *sarvajña* ("omniscient") and the acquisition of insight into *brahman*, in an article by Jan Gonda, "Reflections on *sarva-* in Vedic Texts," in *Indian Linguistics* 16 (1955):53-71; reprinted in Jan Gonda, *Selected Studies*, 4 vols. (Leiden: E. J. Brill, 1975), 2:495-513.

[33] I.157 and I.181.39.

[34] VII.172, especially verses 79-91.

[35] XI.8 and XV.39. Other similar revelations, such as I.61 and XVIII.5, are attributed to Vyāsa but recited in the epic by others.

Vyāsa's appearances and disappearances in the epic are also suggestive of his possession of the powers derived from *yoga*. To his mother, who had summoned him with a thought, "he mysteriously appeared that very instant."[36] Vyāsa and the divine seer Nārada "revealed themselves" suddenly between two converging missiles to prevent their collision.[37] Vyāsa "revealed himself" to the war's survivors, then asked what miracle he should perform for them as a fruit of his *tapas*.[38] Other appearances by Vyāsa were occasioned by his knowledge of events and his desire to intervene in them. For example, he appeared suddenly in an effort to stop the Kaurava raid on the exiled Pāṇḍavas, having seen their advance with his divine eye (III.8.21.-III.11.). With similar suddenness, Vyāsa appeared in the Kaurava court when Saṃjaya needed him to bolster his statements on devotion to Kṛṣṇa (V.65-68.). At times, Vyāsa disappeared quite suddenly also. Awaiting the time for cohabitation with the Bhārata princesses, he vanished from view.[39] After impregnating them, and being acquitted of his debt to the dharma and the dynasty, Vyāsa again vanished.[40] After his sudden appearance during an argument between the Pāṇḍavas, Vyāsa gave them a magic spell (*brahman*), and then vanished.[41] After appearing briefly before his son Dhṛtarāṣṭra to console him, Vyāsa vanished.[42] The same expression was used for Vyāsa's sudden disappearance after a long sermon.[43] The phrase *tatraivāntaradhīyata*, used to describe Vyāsa's sudden disappearances, was used also for Nārāyaṇa's disappearance and immediate reappearance elsewhere (XII.337.27.), and indicates a kind of movement other than simply walking away. Vyāsa's mysterious movements, his sudden appearances and disappearances, are those of the accomplished yogi in full possession of the powers accruing from yoga.

Vyāsa's asceticism also enabled him to perform various literary feats, according to the MBh. "The son of Satyavatī, having arranged the eternal *Veda* by the power of his asceticism and celibacy, composed this holy history" (I.1.52.). He is described as "the blessed lord and *ṛṣi* who, by

---

[36] *prādurbabhūvāviditaḥ* / I.99.22.

[37] *darśayāmāsatuḥ* / X.14.11.

[38] *darśayāmāsa* / XV.34.22.

[39] *antarhito* (*antar* + $\sqrt{}$*dhā*), meaning "disappeared, became invisible, was concealed," from I.99.44.

[40] *tatraivāntaradhīyata*, a different form of *antar* + $\sqrt{}$*dhā* with the same meaning; I.100.29.

[41] III.37.35, using the same phrase.

[42] XI.8.48, using the same phrase.

[43] Vyāsa's sermon is in *Droṇa Parvan* Appendix I, No. 8; he "disappears" in line 914. This passage is excluded from the critical edition text, but is found throughout much of the textual tradition. It might well have been included in the critical edition, as observed by Alf Hiltebeitel in *Ritual*, p. 346.

the power of his asceticism, divided the *Vedas* into four, and hence became in the world Vyāsa..." (I.99.13.). He was an only son, endowed with great *ṛṣi*-power, who, by the power of his *tapas*, divided the *Vedas.*[44] One of his pupils described Vyāsa's composition of the MBh as *tapas*, and described the seer as tired from the exertion (XII.337.10.). According to the MBh, Vyāsa's asceticism enabled him to arrange the Vedic texts and compose the MBh.

Vyāsa is often depicted as expounding on the topic of asceticism to various characters in the epic, and must be regarded as one of its most authoritative spokesmen for *tapas* and *yoga*. All these statements are in the *Śānti Parvan* except for one, the story of Mudgala and the measure of rice which Vyāsa told Yudhiṣṭhira when his enthusiasm for the life he led in the forest had ebbed. He preached to Yudhiṣṭhira on the importance of asceticism as follows: "...nothing is higher than *tapas*; through *tapas* one obtains great things; nothing is out of reach for *tapas*" (III.245.16.). Vyāsa then told the story of Mudgala, a brahmin whose generosity had earned him the reward of heaven. When the envoy of the gods came to take him there, Mudgala questioned him about heaven, and decided to reject that temporary refuge in favor of seeking eternal emancipation through *yoga.*[45] The *Śānti Parvan* contains several sermons by Vyāsa on *yoga* and its underlying philosophy of *sāṃkhya*, the longest being his extended exposition of the evolutionary cosmology of *sāṃkhya* to his son Śuka.[46] Also attributed to Vyāsa is a briefer version of *sāṃkhya* cosmology from the Pañcarātra perspective, in which the worship of Nārāyaṇa figures prominently (XII.334-36.). A short sermon on the religious paths of *pravṛtti* and *nivṛtti* is also attributed to Vyāsa and is found in the *Śānti Parvan.*[47] These are Vyāsa's major teachings on *yoga* in the epic. In general, he is depicted in them advocating the *nivṛtti* path of asceticism leading to *mokṣa*. As will become more apparent below, these sermons are not in accordance with the pattern of his own behavior in the epic; while

---

[44] XII.337.4 and 40-49. Stories of Vyāsa's birth link his ascetic power with his father's; Vyāsa in turn had a son, Śuka, who was inclined toward asceticism and became a great *yogin* (XII.310-20). The MBh seems to be suggesting that ascetic power can be inherited.

[45] III.246-47. In 247.41-43, Vyāsa uses the terms *dhyānayoga* (meditation) and *kevalaṃ* (isolation), which are technical terms for stages in yogic trance. These are said to lead to *nirvāṇa* (extinction), a term not of exclusively Buddhist use; see III.32.24 and the *brahmanirvāṇa* of *Bhagavad-Gītā* 2.72 and 5.24-26 (= MBh VI.24.72 and 27.24-26).

[46] XII.224-46. This passage is too long and diverse to be summarized here. See the translation in Roy, *MBh*, 9:166-237.

[47] As Vyāsa explained in XII.327, *pravṛtti* religion is based on the *Vedas* and the sacrificial rites enjoined therein, and leads to the transitory reward of heaven; *nivṛtti* religion is based on asceticism and the renunciation of ritual activity, and leads to eternal emancipation. *Pravṛtti* is the path of dharma, and *nivṛtti* is the path of *mokṣa*.

he follows the *pravṛtti* path of dharmic activity, he reveals significant aspects of the *nivṛtti* path.

A description of Vyāsa's way of life is provided by his royal son Pāṇḍu (I.110.). After ruling the Bhārata kingdom, Pāṇḍu fell under a curse of celibacy and resolved to seek emancipation through asceticism, which he called "the imperishable good way of life" of Vyāsa. Pāṇḍu's description of the ascetic way of life emphasized the cultivation of equanimity, the eating of donated food only, homelessness, and the abandonment of all ritual activity. Pāṇḍu expressed his intent to follow the renouncer's way of life, wandering as a shaven-headed ascetic "without blessings, without greetings, without choices, without possessions." His two wives, however, persuaded Pāṇḍu to allow them to accompany him into the forest, and to perform rites for the ancestors, and to live by gathering roots and fruits. Rather than shaving his head as he had earlier intended, Pāṇḍu resolved to wear the matted locks emblematic of the ascetic who has not entirely renounced society and the dharma.[48] In short, Pāṇḍu's wives convinced him to adopt the way of life of the forest-dwelling recluse (*vānaprastha-āśrama*) rather than the harsher way of life of the renouncer (*saṃnyāsa-āśrama*). Pāṇḍu refers to both these ascetic ways of life as the way Vyāsa lives (I.110.6. and 29.). If his intention was to live as Vyāsa did, however, his wives were right to persuade him to follow the *vanaprastha* mode, because Vyāsa's way of life corresponds closely to the classical ideal of the forest-dwelling recluse. Vyāsa certainly sacrificed for others, so he had not abandoned all ritual activity as would the *saṃnyāsin*. Vyāsa's head was not shaven like the *saṃnyāsin*'s, but his matted locks are occasionally mentioned.[49] Also, Vyāsa was not a homeless wanderer; he is said to live in a hermitage somewhere.[50] Although Pāṇḍu seems somewhat confused about which category Vyāsa occupied, he described accurately the two different ways of life followed by ascetics, the *vānaprastha* and *saṃnyāsa āśramas*.[51]

Vyāsa in the MBh is a man born to asceticism; in fact, he never had a home to renounce. On the day of his birth, he forced his body to maturity and left for the forest to do *tapas* (I.54.2-4.). The hermitage at which he is said to live is the only home mentioned for Vyāsa. References

---

[48] The *vānaprastha* does not trim his hair, beard, or nails, he leaves them uncut (*Manu* 6.6), while the *saṃnyāsin* shaves off his hair and beard and cuts his nails for his initiation (*Manu* 6.52). See also the Notes to XIII.17.56, in which they are described, respectively, as *jaṭī* (having matted locks) and *muṇḍī* (shaven-headed).

[49] I.100.4; XII.310.23 and 25.

[50] See below for citations on the *āśrama* of Vyāsa.

[51] These are the third and fourth stages of life in the classical Hindu system, described in *Manu* 6.87-89. See *Manu*, chapter 2 on the student stage, 3 on the householder, and 6 on the forest-dweller and renouncer stages.

to it, however, are both few in number and vague, e.g., "...the venerable and wise Vyāsa went back to his hermitage for *tapas*."[52] Vyāsa is occasionally depicted in the company of his pupils at an indefinite location in the Himālayas,[53] and Vyāsa is said to have performed feats of asceticism in the Himālayas (I.107.23.). The location of the hermitage at which Vyāsa lived, however, is not specified by the MBh, nor is any scene set in the hermitage itself. Despite the importance of Vyāsa to the Pāṇḍavas, their pilgrimage to the major sacred sites of India did not include a stop at the *āśrama* of Vyāsa, nor even reference to its location.[54] Vyāsa's solitary *tapas* to obtain the boon of a son took place on Mount Meru (XII.310.), also the site of one of his sermons to his pupils (XII.327.). Mount Meru, though, is more a feature of the sacred, mythical landscape than a definite geographical locale. Likewise of no help in locating the site of Vyāsa's residence is the anomalous passage (II.7.8-11.) which lists Parāśara and Pārāśarya (presumably Vyāsa, his only descendant in the MBh) as among the divine seers living in Indra's heaven. In the MBh, wherever Vyāsa is, he is not at home. He never had a home with his parents, never even had a childhood, never took a wife, and did not live with the royal offspring of the Bhārata dynasty he had fathered. Vyāsa is depicted as a hermitage-dwelling brahmin, though the location of that hermitage is never specified.

One passage in the *Śānti Parvan* (XII.310-20) contrasts the two different approaches to asceticism which Vyāsa and his son Śuka typify. Vyāsa pleased Śiva by his *tapas* and his devotion (*bhakti*), for which he was granted the boon of a son. Later, at the sight of a celestial nymph, Vyāsa was enthralled by desire (*kāmamohita*) and shed his seed, from which was immediately born Śuka. After instruction from Vyāsa and other teachers, Śuka decided to become a *saṃnyāsin*, eschewing marriage and family life altogether in single-minded pursuit of *mokṣa*. Vyāsa, however, had become very attached to his son, and when Śuka attained emancipation and vanished from the earth, Vyāsa was grief-stricken at the loss of his son and ashamed at his own lesser attainment. He was consoled by Śiva, who gave him the boon of having a shadow-image of Śuka for company.

This spiritual biography of Śuka illustrates two different ways in which the life of an ascetic may be shaped by the tension between celibacy and

---

[52] III.247.47; see also I.1.54.

[53] XII.314 and XII.327.

[54] III.80-153. Among the sacred sites are two named after Vyāsa: Vyāsavana (Vyāsa's Grove) and Vyāsasthalī (Vyāsa's Mound, or Land). These may be near the Naimiṣa forest (see III.81.76-82), but as van Buitenen observed, along with one of the sages, some may be accessible only in thought; see *MBh*, 2:186-87, and III.83.88.

passion.[55] Śuka is depicted as free from all passion, unattached, while Vyāsa is subject to desire, grief, attachment, all the passions. That this would be so was predicted by Nārāyaṇa in another passage (XII.337.43-46.); he said that Vyāsa would have a son who would become free from passion (*rāga*), but that Vyāsa, despite being yoked to *tapas*, would not become free from passion. Thus, while Śuka attained *mokṣa*, Vyāsa did not, and did not strive for it.[56] Śuka followed the path of *nivṛtti* and attained *mokṣa*; Vyāsa followed the dharmic path of *pravṛtti*, and did not attain *mokṣa*.

Asceticism could be undertaken in various ways and for various purposes. As van Buitenen pointed out, the ascetics in the MBh seem not to have a clearly stated purpose in doing *tapas* other than the accumulation of ascetic power for themselves; the power acquired by the ascetics made them

> ... new Gods on earth, rivaling and surpassing the Gods, and divinely unpredictable. While in Buddhism and Jainism such self-mortification is directed toward release from transmigration, this is distinctly understated in MBh. The ascetics are bent on their own purposes, but motivation is oddly lacking.[57]

For many of the epic's ascetics this is quite true. Certainly Śuka is an exception since he clearly stated that his purpose was the attainment of *mokṣa*, and the same may be said of Mudgala. The warrior Bhīṣma also clearly stated the reason for his vow of celibacy, though it was considerably more mundane than *mokṣa*; he did not want offspring of his contending for the throne. In most other stories about ascetics in the MBh, however, the purpose for which they did *tapas* was rarely the attainment of *mokṣa*.

Often the acquisition of fame or glory is the apparent purpose for asceticism. Pāṇḍu asked his wife to do *tapas* for this reason:

> For the sake of glory, you must do a very difficult deed—just as Indra, who had already attained sovereignty, offers sacrifices for the sake of glory—just as brahmins who know the mantras and have accomplished difficult ascetic

---

[55] See Wendy O'Flaherty's *Asceticism and Eroticism in the Mythology of Śiva* (London: Oxford University Press, 1973), which discusses this issue with particular attention to the paradigmatic ascetic Śiva; it is cited hereafter as *Śiva*.

[56] The MBh maintains with great consistency that Vyāsa did not attain *mokṣa*. The only hint to the contrary is in XVIII.5.41, where Vyāsa is praised as "never-returning" (*anāgatam*) suggesting that he attained *mokṣa*. A few texts from South India add to this verse the word *mokṣam*, indicating that he was *mokṣa* incarnate, but so few texts say this that it is excluded from the critical edition. Even *anāgatam* is questionable since two important Kashmiri manuscripts omit that word.

[57] van Buitenen, *MBh*, 1:436.

> acts still go to new gurus for the sake of glory, O radiant woman—just as all royal *ṛṣis* and brahmins rich in *tapas* perform many difficult acts for the sake of glory.[58]

Not only the *kṣatriya* was subject to the allure of glory as a reward for *tapas*; Vyāsa found consolation and even joy in the idea that Śuka's asceticism had earned eternal fame for Śuka (XII.320.33-41.). One might well expect to see asceticism depicted as heroic in a text as martial in content as the MBh, but the imagery of conquest and its attendant glory is common for the ascetic in India.[59]

Asceticism is often undertaken for the purpose of obtaining a boon from a deity in the MBh. By his *tapas*, Pāṇḍu sought a son as a boon from Indra (I.114.). Yavakrīta did the most severe *tapas* in order to win from Indra the boon of acquiring the *Vedas* without study (III.135-39.). Arjuna's *tapas* in the Himālayas was undertaken to procure divine weapons as a boon.[60] Vyāsa did *tapas* to obtain from Śiva the boon of a son (XII.310-11.).

Each of these purposes for asceticism, the acquisition of fame or glory, boons, or even *mokṣa*, involves only that individual. As van Buitenen commented, the epic's ascetics for the most part seem to have as their purpose only the accumulation of ascetic power for themselves.

Vyāsa's purpose in being an ascetic was not to attain *mokṣa*, but to support the dharma. The *saṃnyāsin*, such as Śuka, rejects society and its dharma, seeking to escape society's constraints altogether. Obviously society would cease to exist if everyone became a *saṃnyāsin* before having any children to carry on the duties incumbent upon one, as Śuka had done, and consequently Hindu society could never fully accept the *saṃnyāsin*.[61] The radical asceticism which Hindu mythology often depicts as threatening the gods clearly was a threat to Hindu society and its dharma, as well as its gods. At the other end of the spectrum, the householder (*gṛhastha*) does not pursue *mokṣa*, but performs the many duties the dharma demands. Between these two categories is the com-

---

[58] I.115.11-13.

[59] Typically, the Indian ascetic "conquers" his senses, "wins" heaven, etc. Even in Jainism, a tradition in which pacifism is paramount, the fully realized ascetic is a Conqueror (*jina*), and is described in the same martial terminology as the king and Indra.

[60] III.39. His *tapas* pleased Śiva, but the other residents of heaven, not knowing his purpose and thinking that he might win heaven and displace them, wanted to stop his *tapas*. Often the gods are depicted as fearful of ascetics because of the power they accumulate.

[61] This idea is well presented by Patrick Olivelle, "A Definition of World Renunciation," *WZKSO* 17 (1975): 75-82. W. O'Flaherty noted that "...Hindu mythology is generally anti-ascetic." See *The Origins of Evil in Hindu Mythology* (Berkeley: University of California Press, 1976), p. 80; hereafter cited as *Evil*. See also her *Śiva*, pp. 40-82.

promise of the *vānaprastha*[62] in which the individual's connection with his society is not severed altogether, but he becomes liminal, neither fully in nor out of society. The *vānaprastha*, such as Vyāsa seems to be, still performs the duties enjoined by the dharma while pursuing asceticism as well. The MBh tells nothing of Vyāsa's ascetic practices; there are no details given such as his standing on one foot with his arms raised, or heating himself between the five fires. Despite reference to his celibacy (*brahmacarya*) as empowering him to divide the *Veda* (I.1.52.), it was not an unbreakable vow such as Bhīṣma's. For the sake of the dharma, Vyāsa fathered princes for the Bhārata dynasty. Rather than using ascetic power for his own benefit, Vyāsa generally used his ascetic power to benefit others in the epic, through teachings, division of the *Veda*, composition of the MBh, etc. Vyāsa's asceticism, far from being a threat or challenge to the gods, is depicted in the epic as serving the purpose of the gods—by means of his ascetic power, Vyāsa revealed to humanity the subtle course of the dharma in difficult times. Vyāsa used his ascetic power to help others rather than simply for his own benefit, and consequently his asceticism was more acceptable to Hindu society than the *saṃnyāsin*'s. Vyāsa represents the desirability, even the necessity, of acting in the world rather than renouncing it, of being a contributor to the society that created him. Hindus have repeatedly attempted to integrate ascetic values into society as a whole, to find a place for asceticism in society, and Vyāsa represents one paradigm in the Hindu search for the proper role of the ascetic in society.

Asceticism is one of the definitive features of Vyāsa as he is depicted in the MBh. He was born to asceticism, practiced asceticism all his life and acquired remarkable powers from it, powers which he used to the benefit of other people as a *ṛṣi*, priest, and, as will be seen below, as a guru. He follows the path of *pravṛtti*, but reveals important aspects of the *nivṛtti* path to various epic characters. Vyāsa embodies and personifies ascetic ideals in the MBh to such an extent that Kṛṣṇa regarded Vyāsa as an exemplary ascetic. Just before revealing his full divinity in the *Bhagavad-Gītā*, Kṛṣṇa identified himself with the best member of a series of groups, as follows:

> Among the Vṛṣṇis, I am Vāsudeva (Kṛṣṇa);
> Among the Pāṇḍavas, I am Dhanaṃjaya (Arjuna);
> Among the ascetics (*muni*), I am Vyāsa...[63]

[62] But this is an uneasy compromise, characterized by Wendy O'Flaherty as "delicate" and "inadequate" and which, as a way of life, was finally rejected; *Śiva*, pp. 79-82. Going even further, Madeleine Biardeau refers to the *vānaprastha* as an intermediate category that was essentially fictitious ("fictiv") in *Clefs pour la pensée Hindoue* (Paris: Seghers, 1972), p. 81.

[63] *BhG.* 10.37. = MBh VI.32.37.

(4) *Guru*: Vyāsa the Spiritual Preceptor

Vyāsa has a very special relationship with some characters in the epic, for whom he is an advisor on spiritual matters—their guru. The five brahmins who learned *Veda* and MBh from Vyāsa refer to him often as their guru. For the Pāṇḍavas, Vyāsa was a "friendly advisor" (*mantrī priyahito*) and much more (III.13.99.). For the rest of the Bhārata family, too, he was the brahmin who instructed them most fully in matters of religion. Vyāsa advised, taught, granted boons to, and also cursed some members of these three groups.

Vyāsa's position as guru is most explicitly stated in the case of his five brahmin pupils. The MBh's reciter Vaiśaṃpāyana described Vyāsa as "my guru"[64] and, with the other pupils present, as "our guru."[65] The guru is depicted in the company of his students, instructing them in religion, when they asked him for the boon of being his only brahmin pupils (XII.314-15.). Vyāsa agreed to their request, and taught them the rules for proper study of the *Veda* and for selecting suitable students. Then the disciples dispersed to disseminate the *Veda* that Vyāsa had taught them. A later passage (XII.337.) depicts Vyāsa surrounded by his five students who were learning *Veda* and MBh from him, and who questioned their guru about spiritual matters. A major sermon on religion was delivered by Vyāsa to his five pupils (XII.327.). On this occasion, Vyāsa advocated the path of *nivṛtti* be followed, saying that it was superior to the dharmic path of *pravṛtti*.

Vyāsa was the guru for the five brahmins Sumantu, Jaimini, Paila, Vaiśaṃpāyana, and Śuka, and they were his only brahmin pupils in the epic.[66]

Occasionally the MBh portrays Vyāsa interacting with his brahmin pupils individually rather than as a group. For example, Paila was the only one of his pupils to assist Vyāsa in both the Rājasūya and Aśvamedha rites. Vaiśaṃpāyana is unique in that he is the reciter of the epic in the extant version, and he appears together with Vyāsa sometimes. To Śuka, Vyāsa addressed a long discourse on *yoga* practice and *sāṃkhya* philosophy, which Bhīṣma later repeated (XII.224-46). Śuka, in whom the *Vedas* were innate, nevertheless resorted to the divine Bṛhaspati for instruction in the *Vedas* (XII.311.22), and to his father Vyāsa for preliminary instruction in *mokṣa*.[67] Jaimini and Sumantu do

---

[64] e.g., I.55.1 and 3.

[65] e.g., XII.327.15; 334.8; 336.79; 337. passim.

[66] The five appear as a group in the following verses, among others: I.57.74-75; XII.314.24; XII.327.15-16; XII.337.11.

[67] XII.312.

not figure in the epic narrative as distinctive individuals. Through these five brahmins, Vyāsa disseminated his literary works.

Vyāsa's position as the Bhāratas' guru is not as explicitly stated in the MBh as is his relationship with the five brahmins, nor is the title guru applied exclusively to Vyāsa by the Bhāratas. All the warriors in the Bhārata family and many of their allies had learned "the Veda of weaponry" (*dhanurveda*) from two martial brahmins who lived at court, Kṛpa and Droṇa. First they studied with Kṛpa Gautama, a great teacher (*ācārya*) who had learned weaponry from his brahmin father Śaradvat Gautama, but who had been raised at court.[68] Soon, however, another brahmin named Droṇa Bhāradvāja became the guru of the Bhārata warriors, and they refer to him as "guru" throughout the epic.[69] Both these brahmin warriors were counselors at the Bhārata court, as were Vidura and the old *kṣatriya* Bhīṣma. It was Vyāsa, though, who counseled the members of the Bhārata family and their allies in spiritual matters; it was he who guided the dynasty with his religious instruction, his boons and curses.

Vyāsa's importance as an advisor to the court of the Bhārata regent Dhṛtarāṣṭra and his wife Gāndhārī is quite often evident. Vyāsa advised his mother and her two daughters-in-law that the time had come for them to leave the court for a life of asceticism in the forest, predicting disaster in the Bhārata dynasty's future (I.119.). Arriving at court once tired and hungry, Vyāsa was fed and comforted by Gāndhārī, to whom he gave the boon of having 100 sons. When she attempted to abort the fetus in frustration after two years of pregnancy, Vyāsa became aware of her intent and intervened, breaking apart the mass of flesh into 101 pieces. These embryoes, placed in pots to mature, developed into the promised 100 Kaurava warriors, plus a daughter as well (I.107.). These princes grew up to be bitter rivals of their cousins, the Pāṇḍavas, even trying to kill them as they slept in Vāraṇāvata. On that occasion, the Pāṇḍavas were saved by the timely intervention of Vyāsa's third son, Vidura the counselor, who warned them (I.130-37.). Vidura's later comment that Vyāsa had instructed him in dharma in Vāraṇāvata city may be a subtle suggestion that Vyāsa had been instrumental in saving his grandsons' lives.[70] Vyāsa also advised Dhṛtarāṣṭra to restrain his belligerent sons (III.8.21.-III.11.), and told him the story of Surabhī and Indra. Vyāsa

---

[68] See I.120 on Kṛpa; he is called "guru" in a passage at the end of I.119, which was omitted from the critical edition on questionable grounds, and which van Buitenen added to his translation.

[69] See I.121-23 on Droṇa.

[70] II.69.12. Vāraṇāvata figures in the MBh only as the city in which the Kauravas tried to burn the Pāṇḍavas to death in a highly flammable house.

said that, although each of one's sons is equally loved, one's compassion is greatest for the oppressed; thus, said Vyāsa, he was greatly concerned for the welfare of his descendants the Pāṇḍavas.[71] Dhṛtarāṣṭra agreed with Vyāsa, but confessed his inability to control his son Duryodhana. Vyāsa responded that the seer Maitreya would soon arrive and that whatever he said should be done, "for if the task is not done, he shall angrily curse your son" (III.11.). Maitreya's angry curse was soon pronounced (III.11.30-39.), just as Vyāsa had threatened would happen. Maitreya seems to be substituting for Vyāsa in this scene, because Maitreya is not a factor in the epic otherwise. Thus, Vyāsa threatened Duryodhana with the curse of Maitreya for not complying with the demands of Maitreya and not heeding the advice of Vyāsa.

Vyāsa repeatedly advised reconciliation until the fighting actually began. Dhṛtarāṣṭra knew that the Pāṇḍava behemoth Bhīma was stronger than any among the Kaurava troops: "I have heard from the mouth of Vyāsa himself that even as a child the Pāṇḍava was actually like that in form and strength" (V.50.21.). But Duryodhana can also quote Vyāsa, twisting his words to bolster an argument for war. Duryodhana said that he was told by Vyāsa, Nārada, and Rāma Jāmadāgnya that the gods became gods by being impervious to love and hatred, malice and greed, and by ignoring all sentiments (V.60.). Hence, he said, the gods would not act out of love for the Pāṇḍavas, and would not concern themselves with human affairs. On another occasion, Vyāsa, divining the thoughts of Saṃjaya and Dhṛtarāṣṭra, appeared before them to encourage the bard to tell what he knew of Kṛṣṇa and Arjuna (V.65.6-V.67.). Saṃjaya said that Kṛṣṇa was the supreme deity,[72] to whom he offered his devotion (*bhakti*). Vyāsa supported the bard's statements, saying that Saṃjaya knew Kṛṣṇa, both the old and the new (i.e., the eternal deity and the earthly form), and again threatened dire consequences if this advice was not heeded (V.67.). Even the subsequent appearance of Kṛṣṇa himself did not shake the resolve of the Kaurava warriors, but Vyāsa made another appeal for peace (VI.2-4.). As noted earlier, Vyāsa came to Dhṛtarāṣṭra and told him the ominous portents he saw which clearly indicated that the outcome of the war would be devastating for the Bhāratas, and urged reconciliation. Vyāsa offered the boon of divine sight to blind Dhṛtarāṣṭra, who asked that instead it be given to his bard Saṃjaya. Vyāsa, "the lord of boons," by means of his energy (*tejas*), gave Saṃjaya the divine eye and the boon of battlefield invulnerability

---

[71] III.10; similar concern is also voiced by Vyāsa in I.144.

[72] Kṛṣṇa is called *puruṣottamaḥ* (V.66.5 and 10); the whole chapter is a paean to Kṛṣṇa as the supreme deity, prefiguring the revelation of the *BhG*.

so that he could describe the conflict in detail to Dhṛtarāṣṭra.[73] Vyāsa's advice, however, was not heeded, and soon the Bhāratas were killing each other.

Even during the war, Vyāsa made an attempt to reconcile the combatants. He appeared before Aśvatthāman, son of the martial arts guru Droṇa, after the death of his father, and responded to his anguished questions (VII.172.). Vyāsa told the brahmin warrior that his enemy Kṛṣṇa was the eternal Nārāyaṇa whose companion Nara was beside him as Arjuna Pāṇḍava. Reciting for him the Śata Rudrīya hymn and recalling Śiva's great deeds, Vyāsa revealed to Aśvatthāman that in his previous lives he had been a devotee of Śiva. After most of the combatants had died, Aśvatthāman and Arjuna met on the battlefield and released their powerful weapons which threatened to destroy the whole world (X.14-16.). Vyāsa and Nārada suddenly appeared between the converging missiles, preventing their collision, and Vyāsa demanded that the warriors withdraw them. By virtue of his perfect adherence to his vows, Arjuna was able to do as Vyāsa ordered, but Aśvatthāman was not. Aśvatthāman's weapon, empowered by the curse he spoke when releasing it, was allowed by Vyāsa to kill the Pāṇḍavas' offspring, but Kṛṣṇa revived one Pāṇḍava heir, Parikṣit. Kṛṣṇa then cursed the brahmin warrior to wander the earth friendless for 3,000 years and Vyāsa seconded the curse, emphasizing the evil of adopting the warrior's dharma if born a brahmin.[74] Despite Vyāsa's direct intervention and his religious teachings, the Pāṇḍavas and the Kaurava ally Aśvatthāman could not be reconciled.

Occasionally in the course of conversation, the counselor Bhīṣma referred to something he had been taught by Vyāsa, e.g., that Vyāsa and Nārada agree no man can escape what is fated for him (V.187.15-17.). As Bhīṣma later lay wounded on the battlefield, he repeated for the edification of the new king Yudhiṣṭhira some of Vyāsa's teachings about dharma. The most extensive discourse by Vyāsa in the MBh is actually Bhīṣma's recitation of his views on *yoga* and *sāṃkhya* (XII.224-46.). Still teaching his protege days later, Bhīṣma said that Nārada and Vyāsa had told him that Kṛṣṇa is Nārāyaṇa (XIII.153.42.). Some MBh texts explain Bhīṣma's vast knowledge with a long account of his instruction about the gods by Vyāsa.[75]

---

[73] VI.2.6-14. Cf. VI.40.75 (= *BhG.* 18.75), where Saṃjaya refers to the divine eye as a boon from Vyāsa. See also section (1) of this chapter for discussion.

[74] X.15-16. Kṛṣṇa's curse is in 16.8-15; Vyāsa's seconding speech follows, in 16.16-17. Notes in the critical edition show a second reading in which Vyāsa is condemning Aśvatthāman's adoption of the warrior's way of life (*kṣatradharma*) not just his evil act (*kṣudrakarman*).

[75] See *Anuśāsana Parvan* Appendix I, No. 14; he says that Vyāsa told him all this in lines 7 and 555.

Vyāsa often counseled distressed or grieving members of the Bhārata dynasty. After Pāṇḍu's death, Vyāsa consoled Kuntī with the prediction that the Pāṇḍavas would be powerful rulers of their father's kingdom and offer up great sacrifices (I.144.). Vyāsa consoled Gāndhārī and Dhṛtarāṣṭra on the loss of their sons (IX.62.) and, with Kṛṣṇa, consoled Gaṅgā when Bhīṣma finally died (XIII.154.). After the war, Vyāsa advised Gāndhārī not to curse the Pāṇḍavas for their role in the death of her sons, but to recognize the culpability of the Kauravas and to forgive the Pāṇḍavas (XI.13.). He gave her the boon of divine sight to survey the battlefield (XI.15.).

Vyāsa appeared before the few survivors of the battle and, after some religious instruction, asked what he could do for them (XV.34-35.). As a boon for Dhṛtarāṣṭra and the other survivors, and to dispel their grief, Vyāsa summoned the deceased warriors from the heavens they had won and reunited them for a night with their loved ones.[76] For that one night, Vyāsa gave Dhṛtarāṣṭra sight to see his 100 sons for the first time, and revealed the divine identities of the participants in the conflict. He reconciled all the warriors to one another and at dawn sent the widows with their husbands back to heaven. Afterwards, he advised Dhṛtarāṣṭra and Gāndhārī to retire from society and cultivate asceticism. Generations later, Janamejaya was so thrilled upon hearing this story that he asked Vyāsa to summon from heaven his father Parikṣit, and Vyāsa granted this boon as well (XV.43.).

Vyāsa was the guru not only for the Kauravas, but for his other grandsons, the Pāṇḍavas, as well. Vyāsa's role in supervising the Pāṇḍavas' transition from one stage of life to another is particularly revealing of their guru/pupil relationship. Vyāsa advised the Pāṇḍavas to marry a Pañcāla princess, Kṛṣṇā Draupadī, and told them why she was destined to be the wife of them all (I.157.). Because such a marriage was unprecedented, her father balked at giving his permission until Vyāsa revealed to him that she was Śrī incarnate, and that the Pāṇḍavas were five former Indras, ordained to be her husbands (I.188.). He went on to say that in her former life she had won the boon from Śiva of having five husbands in this life (I.189.). With these revelations, Vyāsa swept aside all opposition to their marrying Draupadī, effectively guiding the Pāṇḍavas from the student to the householder stage of life. Vyāsa later advised the Pāṇḍavas that the time had come for them to retire from administering the realm and to make the final journey, thus guiding them from being householders to being ascetics.[77] In supervising these

---

[76] XV.36-44, the *Putradarśana Parvan.*

[77] See XVI.9. In the MBh, the Pāṇḍavas walk north, ascending the Himālayas to heaven. The term used for this departure is *prasthāna*, the term for the "departure" from society of a renouncing *saṃnyāsin*; see XVII.1.2.

transitions in the Pāṇḍavas' lives, Vyāsa clearly functioned as their guru.

Vyāsa also provided guidance for the Pāṇḍavas in a purely physical sense by controlling their movements. As noted earlier, he may have saved the Pāṇḍavas' lives by his instruction to Vidura (II.69.12.). Immediately thereafter, Vyāsa advised the Pāṇḍavas to go live in disguise as brahmins in the city of Ekacakrā to which he led them.[78] Ekacakrā means "the single wheel," and is an image symbolic of imperial power; their disguises prefigure their disguises while in the kingdom of Virāṭa (Book V.). While in Ekacakrā, Vyāsa told them that they were to marry Draupadī, and they soon set out for the Pañcāla capital to find her (I.157). During the Pāṇḍavas' exile in the forest, Vyāsa appeared to them, accompanied by the divine seers Nārada and Parvata, and these three great seers encouraged them to tour the sacred sites (III.91.17-25). One pilgrimage site was particularly advocated by Vyāsa, according to Pulastya: "It has been said by Sanatkumāra and the great-spirited Vyāsa, and it is enjoined in the *Veda*, O king, that one should go to Pṛthūdaka" (III.81.127). Vyāsa also helped prepare the Pāṇḍavas for the impending war while they were in exile by teaching Yudhiṣṭhira a magic spell for Arjuna to use in acquiring weapons from the gods (III.37-38). The *brahman* imparted by Vyāsa on this occasion resulted in the Pāṇḍavas obtaining the weapons they needed to defeat the more numerous Kauravas. Vyāsa told the Pāṇḍavas to leave the Dvaita forest "because a long stay in the same place does not add to one's own happiness and might disturb the serene ascetics; the deer are eaten up and the plants and herbs depleted" (III.37.30-35). Although the Pāṇḍavas were Vyāsa's grandsons and were very dear to him on that account, the extent of his control over their lives indicates that he was much more than merely their respected grandfather.

Throughout the epic, Vyāsa instructs the Pāṇḍavas in religion. Vyāsa told Yudhiṣṭhira that Arjuna was Nara, the divine companion of Nārāyaṇa (III.37). Yudhiṣṭhira later told others that Vyāsa was aware that Arjuna and Kṛṣṇa were the eternal ascetics Nara and Nārāyaṇa (III.84.4). Vyāsa taught Yudhiṣṭhira about the different rewards of generosity (*dāna*) and *tapas*, particularly *yoga*, with his narration of the story of Mudgala (III.245-47). Yudhiṣṭhira was once more his pupil for a discourse on Nārāyaṇa and the devotional religion of Pañcarātra.[79] Vyāsa also encouraged Yudhiṣṭhira to recite the 1,008 names of Śiva, as he himself had done when seeking a son from Maheśvara Śiva (XIII.18).

---

[78] I.144; see also van Buitenen, *MBh*, 1:462.

[79] XII.335-36, which is one of the few occasions on which Vyāsa is said to have learned something from someone else, Nārada in this instance; see XII.336.60 and 79.

Yudhiṣṭhira's grief over the death of his kinsmen, and his sense of guilt for his role in the war, were mitigated by Vyāsa's reassurances that his actions had been in accord with dharma, and by Vyāsa's supervision of a sacrificial rite.[80] Vyāsa gave religious instruction to Arjuna as well. After Arjuna asked about the fiery being he had seen preceding him in battle and killing the other warriors, Vyāsa revealed to him that it was Śiva who went before him, and told him the god's myths and attributes (VII.173). In the *Bhagavad-Gītā*, Arjuna exclaimed that all the seers knew Kṛṣṇa to be the primordial god, and specifically named Nārada, Asita Devala, and Vyāsa as seers who knew this.[81] Kṛṣṇa described Vyāsa as the guru of Yudhiṣṭhira (XII.38.24), a doubly meaningful term signifying both "elder" and "spiritual preceptor." Clearly, Vyāsa was the preceptor of all the Pāṇḍavas, instructing them in religious matters.[82]

In summary, Vyāsa is depicted as the spiritual preceptor of five brahmins who learned from him the *Vedas* and MBh, and whom he instructed in religion. He also gave spiritual counsel to members of the Bhārata family, both Pāṇḍavas and Kauravas, exercising control over their lives. That he was their spiritual preceptor as well as their concerned elder is particularly evident in the case of the Pāṇḍavas, in whose lives the major events were supervised by Vyāsa. He granted various boons to deserving members of the Bhārata family and to his brahmin pupils. He cursed Aśvatthāman, one of the staunch supporters of the Kauravas, and perhaps others as well. Though Vyāsa's curse, or the threat of it, is at times significant, his boons are awarded more often,[83] and the power of his speech was legendary.[84] As the guru of many prominent characters in the epic, Vyāsa's influence is omnipresent, though he himself is not.

The comprehensive picture drawn here of Vyāsa in the MBh includes his functions as seer, priest, ascetic, and spiritual preceptor. Of all the

---

[80] See above, section (2) on Vyāsa as a priest.

[81] *BhG.* 10.13. = MBh VI.32.13.

[82] The *purohita* Dhaumya, however, performed the *saṃskāras* (initiatory rites) for the Pāṇḍavas' children, and Arjuna was their teacher in weaponry (I.213.79-82).

[83] Hence Vyāsa is called "the foremost granter of boons" (I.57.74) and "the lord of boons" (VI.2.8).

[84] Vyāsa's words had transformative power, according to legend. A group of people in Bengal regard themselves as brahmins because Vyāsa once called them brahmins; hence they are "Vyāsokta" brahmins. The myth of their origin tells how Vyāsa once hailed some people on the opposite bank of a river, mistaking them for brahmins in the early-morning mist. In fact, they were fishermen mending their nets rather than brahmins doing their morning worship rites, but because he had greeted them as brahmins and his words could not be false, his speech transformed them into brahmins. (Thanks to Prof. Ralph Nicholas of the Anthropology Department at the University of Chicago for his field notes).

epic's brahmins, Vyāsa is the one who most closely corresponds to the ideal of brahminhood promulgated by the dharma literature and the MBh's *Śānti Parvan*, the section of the epic having the greatest similarity to the dharma literature.

The MBh includes many discussions of the duties of brahmins, kings, *kṣatriyas*, and other social groups. In one such passage (XII.60.8-12), the epic presents the idea that the brahmin should first attain self-control (*dama*), and that then he should study the *Veda* and teach the *Veda* for his livelihood. If the brahmin somehow obtains wealth, the text continues, he should raise a family, but the wealth should be distributed through sacrifice and charity. By mastery of the *Veda*, the brahmin does what should be done.

More precise and specific articulations of the proper role of the brahmin occur in dharma texts, which are roughly contemporaneous with the MBh. In fact, the MBh and dharma texts, particularly the *dharmaśāstra* of Manu, have many parallel passages.[85] The classic statement on the brahmin's role in society is Manu's dictum that a brahmin should study and teach the *Veda*, sacrifice for himself and for others, and give and receive gifts.[86] Very similar statements are found in other dharma texts also.[87] The brief passage from the epic paraphrased above is clearly in agreement with the ideals expressed in the dharma literature on the proper role of the brahmin, namely, that he should be preoccupied with the *Veda*, sacrifice, and gifts.

Vyāsa's activities in the MBh cover the full range of activities traditionally deemed appropriate for a brahmin. Unquestionably, Vyāsa is the epic's foremost expert on the *Veda* and the ritual activity enjoined by the *Veda*. Having rearranged the one *Veda* into four texts, Vyāsa taught those to his five pupils along with the MBh as the fifth *Veda*. Vedic students traditionally provided food for their teachers, and although the epic does not depict such an exchange involving Vyāsa and his students, presumably they gave their guru material support while he taught them.

---

[85] Scholars have long noted the parallels. Georg Bühler, in *The Laws of Manu* (Oxford: Clarendon Press, 1886), p. xc, wrote that the authors of the MBh and *Manu* must have drawn upon a common source because the two texts have so many parallel passages. Similar views were expressed by E. W. Hopkins in "Professed Quotations from Manu found in the *Mahābhārata*," *JAOS* 11 (1885): 239-75. Most of the parallels are in the *Śānti Parvan*. P. V. Kane disagrees with them, saying that the MBh drew upon an already extant *Manu*; see his *History of Dharmaśāstra*, 5 vols., 2d ed. (Poona: B.O.R.I., 1968-77), 1:335-49. See the discussion in Robert Lingat, *The Classical Law of India* (Berkeley: University of California Press, 1973), pp. 87-96; he describes them as contemporaneous.

[86] *Manu* 1.88 and 10.74-76.

[87] *Baudhāyana Dharmaśāstra*, ed. E. Hultzsch (Leipzig: Brockhaus, 1884), 1.18.1-4; *Gautama Dharmasūtra*, ed. Veda Mitra (Delhi: Veda Mitra, 1969), 10.1-7 and 49. See also the other citations in Bühler, *The Laws of Manu*, p. 419.

Interestingly, the MBh does not depict Vyāsa himself studying the *Veda* with a guru,[88] the traditional method of acquiring knowledge of the *Veda*, but he certainly is the greatest teacher of the *Veda* known to the MBh. The epic also does not to any great extent depict Vyāsa sacrificing for himself,[89] but he does preside at the sacrifices of others. Finally, there are in the epic many instances of gift-giving involving Vyāsa, e.g., his giving boons to kinsmen and pupils, and receiving food and shelter at times. The most significant exchanges of gifts involving Vyāsa, however, took place in the context of sacrifice. As previously observed, he received a gift of gold as his *dakṣiṇā* after the Horse Sacrifice, and Vyāsa immediately gave it all away to deserving recipients (XIV.91). At another sacrificial site, King Janamejaya gave Vyāsa a cow as a gift, and Vyāsa set it free (I.54.10-15). Thus, Vyāsa is depicted in the MBh as subsisting by means of teaching the *Veda* to qualified pupils, by presiding at the sacrifices of a qualified king (King Dharma as he is known), and by accepting gifts from appropriate benefactors.

Other brahmins in the MBh either have less important roles in the narrative or adhere less closely to the traditional ideal of brahminical behavior than does Vyāsa. Among the minor characters in the epic who are brahmins, the Pāṇḍavas' *purohita* Dhaumya, as seen earlier, though usually with the Pāṇḍavas, is mentioned only occasionally, says little, and does even less to distinguish himself. Nārada and Mārkaṇḍeya figure in the narrative as infrequent visitors to the Pāṇḍavas, but they are celestial brahmins who describe the activities of the gods to the Pāṇḍavas and do little themselves to affect events on earth. Other than Vyāsa, the most important brahmins in the MBh all lived as warriors, including Aśvatthāman, Droṇa, and Kṛpa. The epic poets apparently were not bothered by depicting some brahmins adopting the way of life of *kṣatriyas*, for no condemnation of them or justification of their behavior appears in the MBh.[90] Even dharma texts allow a brahmin in times of distress to

---

[88] As noted above, knowledge of the *Veda* is said to have been innate for Śuka, the son of Vyāsa. Perhaps Vyāsa also had knowledge of the *Vedas* from birth; the *Vedas* dwell in Śuka in the same way they dwell in Vyāsa (XII.311.22):

utpannamātraṃ taṃ vedāḥ sarahasyāḥ sasaṃgrahāḥ /
upatasthur mahārāja yathāsya pitaraṃ tathā //

[89] When Śuka was born, Vyāsa may have been making a fire for sacrifice, however (XII.311). Śuka's *tejas*, it is said, blazed like the sacrificial fire when an oblation of ghee is poured on it.

[90] The exception to this is Aśvatthāman, who was cursed by Kṛṣṇa and Vyāsa after he had killed the Pāṇḍavas' descendants in the womb (X.16). Vyāsa chastised him for his deed and, in a variant reading, for living as a warrior though born a brahmin; see section (4) of this chapter.

support himself as a warrior or in other ways.[91] Other characters in the epic, whatever their social standing or means of subsistence, treat these brahmin warriors with respect and deference.[92] Droṇa was particularly revered as the instructor in weaponry for many of the epic's warriors, and was often addressed by his erstwhile pupils as "guru." Among all the brahmins in the MBh, however, the peerless authority on the *Veda* and on the Vedic sacrificial rites is clearly Vyāsa. He is the most prominent brahmin in the MBh who is engaged in the activities traditionally held to be appropriate for a brahmin. In terms of the injunctions of the dharma literature, and of the dharma passages of the MBh itself, Vyāsa is the epic character most representative of the ideal of brahminical activity.

Nevertheless, from that same orthodox Hindu perspective that the dharma literature represents, Vyāsa's status as a brahmin might not be unimpeachable. Vyāsa is depicted in the MBh as the son of a brahmin man and a non-brahmin woman who was from a community of fishermen.[93] That such a union, in which the customary distinctions between *varṇas* was not observed, should produce in Vyāsa the epic's most respected brahmin, its most authoritative teacher of the *Veda* and a paradigm of brahminhood, is striking indeed. However, the epic does not raise the question of *varṇa*-mixing in Vyāsa's heritage at all, nor is there any hint that his status as a brahmin was suspect because of his parentage. He was the son of two people regarded as admirable, Parāśara and Satyavatī, and was a great brahmin. Of course, miraculous and mixed-*varṇa* births abound in the epic, so the miraculous birth of the brahmin Vyāsa from a non-brahmin woman is by no means unique. In fact, many epic characters of mixed-*varṇa* heritage have prominent roles.[94] Moreover, Brahmanical orthodoxy as represented by the dharma

---

[91] *Manu* 10.80-117; similar passages in other dharma texts are cited by Bühler in *The Laws of Manu*, p. 420.

[92] Droṇa and Kṛpa themselves, however, expressed their feelings of regret for the path they had chosen, describing themselves as captives of the Kauravas' wealth and powerless as eunuchs because they had accepted support from those evil *kṣatriyas*, and were thus obligated to fight alongside them (VI.41).

[93] Vyāsa's mother Satyavatī was born of the seed of King Vasu Uparicara, which dropped into the Yamunā River and impregnated a fish. Twins were conceived and, while the boy became king of the Matsya people, the girl eventually married the king of the Bhārata people, after giving birth to Vyāsa by the brahmin Parāśara. See the beginning of this chapter for details. Vyāsa's mother was thus no brahmin; she was a *kṣatriya* at best. Only those children born to properly wed women of the same *varṇa* as the husband were to be regarded as belonging to that *varṇa*, according to *Manu* 10.5. Vyāsa's mixed-*varṇa* heritage deviates from the orthodox ideal.

[94] Vyāsa fathered two princes with *kṣatriya* women and the counselor Vidura with a *śūdra* woman. Yuyutsu was Dhṛtarāṣṭra's son by a *vaiśya* women, was the only Kaurava to join the Pāṇḍava side, and eventually was named regent for the minor Parikṣit. Bhīma

literature held in highest esteem the married householder stage of life, while Vyāsa never married.[95] He had a family in the Bhārata warriors and Vidura, and even a son, Śuka, created through *tapas*, but did not raise his own offspring, and had no home. Apparently, however, there is no explicit criticism of Vyāsa in Hindu literature for his decision to remain unmarried. Though born of a mixed-*varṇa* union and never married, Vyāsa's greatness was such that his status as a brahmin was beyond dispute.

If Vyāsa's social standing as a brahmin was not questioned, misgivings about his morality did occasionally find expression, and centered on one incident in his career. His willingness to father children for the Bhārata dynasty with his deceased half-brother's two *kṣatriya* widows, and even a *śūdra* woman, is matter-of-factly treated in the epic and is clearly regarded as dharmic; Vyāsa says that he will do what is needed with respect to the dharma so that the kingdom would be spared the disaster of having no heir (I.99.36-43).

In texts other than the MBh, Indian civilization has recorded a variety of views on Vyāsa's behavior. Aśvaghoṣa, a brahmin who converted to Buddhism, wrote two poems in which Vyāsa's behavior in this incident was denigrated quite explicitly. In the *Buddhacarita*, a brahmin *purohita*'s son makes reference to famous sages who were involved in questionable ways with women, first among whom he describes Vyāsa: "Formerly, for instance, the prostitute Kāśisundarī kicked with her foot the great *ṛṣi* Vyāsa, with whom even the gods could hardly contend."[96] The poet, in building toward the literary climax of the Buddha renouncing the world

---

Pāṇḍava married a *rākṣasī* who bore Ghaṭotkaca. The bard Saṃjaya was a *sūta*, considered a mixed-*varṇa* group (see *Manu*, 10.11).

Regarding Vyāsa himself, the *Vajrasūcika Upaniṣad* observes that he was born from a fisher-maiden, but that the births of many great sages were irregular, and concludes that the true brahmin is the one who perceives the Self (*ātman*) to be *brahman*. See verse 5 of the text and translation in S. Radhakrishnan, trans., *The Principal Upaniṣads*, pp. 933-38.

[95] See section (2) of this chapter for discussion.

[96] *Buddhacarita*, 4.16; see the text and translation by E. H. Johnston. The same poet describes Dvaipāyana the *Veda*-Divider, son of Parāśara and Kālī, as once having intercourse with Kāśisundarī the prostitute, in *Saundarananda*, ed. and trans. E. H. Johnston (Lahore: Motilal Banarsidass, 1928), 7.29-30. Johnston observes that the story referred to is otherwise unknown, and that it is not certain that Kāśisundarī is a name. The poet may well be referring here to the well-known account of Vyāsa and the Bhārata princesses. Bhīṣma obtained them from Kāśi to be Vicitravīrya's wives, and when they were left childless widows, Vyāsa was summoned to give sons to the family (I.96-99). One of these princesses rejected Vyāsa when a second attempt at procreating had been arranged (I.100), though the epic contains no scene of her kicking Vyāsa. Either of the princesses could be called *kāśisundarī* ("the beauty from Banaras"). The poet may be referring to a popular tradition about her encounter with Vyāsa. In any case, the poet is censuring Vyāsa for his involvement with the woman.

to attain *nirvāṇa*, has cited Vyāsa as an example not to be followed. Another work in the *kāvya* genre, Daṇḍin's *Daśa Kumāra Carita*, which was composed by a Hindu rather than a Buddhist, derides both Vyāsa's origins and morals. A prostitute in this poem bolsters her position in an argument about dharma with an ascetic by observing that "Parāśara violated a non-Āryan maiden, while his son had intercourse with a brother's wife..."[97] Daṇḍin is trying to get a laugh from his audience, and Aśvaghoṣa is trying to proselytize his audience, both at Vyāsa's expense.

The orthodox Hindu tradition responded to those who called into question the propriety of Vyāsa's behavior. Kumārila's *Tantravārtika* discusses the transgressions of dharma by twelve great men in former times.[98] Vyāsa, though avowedly celibate as a *brahmacārin*, procreated by the law of levirate (*niyoga*) and because his mother asked him to do so, both reasons for which Kumārila cites legal precedent and sanction. Moreover, he continues, because of Vyāsa's vast *tapas* and the power obtained thereby, he was strong enough to do this; for the strong, everything is permissible.[99] However, the behavior of such an extraordinary person should not be regarded as establishing a precedent for others to follow in later ages. This Mīmāṃsā apologist's response, while providing justification for Vyāsa's behavior, removes him from consideration as an exemplar of the brahminical tradition; Vyāsa is too extraordinary to be a model for others to emulate, according to Kumārila.

Kumārila, however, was looking back at a story formulated a millenium earlier, in the course of which millenium the dharma had been codified in great detail in many *śāstras*,[100] and applying those standards to the epic. However, despite the passages in the MBh's *Śānti Parvan* which parallel the *dharmaśāstra* literature, the epic is not itself a *dharmaśāstra* and was not composed merely as a narrative exposition of the dharma.[101] The MBh might be better described as a meditation on the difficulty of resolving the perceived conflicts between the various injunc-

---

[97] *Daśa Kumāra Carita*, H. H. Wilson, ed. (London: Asher, 1846), p. 64: "...parāśarasya dāsakanyādūṣaṇaṃ pārāśaryasya bhrātṛdārasaṃgatir..."

[98] P. V. Kane, in *The History of Dharmaśāstra*, 3:843-46, discusses *Tantravārtika*, pp. 205-8 of the Ānandāsrama Press edition, which is a commentary on Jaimini's *Pūrvamīmāṃsāsūtra* 1.3.7.

[99] Kumārila is quoting MBh XV.38.23:
sarvaṃ balavatāṃ pathyaṃ sarvaṃ balavatāṃ śuci /
sarvaṃ balavatāṃ dharmaḥ sarvaṃ balavatāṃ svakam //

[100] Kumārila lived about A.D. 700, according to Winternitz, *History*, 3:478.

[101] Dahlmann's assertion thus cannot be accepted; see Chapter. 1. The prominence of brahmin warriors, mixed-*varṇa* heroes, and Vyāsa himself emphasize the point.

tions of the dharma. Vyāsa's dilemma in the case of the Bhārata princesses pitted his personal dharma as a celibate *brahmacārin* against the dharma of his family, which needed sons to continue the lineage, and society as a whole, which needed an heir to the throne. Vyāsa responded to this dharmic riddle in a way that produced the greater good for the greater number of people, rather than simply for himself, and of course also produced a good story, the epic battle between the Bhāratas.

Vyāsa is the epic character who, other than Kṛṣṇa himself, most clearly perceives the dharma at all times and knows what should be done in all cases. For the epic, Vyāsa's actions, including fathering the Bhārata princes, are always in accord with the dharma; indeed, he defines the dharma. Vyāsa knows the higher and lower dharmas (I.99.36); he knows all of dharma (XII.224.10). Vyāsa is the foremost dharma-knower (XII.315.22), one who has reached perfection by dharma alone (III.32.10-11). Vyāsa perceived the subtle dharma in the marriage of Draupadī to the five Pāṇḍavas and revealed it to Drupada and the others.[102] Hence, it may well be said of Vyāsa that he speaks dharmically and his very Self is dharma (XII.314.39).

Vyāsa is depicted in the epic as a brahmin whose activities encompass the full range of activities traditionally deemed appropriate for a brahmin. He is the foremost master of the Vedic tradition, both in its textual and ritual aspects, and is thus a paradigm of the *pravṛtti* path of dharmic action. One also sees in Vyāsa the emergence of other ideals of brahminical behavior involving *tapas*, and the practice of religious devotion. The classical Vedic model of brahminhood is not supplanted by a different model in the MBh, but is clearly undergoing some modification through the adoption of these other traditions to the brahmin's repertoire. The brahmin is a figure in transition in the MBh, a figure whose role was being redefined. Vyāsa reflects the Hindus' struggle to define the proper role of the brahmin and to integrate into society the practices of *tapas* and *bhakti*, to integrate into the life of the brahmin both family concerns and asceticism. For the MBh, Vyāsa is the epitome of the dharmic brahmin.

---

[102] I.187-90. As Yudhiṣṭhira says (I.187.28), the dharma is subtle (*sūkṣma*).

CHAPTER THREE

THE DIVINE PLAN IN THE EPIC

The MBh portrays Kṛṣṇa Dvaipāyana Vyāsa as the very symbol of brahminical orthodoxy, the foremost master of the Vedic texts and rituals, a great ascetic, and the guru of brahmins and Bhārata warriors. He is the MBh's leading brahmin, the one most in harmony with the dharma. Nevertheless, his actions in the MBh in three particular crises have disastrous consequences, suggesting that, paradoxically, this powerful brahmin failed in his most important undertakings. My interpretation of Vyāsa's role in the epic is set in the context of the epic's central myth, the conflict between the gods and demons. To combat the demons who were overrunning the earth, Brahmā formulated a plan according to which all the gods would become incarnate. Hence, many of the epic's major characters are depicted as either incarnate gods or demons, and the characters re-enact much of the mythology of the gods and demons of whom they are incarnations. Vyāsa is regarded as an incarnation of Nārāyaṇa in the *Purāṇas*, and this idea is not unknown to the MBh; however, it is stated very rarely. The depiction of Vyāsa in the MBh is not inconsistent with the role of an incarnation of Nārāyaṇa, particularly with regard to his mediating oppositions and cooperating with Kṛṣṇa Vāsudeva, who is very often said to be a Nārāyaṇa incarnation. Although Vyāsa, like many other epic characters, may be seen as an incarnation of a deity, it is by no means certain that he is depicted in the MBh as an incarnation of Nārāyaṇa exclusively or consistently.

In the plot of the epic narrative, there are three major crises in which Vyāsa is intimately involved, and in all three the Bhārata dynasty suffered disastrous consequences. Thus, despite being the epic's most dharmic brahmin, a priest of unexcelled expertise, and an ascetic of considerable power, Vyāsa's actions were to a large degree responsible for the ruination of his relatives, the Bhārata family. An examination of the three epic crises, and the role of Vyāsa in those crises, follows.

(1) Fathering the Flawed Princes

Asked by his mother to produce qualified heirs to the throne with the two widows of his half-brother, Vyāsa promised the Bhārata dynasty princes "the likes of Mitra and Varuṇa."[1] The first princess called upon, however, could not bear to look at the frightening ascetic's matted orange hair and beard, and his fiery eyes, so she closed her eyes (I.100.4-6). Vyāsa declared of the son they had produced that

> He will be a man with the strength of a myriad elephants, a wise and great royal *ṛṣi*, of great fortune, great power, and great intelligence. And 100 powerful sons will be his, but because of his mother's lack of virtue, he shall be born blind.[2]

So, in time, Dhṛtarāṣṭra was born blind, and Vyāsa was asked to father another son for the dynasty, one better qualified to be king. The second widowed princess paled at the sight of the ascetic, and Vyāsa declared, "Because you paled on seeing my ugliness, your son shall be pale (*pāṇḍu*), and that will be his name, O woman with the beautiful face" (I.100.17). Still not satisfied that a qualified prince had been born to the dynasty, Satyavatī prevailed upon her son Vyāsa to try a third time. It was again the turn of the first princess, but she, aghast at the prospect of another encounter with Vyāsa, sent to him as her substitute a servant woman. Vyāsa and this servant woman, both substitutes, conceived Vidura, who became the wise counselor at the Kaurava court, said to be an incarnation of the god Dharma (I.101). Rather than princes similar to those ancient paradigms of the royal virtues, Vyāsa produced for the Bhārata dynasty three defective candidates for the inheritance, one blind, one afflicted with abnormally pale skin, and the third, arguably the best of the trio, was disqualified for kingship because he was not a *kṣatriya*. The two princes Vyāsa fathered were flawed because of the defects of their mothers, as the seer had predicted before their births. As another passage (I.61.78) informs us, however, Dhṛtarāṣṭra was born blind because of the anger of the seer, thus emphasizing the responsibility of Vyāsa for the Bhārata princes' flaws.

Because Dhṛtarāṣṭra was blind, his younger brother Pāṇḍu ruled the kingdom first and ruled well, finally retiring with his wives to the forest, where he had five sons, the Pāṇḍavas. Dhṛtarāṣṭra succeeded to the throne, and at that point the problems of the Bhārata dynasty began to be unmanageable. Both Dhṛtarāṣṭra and Pāṇḍu had produced sons, and it was unclear to whom kingship rightfully belonged, whether to the eldest son of Pāṇḍu, who had ruled first, or to the eldest son of Dhṛtarāṣṭra, who was ruling at the time and was actually the elder of the

---

[1] Mitra and Varuṇa are Vedic gods who represent two types of ideal ruler, and are often associated with one another, as in *Ṛg Veda* 7.61. See also Georges Dumézil, *Mitra-Varuṇa*, 2d ed. (Paris: Éditions Gallimard, 1948).

[2] I.100.9-10.

brothers. To complicate the problem further, the eldest son of Pāṇḍu, Yudhiṣṭhira, was born before the eldest son of Dhṛtarāṣṭra. As van Buitenen observed, "The succession rights of the male descendants are a genealogist's nightmare, and, to me at least, there is little doubt that the story was in part *designed* as a riddle."[3] The question of succession to the throne divided the Bhārata family, pitting against each other as rivals the Pāṇḍavas and their cousins, the Kauravas. The rivalry between the two groups, Vyāsa's grandsons, escalated to a total rupture in the ruling family, and open warfare. This split in the Bhārata dynasty and the wholesale slaughter that followed were the lasting legacies of Vyāsa's fathering flawed princes a generation earlier.

(2) The Ritual Gone Wrong

The conflict between the Bhārata cousins became so acrimonious that the difficult decision was made to divide the kingdom and give the Pāṇḍavas a small tract of wilderness to rule. The establishment of the Pāṇḍavas' city of Indraprastha under Yudhiṣṭhira's leadership was followed quickly by their performance of the Royal Consecration ritual (*rājasūya*). This grand Vedic ceremony celebrated the sovereignty of the royal patron, and was used for a new king's installation or as a periodic reaffirmation of his sovereignty.[4] The dramatic possibilities of this rite were not lost on the epic poets, who patterned the narrative of the MBh's second book, the *Sabhā Parvan*, on the very ritual which was their subject. The structure of the *Sabhā Parvan* narrative was inspired by the events in the Rājasūya rite; "it is structurally an epic dramatization of the Vedic ritual."[5] The ritual's "establishment of the four quarters" (*digvyāsthāpanaṃ*), in which the king was to take possession of his domain symbolically by stepping in the four directions, became in the epic an account of the "conquest of the four quarters" (*digvijaya*) by his four Pāṇḍava brothers while Yudhiṣṭhira occupied the center of the realm.[6] Similarly, the ritual "challenge" from a warrior during the king's triumphant chariot ride became in the epic a serious challenge to the completion of the rite from a dissident *kṣatriya*, Śiśupāla.[7]

---

[3] van Buitenen, *MBh*, 1:xvi.

[4] See Jan Heesterman, *The Ancient Indian Royal Consecration*; hereafter cited as *Consecration*.

[5] van Buitenen, *MBh*, 2:6. He has discussed the numerous structural correspondences between the ritual and the epic narrative in his *MBh*, 2:3-30. An earlier version of his argument is his "On the Structure of the Sabhāparvan of the Mahābhārata," in *India Maior*, pp. 68-84.

[6] Heesterman, *Consecration*, p. 103; van Buitenen, *MBh*, 2:18-19.

[7] Heesterman, *Consecration*, pp. 127 ff.; van Buitenen, *MBh*, 2:22-24. See also the interesting analysis of Śiśupāla in Georges Dumézil, *Stakes*.

As depicted in the MBh, however, the consecration of Yudhiṣṭhira was more than the installation of a new king; it was his proclamation of his universal sovereignty (*saṃrājya*) over all other kings. The Kaurava side of the family participated in the ritual, but not all the Kauravas were supportive of Yudhiṣṭhira's imperial ambitions. The eldest of the Kauravas, Duryodhana, also cherished the hope of imperial sovereignty, and conspired against Yudhiṣṭhira. He challenged his cousin to a gambling match, naming as the Kaurava champion his maternal uncle Śakuni. Not only was Śakuni masterful with the dice and Yudhiṣṭhira a novice, but the game was rigged; Śakuni cheated to win.[8] In the gambling match, Yudhiṣṭhira successively staked and lost everything, not only his possessions but even the freedom of his brothers and their wife. Over the protests of Duryodhana and his clique, Dhṛtarāṣṭra restored their freedom and possessions to the Pāṇḍavas, but a second challenge was issued and accepted, this one an all-or-nothing gamble for the Bhārata throne. The losing side was to go into exile in the forest for twelve years, and then to wander incognito a thirteenth year before returning. Again Yudhiṣṭhira lost, so the Pāṇḍavas went into exile, but not before vowing to return and avenge their mistreatment by killing the principal Kaurava offenders.[9]

As van Buitenen has so convincingly shown, Yudhiṣṭhira was not gambling simply out of folly or greed, but of necessity; he was still bound by the ritual requirements of the Rājasūya, which included a dice match after the consecration and installations of the king.[10] Of course, the ritual envisioned the king being victorious in the dice game, just as in the "challenge" from the dissident warrior, but in the epic's rigged game King Yudhiṣṭhira lost to the Kauravas. Although at times an epic character will refer to the dice match so as to suggest that Yudhiṣṭhira could have avoided it, clearly it was an integral component of the Rājasūya ritual itself.[11] According to Baladeva, Yudhiṣṭhira challenged Śakuni but was defeated because the dice were hostile (V.2.8-12). Given the requirement of a dice match to conclude the Rājasūya, Yudhiṣṭhira did, in a sense, issue a challenge simply by sponsoring the imperial ritual.

---

[8] See II.53-54; II.56.10; III.9.2.

[9] The dicing and its sequel are found in II.43-72.

[10] On the rite's dice match, see *Śatapatha Brāhmaṇa* 5.4.4; Heesterman, *Consecration*, pp. 140 ff.; van Buitenen, *MBh*, 2:27-30. Although the MBh (II.42.32-49) indicates that the ritual had been completed before the dicing episode, and that most of the participants had departed, the dicing follows immediately (II.43-65) and was, in fact, part of the ritual itself.

[11] Kṛṣṇa calls dicing a vice sprung from desire, and says that he would have stopped it if he had been there (III.14).

Vyāsa was the presiding priest at Yudhiṣṭhira's Rājasūya; he chose the other priests involved in the rite, and himself performed the role of *brahman* priest. The *brahman* was the supervising priest who oversaw the activities of all the other priests involved in the ritual.[12] It was the responsibility of the *brahman* priest to correct any errors made by the other priests so as to avoid the disastrous consequences of incorrect performance of the ritual.[13] It was, therefore, specifically Vyāsa's responsibility as *brahman* priest to see that the Rājasūya of Yudhiṣṭhira was properly completed and the sovereignty of the king established. However, the Pāṇḍavas' attempt to establish Yudhiṣṭhira's sovereignty through the Rājasūya failed, resulting in their exile. Thus, the fact that the ritual went wrong for the Pāṇḍavas means that Vyāsa failed to carry out his responsibilities at the rite. Charged with the duty of overseeing the sacrifice to its proper conclusion, Vyāsa instead presided over a ritual fiasco.

(3) Failure to Reconcile the Combatants

After the disastrous Rājasūya rite which resulted in the exile of the Pāṇḍavas, Vyāsa attempted to prevent the family feud from becoming open warfare. Hardly had the Pāṇḍavas reached the forest that was to be their only home for twelve years when Vyāsa had to go to the Kaurava court in an effort to preserve the uneasy peace. He warned Dhṛtarāṣṭra to restrain his son Duryodhana: "King, if you want the Kauravas to live, have your son go make peace with the Pāṇḍavas!" (III.10.24). Vyāsa's forceful counsel was not heeded, and his effort to mediate the dispute between his bellicose grandsons was unsuccessful.

After the Pāṇḍavas had completed their term of exile and returned to claim their inheritance, the Kauravas were still not inclined to share the kingdom with them. Saṃjaya the court bard was sent to the Pāṇḍavas to inform them of this, and returned with messages from Kṛṣṇa (V.58.18-28) and Arjuna (V.64) announcing their willingness to fight. Dhṛtarāṣṭra questioned Saṃjaya about the Pāṇḍavas and their ally Kṛṣṇa, and authoritative support was given to the bard's statements by Vyāsa, who had just appeared (V.65.8-9). The bard said that Kṛṣṇa was

[12] See Eggeling's introduction to *Śatapatha Brāhmaṇa*, 1:xx-xxi, describing the *brahman* as "the very embodiment of the sacrificial art and Vedic lore in general..."

[13] The following summaries of *Śatapatha Brāhmaṇa* verses concern the *brahman* priest's role: the most learned brahmin is the strongest and is to be made the *brahman* (4.6.6.5); he heals the sacrifice using all three *Vedas* (11.5.8.1-7); he is the guardian of the sacrifice (14.1.3.3); he is the heart of the sacrifice (12.8.2.23); he is the entire sacrifice (6.2.2.40). The choice of Vyāsa as the *brahman* was particularly appropriate since the *brahman* was originally always a descendant of Vasiṣṭha (12.6.1.37-41), as was Vyāsa himself.

none other than the Supreme Deity come to earth, and that this was known to him because of his devotion to Kṛṣṇa (V.66.-V.67.5). Vyāsa encouraged Dhṛtarāṣṭra to listen to his bard, who would bring him out of danger (V.67.11-15). Saṃjaya spoke further to Dhṛtarāṣṭra about Kṛṣṇa, and about the attainment of serenity through yoga (V.67.17-V.68). Immediately thereafter, Kṛṣṇa himself came to the Kaurava court in a last effort to avert warfare through compromise. The statements of Saṃjaya and Vyāsa were preparatory to this embassy of Kṛṣṇa to the Kauravas, but this effort to resolve the conflict also failed.

War broke out after the Kauravas rejected the offer of compromise Kṛṣṇa brought. Several days of bloody but inconclusive fighting resulted in the wounding of the patriarch Bhīṣma and the death of the guru Droṇa, after which Droṇa's son Aśvatthāman confronted Arjuna in a duel (VII.172). Defeated and discouraged, Aśvatthāman ran from the battlefield and suddenly encountered Vyāsa. He asked the sage how it was possible that his weapon had not killed Arjuna and Kṛṣṇa, who have mortal natures (VII.172.42-49). Vyāsa told him that Arjuna and Kṛṣṇa were the eternal yogis Nara and Nārāyaṇa; "... those two *ṛṣis*, first of the gods ... are born in age after age for the purpose of ordering the affairs of the world" (VII.172.81). Vyāsa's revelation to him of his devotion to Śiva in previous lives, and of the mutual respect Śiva and Nārāyaṇa have for each other, caused Aśvatthāman to regard Kṛṣṇa with newfound esteem, but did not induce him to make peace (VII.172.90-93). This confrontation between Arjuna and Aśvatthāman foreshadows their horrific combat at the war's end in which, once again, Vyāsa figures prominently.

The virtual annihilation of the Kaurava forces placed victory out of their reach. Only three Kaurava warriors survived: Kṛtavarman, the brahmin warrior Kṛpa and their leader Aśvatthāman. This pitiful remnant of an army, however, mounted a night attack on the Pāṇḍava camp and killed in their sleep most of the allies of the Pāṇḍavas and even the five Draupadeyas, the Pāṇḍavas' sons. The enraged Pāṇḍavas charged toward Aśvatthāman, intent on revenge. The brahmin warrior released a deadly missile (X.13), and, encouraged to do so by Kṛṣṇa, Arjuna released a similar weapon to neutralize Aśvatthāman's (X.14). At that critical moment, the two great seers Vyāsa and Nārada appeared there, standing between the two blazing weapons and preventing them from colliding with destructive results. Arjuna immediately acquiesced to their request and withdrew his weapon, but his opponent Aśvatthāman confessed his inability to recall his missile due to his non-observance of his vows, particularly the vow of chastity (*brahmacarya*). Vyāsa mediated the conflict in an effort to preserve the lives of the few survivors of the

Bhārata war, but the compromise Vyāsa negotiated in this life-threatening crisis was very costly for the Pāṇḍavas. The five Pāṇḍava brothers were spared the effects of Aśvatthāman's missile and the mantra that empowered it, but all the descendants of the Pāṇḍavas were killed in the womb. Moreover, Aśvatthāman himself was allowed to escape the wrath of the Pāṇḍavas by the symbolic act of surrendering his crest-jewel. In Vyāsa's presence and with his explicit consent, Aśvatthāman then redirected his weapon into the wombs of the Pāṇḍavas' women, killing the unborn generation (X.15). Though Kṛṣṇa subsequently revived one Pāṇḍava fetus, born as Parikṣit, grandson of Arjuna and heir to the Bhārata throne, the destruction of the Bhārata family was almost complete. Not only did Vyāsa not succeed in resolving the feud, but in the final duel of the ensuing war, Vyāsa consented to the grotesque slaughter of the most inappropriate victims imaginable, the Pāṇḍavas' unborn descendants.

These three epic crises have in common the intimate involvement of Vyāsa and disastrous consequences for the Bhārata dynasty. In each of the three crises, Vyāsa has expressed a desire to benefit his relatives, yet the outcome in each case has been detrimental to the Bhāratas. Vyāsa announced his intention to father princes for the dynasty "the likes of Mitra and Varuṇa," but the first one was blind and the second abnormally pale, so that neither was ideally qualified to rule. Vyāsa supervised a rite intended to secure sovereignty for Yudhiṣṭhira, but the result was exile for all the Pāṇḍavas. Vyāsa repeatedly tried to reconcile the Pāṇḍavas and Kauravas to no avail, and after many warriors had died, he saved the five Pāṇḍava brothers from death at the price of allowing the weapon to kill all the unborn Pāṇḍava offspring. In several of his most important undertakings in the epic, Vyāsa's actions resulted in disaster for the Bhāratas. Yet Vyāsa is certainly the leading brahmin in the MBh, where he is depicted as drawing upon a store of accumulated ascetic power to affect and even control events. In situations other than these three crises, Vyāsa's power was considerable; for example, after the war he summoned from heaven all the slain warriors for one night of reconciliation. Thus, only after their death did Vyāsa succeed in reconciling the enemies. One is presented with the paradox of a powerful brahmin whose actions at times have truly catastrophic consequences for his relatives, the Bhārata family.

Vyāsa's paradoxical failures in these three epic crises suggest comparison with the "three sins of the warrior" on which Georges Dumézil has written extensively.[14] In his analysis, the life of the warrior in Indo-

[14] See Georges Dumézil, *The Destiny of the Warrior* (Chicago: The University of Chicago Press, 1970), hereafter cited as *Warrior.* See also his *Stakes.*

European traditions is characterized by the commission of three "sins" which are distributed in each of three categories, his first, second, and third "functions," as follows: (1) administration of the sacred, (2) physical force, and (3) abundance and fecundity.[15] Each sin by the warrior entails a penalty for the warrior which is appropriate to that function. In the case of Indra, the sin of killing a brahmin causes his loss of spiritual force (*tejas*, the first function quality); a cowardly breach of promise causes his loss of physical power (*bala*, the second function quality); and his adultery causes loss of beauty (*rūpa*, the third function quality).[16] Vyāsa's actions in the epic, analyzed according to Dumézil's vision of the warrior hero's destiny, reveal a pattern similar to that of the warrior's life. (1) Vyāsa's failure to produce a qualified heir to the Bhārata throne, a failure in fecundity, caused a loss of *rūpa* for the Bhāratas; both Pāṇḍu and Dhṛtarāṣṭra had physical defects. Further paternity problems ensued, with Pāṇḍu unable to conceive offspring without dying from a curse immediately, and Dhṛtarāṣṭra's wife delivering a misshapen mass, only due to Vyāsa's aid, that developed into the 100 evil Kauravas. (2) The failure of the Rājasūya rite at which Vyāsa presided and for which he was responsible, a failure in the administration of the sacred (first function), resulted in the humiliation of the Pāṇḍavas, their momentary loss of freedom, their exile and loss of sovereignty for thirteen years. Loss of sovereignty is a loss of *tejas* for the Pāṇḍavas, and their exile and disguises constitute a covering or hiding of their *tejas*. In their absence, the demonic Kauravas enjoy a flawed sovereignty; Śrī, embodied in Draupadī, is not with them. (3) The failure to reconcile the combatants and the death of inappropriate victims, a failure in the domain of physical force (second function), results in loss of force for the Bhāratas; only the Pāṇḍavas and a few others survive the holocaust. Vyāsa's career in the epic thus may be seen as characterized by three failures, with one failure per function. The striking difference, however, between the career of the brahmin Vyāsa and that of Dumézil's warrior is that the penalty for each transgression or failure is paid not by Vyāsa himself, but by the Bhārata family.

How may we account for the similarity in structure of the mythology of the Indo-European warrior with that of Vyāsa, and for the inversion just noted? Dumézil's comparative study of the three sins of the warrior in the literatures of several cultures had led him to the hypothesis that each culture had preserved an inheritance of ancient Indo-European

---

[15] As defined by Dumézil in *Warrior*, p. ix.

[16] Dumézil, *Warrior* pp. 72-81.

mythology about the warrior hero.[17] Apparently no other Indo-European cultures present figures who are both comparable to Vyāsa and have similar structures in their mythology, so there is no evidence that Vyāsa is another example of the preservation of the Indo-European heritage. Nonetheless, it is interesting to consider the possibility that the poets of the MBh employed the structure of the warrior hero's mythology in telling the story of a very different kind of hero, transforming the three sins of the warrior into the three failures of the brahmin Vyāsa. The warrior and the brahmin have very dissimilar roles, however. The brahmin presides over a sacrificial ritual sponsored by the *kṣatriya* warrior, to whom the results, good or ill, accrue; the brahmin receives a fee for the services he renders for others. Thus, the inversion whereby the Bhārata warriors pay the penalties for Vyāsa's actions replicates the roles of *kṣatriya* patron and brahmin priest in the sacrifice. One way of understanding Vyāsa's career in the MBh may be as a specifically Indian adaptation of the ancient Indo-European myth of the warrior hero and his three sins.

Interpretation of the paradoxical career of Vyāsa must emphasize the MBh's eschatological dimension. Several recent interpreters of the epic, while not focusing on Vyāsa, have stressed in different ways the fact that the epic depicts the transition of the world from one age to another. Georges Dumézil and Stig Wikander have shown structural parallels between the MBh and Scandanavian mythology and have argued that both apparently conserve an earlier Indo-European eschatological drama in which the forces of good and evil fight an age-ending battle.[18] However much the epic poets of India may have inherited from the Indo-European past, apparently they developed and elaborated upon this theme. The epic poets perceived correspondences between the *yuga*-ending Bhārata

---

[17] See Dumézil's argument in *Stakes*, pp. 74-78, for example, in which, after documenting the parallelism between a Scandanavian and an Indian tale, he discusses the possibility that their similarities are due to the preservation of a common inheritance.

Jan Gonda has repeatedly cautioned that the idea of a common inheritance, and indeed Dumézil's entire thesis regarding Indo-European social structure, are far from proven; e.g., see his *Triads in the Veda* (Amsterdam: North-Holland, 1976), Chapter III "The three social classes," and Chapter IV "The tripartite ideology." While here describing Dumézil's ideas as "not wholly untenable and rejectable," he poses the question whether perhaps the basic principle has been not the social structure but the "triadic mode of thought" (p. 127).

[18] See Stig Wikander, "Germanische und Indo-Iranische Eschatologie," *Kairos* 2 (1960):83-87, and "Fran Bravalla till Kurukṣetra," *Arkhiv för Nordisk Filologi* 75 (1960):183-93. See also Georges Dumézil, *Gods of the Ancient Northmen* (Berkeley: University of California Press, 1973), especially chapters 1 and 3, as well as his more recent *Mythe et épopée*, 1:208-37. Hiltebeitel discusses their contributions in *Ritual*, especially pp. 299-353.

war, which initiated the *Kaliyuga,* and the myth of the cataclysmic destruction of the world (*pralaya*) preparatory to its recreation. So frequent and suggestive are the references to the destruction of the world that Madeleine Biardeau has hypothesized that the structure and meaning of the epic as a whole are dependent on the *pralaya* myth: "The cosmic crisis which forms the plot of the epic... (has) its model in the Purāṇic account of the reabsorption and recreation of the world."[19] Biardeau's approach to the MBh draws attention to the activity and complementarity of the epic's primary deities, Nārāyaṇa and Śiva. They, aided by all the other gods, effected the transition from *Dvāparayuga* to *Kaliyuga.* Both the Wikander-Dumézil and Biardeau approaches to the MBh emphasize the eschatological setting of the epic tale.

While the structure of the MBh may have Indo-European roots and may, to some extent, have as its mythic model the *pralaya,* the MBh's explicit expression of the eschatological crisis is in terms of the war between the gods and demons. Their recurrent struggle for sovereignty in this instance had as its battlefield the earth, due to the incarnation of the demons as powerful kings and warriors among men. Brahmā formulated a plan which called for the gods also to become incarnate so as to combat the demons. As a result of the gods and demons contending for sovereignty, the *Dvāparayuga* was brought to an end and *Kaliyuga* begun. Thus, the presence on earth of the gods was neither a fortuitous circumstance nor a haphazard series of theophanies, but was the plan ordained by Brahmā. Vyāsa's activity in the MBh can most fruitfully be examined in the context of Brahmā's plan for the incarnation of all the gods. Several chapters of the epic present discussions among the gods of Brahmā's plan or revelations of it to mankind, brief summaries of which follow.

In the *Ādi Parvan* (I.58.25-I.59.6), Earth, tyrannized by the demonic *asuras,* approached the god Brahmā, who already knew her request. Brahmā said to the gods, "To throw off Earth's burden, you must each be born with a part of yourselves on her to oppose them."[20] Impatient to go to earth with portions of themselves, they went to Nārāyaṇa, and for the purpose of cleansing the earth, Indra said to him, "Descend with a portion of yourself," to which Nārāyaṇa agreed.[21] Indra made a covenant with Nārāyaṇa that they would each descend with a portion of

---

[19] Madeleine Biardeau, "Conférence de Madeleine Biardeau," *EPHE Annuaire* 77 (1969-70):169; my translation.

[20] asyā bhūmer nirasituṃ bhāraṃ bhāgaiḥ pṛthak pṛthak /
asyām eva prasūyadhvaṃ virodhāyeti cābravīt //
I.58.46.

[21] aṃśenāvatarasveti / I.58.51.

themselves from heaven to earth, together with the gods.[22] Indra gave the command, and then left Nārāyaṇa's dwelling. One after another, the gods descended (*avateruḥ*) for the destruction of the demons and for the well-being of all humanity (I.59.3).

The most complete account of the incarnation of the gods and demons among humanity follows this scene in which the divine plan was first presented. The epic gives an account of the origin of the various kinds of creatures, including gods, *gandharvas*, *apsarās*, the primordial seers, the several types of demons, etc. (I.60), then lists the incarnations among humanity of the gods and demons in the days of the Bhārata war (I.61). First are listed the incarnations of many demons as kings on earth who are minor figures in the MBh.[23] Listed after the demon-kings are the major epic figures and their divine identities, among them Vāsudeva (Kṛṣṇa), who was a portion (*aṃśa*) of Nārāyaṇa among mankind (I.61.90). This passage also states that from Kṛṣṇa Dvaipāyana was born Dhṛtarāṣṭra; "because of his mother's fault and the seer's anger, he was born blind."[24] Thus, Vyāsa is named in this chapter as if he were one of the gods who sent portions of themselves down to earth! This surprising and anomalous statement is not supported by any other passage in the MBh.

A complementary glimpse of this divine planning session in heaven was given by Vyāsa in the *Strī Parvan.*[25] Earth said, "What is to be done for me has been promised by you all previously in Brahmā's abode, O Eminent Ones. Let it be done quickly!" Viṣṇu (Nārāyaṇa) replied that when Duryodhana became king, Earth's request would be fulfilled since for his sake kings would come to Kurukṣetra and kill one another, thereby relieving Earth of her burden. Vyāsa went on to tell Dhṛtarāṣṭra that his son Duryodhana was a portion (*aṃśa*) of Kali, born for the purpose of destroying humanity. As a consequence of fate, brothers like him

---

[22] avatartuṃ mahīṃ svargād aṃśataḥ sahitaḥ suraiḥ //
I.59.1.

[23] I.61.3-61; chief among these are the demons Vipracitti, born as Jarāsaṃdha, and Hiraṇyakaśipu, born as his deputy Śiśupāla.

[24] I.61.78. Southern manuscripts tend to eliminate reference to the seer's anger, as if it were considered unseemly, but this leaves a verse in which the fault lies both in the mother and in the seer. Although the critical edition has omitted reference to Pāṇḍu, many Northern manuscripts have a verse here in which Pāṇḍu is similarly born from Vyāsa, while many Southern manuscripts have a verse in which his birth is from the troop of Maruts; see Notes *560 and *561. A further oddity in this passage is verse 79's statement that Vyāsa's third son Vidura is "Atri's son." Nīlakaṇṭha's commentary refers to a myth in which Atri once substituted for Sūrya. Sūrya's son is Dharma, thus Vidura is here, as elsewhere, seen as Dharma incarnate.

[25] XI.8. See Appendix for a translation.

were born; they were all evil-natured, and by them this earth has been caused injury. They and many other kings were born on earth for the purpose of destruction. Vyāsa said that all he had told Dhṛtarāṣṭra was an eternal mystery of the gods.

Later, in the *Āśramavāsika Parvan*, Vyāsa revealed to the survivors of the Bhārata war that the gods had taken on human forms to accomplish a specific purpose. The sage said, "The purpose of the gods is not to be denied; inevitably, it will come to pass. All the gods with their portions have descended to the surface of the earth."[26] "The gods, having become human and having accomplished their works, then returned to heaven" (XV.39.16). Vyāsa also revealed the earthly identities of many of the gods, who had become incarnate as major figures in the dynastic conflict of the Bhāratas.[27] Vyāsa said that Hṛṣīkeśa (Kṛṣṇa) was Nārāyaṇa and that Arjuna was the divine seer Nara, but on this occasion he did not say anything about himself. In the epic's final chapter (XVIII.5.9-25), a similar revelation of the divine identities of the participants is made by Vaiśaṃpāyana, who says that Vyāsa told him all this.

Despite the fact that these passages in which Brahmā's plan to combat the demons come from widely separated sections of the MBh, they agree with one another almost completely regarding the divine and demonic identities of the major characters. The *Ādi Parvan* passage shows Brahmā formulating and revealing the plan, and Indra marshalling the forces of the gods for the fight. Indra's covenant with Nārāyaṇa in this passage, and their leadership in the implementation of the plan, foreshadows the partnership of Arjuna and Kṛṣṇa, their incarnations, in the epic. The *Strī Parvan* passage makes reference to the plan agreed upon in Brahmā's abode, and focuses on Nārāyaṇa's leadership of the gods in this plan to combat the demons. The *Āśramavāsika Parvan* passage depicts the gods acting in concert and does not single out one deity as foremost. All three passages state that the incarnation of the gods was necessitated by the overrunning of the earth by demons. Brahmā's plan was to relieve the earth of its burden by bringing most of the incarnate demons to the battlefield where they could be killed. Thus, the MBh is patterned on the

---

[26] bhavitavyam avasyaṃ tat surakāryam anindite /
avaterus tataḥ sarve devabhāgair mahītalam //
XV.39.5.

[27] The Pāṇḍavas and their allies, as well as Bhīṣma, Droṇa, and Karṇa, were each a portion (*aṃśa* or *bhāga*) of a deity. Droṇa's son Aśvatthāman was born of Rudra (*rudrajam*). All the Kauravas were *rākṣasas* incarnate, with Duryodhana as the demon Kali incarnate, and Śakuni as the demon Dvāpara. Thus, the Pāṇḍavas' two main antagonists in the dicing episode are depicted as embodying the demons named after the current age and the imminent *Kaliyuga*.

recurrent war between the gods and demons, this time transposed to earth.[28]

The MBh uses many different expressions for the incarnation of a god in human form. *Aṃśa* and *bhāga* are used interchangeably to refer to a deity's manifestation on earth while he also remains in heaven.[29] *Putra*, meaning "son," is sometimes used quite similarly, as when Vyāsa is described as Nārāyaṇa's *aṃśa* and *putra*,[30] or when Arjuna is described as Indra's *aṃśa* and *putra*.[31] Of course, a son is a portion of his father. Another word used in Sanskrit texts to describe the incarnation of divinity is *avatāra*, which has come into English as avatar. The word *avatāra* seems not to occur in the MBh at all, though many closely related forms are used to convey the idea.[32] All these words are the poets' metaphors for the mystery of divinity's manifestation among humanity. A particularly important figure may have more than one such metaphor applied to him. Thus, at various times, or even simultaneously, Arjuna can be considered a son or portion of Indra, an incarnation of a former Indra, and an incarnation of Nārāyaṇa's companion Nara. Epic characters who are regarded as divine incarnations not only embody many of the attributes of the gods of which they are incarnations, they also to some extent reenact the mythology of those gods. Expressions such as these are not used in the epic with the doctrinal precision that would later be developed by theologians such as the Gosvāmins. Clearly, the concepts of divine incarnation were still in their infancy during the epic's composition, and many different expressions for incarnation were used.

Like many of the main characters in the MBh, Vyāsa is regarded as an earthly incarnation of a deity. However, unlike the other incarnations, Vyāsa does not appear in the lists of *aṃśas*. While he is explicitly said to be an incarnation of Nārāyaṇa in the MBh, the references are both separate from the lists of incarnations and very few in number. This, of course, contrasts sharply with the frequent identification of

---

[28] The idea that the gods take on human forms to kill the demons who periodically overburden the earth is the kernel of all the Hindu myths of divine incarnation according to Paul Hacker; see "Zur Entwicklung der Avatāralehre," *WZKSO* 4 (1960):47-70. Of course, the killing of the demons entails the deaths of many human warriors and even some of the incarnations of the gods as well, a point which O'Flaherty has emphasized in *Evil*, chapters 4 and 9.

[29] Jan Gonda translates *aṃśa* as "part, portion, share" and *bhāga* as "share," and notes the epic uses of them (e.g., MBh V.56.22-23) as nearly synonymous in his "The Vedic Gods Aṃśa and Bhaga," in *Monumentum H. S. Nyberg* (Leiden: E. J. Brill, 1975), pp. 291-310; see especially pp. 292-93.

[30] XII.337; see the Appendix for a translation.

[31] Arjuna is Indra's son throughout the epic; see I.114. for the account of his birth from Indra. Arjuna is Indra's *aṃśa* at I.189.32.

[32] See the use of *avataraṇa*, *avatartuṃ*, etc. in the passages above on Brahmā's plan.

Kṛṣṇa with Nārāyaṇa in the epic. In fact, only in two chapters of the MBh's critical edition are there explicit references to Vyāsa as an incarnation of Nārāyaṇa.

The first reference to Vyāsa as Nārāyaṇa incarnate is Vaiśaṃpāyana's statement (XII.334.9) which ends with a rhetorical question.

> Know that Kṛṣṇa Dvaipāyana Vyāsa is Nārāyaṇa the Lord, for who other than the Lord could be the author of the *Mahābhārata*, O tiger among men, and who other than the Lord could enunciate truly the manifold dharmas?[33]

In this single verse, Vyāsa's pupil clearly expresses the idea that his master is Nārāyaṇa incarnate; the composition of the epic is evidence enough for him. No other evidence is adduced, no story told, and nothing else is said about Vyāsa here.

A few chapters later, Vyāsa himself expounds upon his relationship to Nārāyaṇa. When Vaiśaṃpāyana extolled his guru Vyāsa as "born a portion of Nārāyaṇa" and as Nārāyaṇa's son,[34] the interlocutor asked for an explanation of Vyāsa's birth and his relationship to Nārāyaṇa. In response, the bard told the account Vyāsa had given his disciples when questioned by them on this matter (XII.337.16-57). Vyāsa said that Nārāyaṇa, having thought of various forms with which to strike down the enemies of the gods, then spoke a syllable from which was created a seer known as Sārasvata ("son of speech") or Apāntaratamas ("one free of inner darkness"). Nārāyaṇa foretold that this *ṛṣi* would be the divider of the *Veda* in every creation, and that as the *Kaliyuga* arrived, he would be born as the son of Parāśara.

> When Tiṣya (*Kaliyuga*) has arrived, Bhāratas named Kuru will be great-spirited kings spread over the earth. Among offspring of them who are descended from you there will be a split in the family resulting in their killing one another, except for you, O best of the twice-born. In that time, you, being endowed with asceticism, will divide the *Vedas* severally, and in that black age you will be black colored.[35]

Vyāsa went on to explain to his disciples that he was the *ṛṣi* Apāntaratamas, born long ago of Nārāyaṇa, born as a portion of the god by the god's grace, and that he was now the son of Parāśara whom they knew as Kṛṣṇa Dvaipāyana Vyāsa. The passage recapitulates the career of Vyāsa in the MBh, emphasizing his division of the *Veda* and his connection to the Bhārata dynasty as the grandfather of the Pāṇḍavas and

---

[33] kṛṣṇadvaipāyanaṃ vyāsaṃ viddhi nārāyaṇaṃ prabhum /
ko hyanyaḥ puruṣavyāghra mahābhāratakṛdbhavet /
dharmānnānāvidhāṃścaiva ko brūyāttamṛte prabhum //

[34] nārāyaṇasyāṃśajam ... sasarja putrārtham ... vyāsaṃ / XII.337.3-5.

[35] XII.337.42-44.

Kauravas. Regarding the timing of his incarnation, "when Tiṣya has arrived" must be understood as "when *Kaliyuga* is imminent" to be in accord with other epic passages; his blackness was a "sign of the times"[36] which signaled the impending transition to the next age, *Kaliyuga*, which he lived to see. More significantly, however, the passage reveals that Vyāsa was to be regarded as an incarnation of Nārāyaṇa, on earth to divide the *Veda* but also to participate in and survive the Bhārata war.

These are the only passages in the MBh which refer explicitly to Vyāsa as an incarnation of Nārāyaṇa.[37] The epic associates Vyāsa with Nārāyaṇa, however, in certain instances. Vyāsa is depicted as teaching various epic characters about Nārāyaṇa and how to worship the god or his incarnation Kṛṣṇa.[38] Another possible way in which Vyāsa may be associated with Nārāyaṇa has been suggested by Madeleine Biardeau. She has written that the divine companions Nara and Nārāyaṇa gave rise to a series of mythic reinterpretations in which complementary pairs represented the dualities *kṣatra/brahman*, human/divine, and pupil/teacher. Among these later reinterpretations were the warrior duo Arjuna/Kṛṣṇa and the brahmin duo Vaiśampāyana/Vyāsa.[39] While Vaiśampāyana and Vyāsa obviously typify the pupil/teacher duality, they embody the other two dualities to a lesser extent. As this chapter shows, Vyāsa's identity with Nārāyaṇa is not much articulated in the MBh, hence his divinity is much less apparent than is Kṛṣṇa's in the epic. With regard to the *kṣatra/brahman* duality, both Vaiśampāyana and Vyāsa are said to be brahmins, so they are not explicitly differentiated.[40] Moreover, the MBh never expresses a comparison of Vaiśampāyana and Vyāsa with Nara and Nārāyaṇa. Thus, one can give only qualified assent to Biardeau's suggestion, and say that perhaps Vyāsa is associated with Nārāyaṇa as

---

[36] See Hiltebeitel, *Ritual*, pp. 62-68. He discusses the simultaneous appearance of Kṛṣṇa Vāsudeva, Kṛṣṇa Dvaipāyana, and Kṛṣṇā Draupadī as a sign of the onset of *Kaliyuga*, a "Vaiṣṇava triad" of black avatars associated with Nārāyaṇa who effect the transition to the black age, *Kaliyuga*. See also Hiltebeitel's article, "Two Kṛṣṇas,...".

[37] Three manuscripts insert the lines of XII.334.9 into the epic's first book as well; see *Ādi Parvan* Appendix I, Nos. 2 and 3. The two references quoted are the only such citations in the critical edition, however.

[38] Saṃjaya's Kṛṣṇa-*bhakti* is supported by Vyāsa (V.65-68); Vyāsa tells Aśvatthāman that Kṛṣṇa is Nārāyaṇa and Arjuna is Nara (VII.172); Vyāsa lectures on Nārāyaṇa and Pañcarātra (XII.335-36); see also III.84.4; VI.32.13 = *BhG.* 10.13; XIII.153.42.

[39] See Biardeau's "Études" (1968):35, note 1, and (1969):82, note 1.

[40] The only hint that Vaiśampāyana might be anything other than a brahmin is his name, which would presumably be derived from *viśampa*, a word which would mean "king" but which is not attested in any text. Thus, his name would mean "king's descendant" and give Vaiśampāyana some affiliation with the *kṣatra* half of the duality.

one of the "réinterprétations mythiques" of the complementary pair Nara and Nārāyaṇa.[41]

Vyāsa is also associated with Nārāyaṇa's incarnation Kṛṣṇa in various ways. Of course, the shared name Kṛṣṇa is an obvious pairing of the two. In the *Bhagavad-Gītā*, Kṛṣṇa identifies himself with Vyāsa by saying "among the ascetics, I am Vyāsa."[42] Out of context, this comment appears more significant than it does in context. In this one chapter of the *Gītā*, within twenty verses, Kṛṣṇa identifies himself with the best and most prominent individual or entity of some sixty groups. The point of so doing is to glorify Kṛṣṇa. Although the identification is complimentary to Vyāsa, and one can say that it was considered not inappropriate that the two of them be so identified, one cannot put much emphasis on this verse in formulating an understanding of Vyāsa. Hiltebeitel has stressed the cooperation in matters of dharma between these two Kṛṣṇas;[43] they are, in fact, the epic characters who most clearly perceive the dharma in all its subtlety, who know what to do in every instance and tell others what they should do. Vyāsa and Kṛṣṇa are not depicted in conflict with or opposing one another, so the characterization of their relationship as cooperative is apt. The way in which the two Kṛṣṇas cooperate can be illustrated by examining particular incidents in the MBh.

When Kṛṣṇa cursed Aśvatthāman for killing the unborn generation of Pāṇḍavas, Vyāsa seconded the curse, as we have seen, saying that he did so because Aśvatthāman had adopted the way of life of the warrior though born a brahmin (X.16). While Kṛṣṇa's motive apparently was revenge against the attacker of his kinsmen, Vyāsa displayed the concerns of an orthodox brahmin in seeking to keep the social categories distinct and their boundaries clearly defined. Vyāsa cooperated with Kṛṣṇa, concurring with and reinforcing the curse, but Vyāsa is not Kṛṣṇa's mere doublet or echo.[44] Each had his own reason, appropriate

---

[41] Biardeau has also written that it would be tempting to see Dvaipāyana as synonymous with Nārāyaṇa by deriving Dvaipāyana from *dvipad* or *dvipāda* ("biped," i.e., man). However, she admits that the name would have to be derived from *dvipa* or *dvīpa*, words with different meanings; hence, the name is not derived from a synonym of *nara* and is not synonymous with Nārāyaṇa. See "Études," (1968): 35, note 1. There is no evidence that such an etymology was ever proposed in any Sanskrit text.

[42] munīnām apy ahaṃ vyāsaḥ / VI.32.37 = *BhG.* 10.37.

[43] See Hiltebeitel, *Ritual*, Chapter 2, especially pp. 84-85.

[44] Biardeau has called Vyāsa a doublet of Kṛṣṇa; see her "Études" (1968):35, note 1 where she writes that "Kṛṣṇa a une sorte de doublet dans l'épopée: Vyāsa, qui est 'une partie de Nārāyaṇa' ... et dont l'enseignment se borne souvent à répetér ce que dit Kṛṣṇa ailleurs." Her analysis of the *avatāra* theme has led her to see the *avatāra* as having *kṣatriya* and brahmin affinities, with Vyāsa as "le complémentaire brāhmaṇe du kṣatriya Kṛṣṇa" (p. 237, *Clefs pour la pensée hindoue*). She continues to describe Vyāsa as the brahmin aspect of the *avatāra* in her more recent work; see Péterfalvi, *MBh*, 1:90, 1:173, and 2:379.

to his character, for acting as he did. Similarly, at Draupadī's wedding (I.186-89), Vyāsa and Kṛṣṇa had different roles. While Kṛṣṇa sanctioned the wedding, Vyāsa's revelations actually resolved the doubts about it, and he then presided at the marriage ceremony. In both these episodes, Vyāsa and Kṛṣṇa cooperated in a common cause, but Vyāsa did what Kṛṣṇa could not do, and vice versa. Vyāsa taught the *Vedas* and presided at Vedic rituals, while Kṛṣṇa drove Arjuna's chariot and advocated battlefield tactics which were morally reprehensible but were necessary if the Pāṇḍavas were to triumph. Vyāsa the brahmin and Kṛṣṇa the warrior, having different capabilities and fields of action, are complementary figures who cooperate in the divine plan.

Kṛṣṇa's role in the divine plan, his purpose in becoming incarnate, is very clearly stated as the destruction of the demons who threatened the dharma.[45] He accordingly instituted a "sacrifice of battle" in which the offerings were warriors, many of whom were demons incarnate.[46] Given Hiltebeitel's insight regarding the cooperation between the three Kṛṣṇas, the Vaiṣṇava triad, in carrying out Brahmā's plan for defeating the demons, what were the contributions of the other two, Draupadī and Vyāsa? At first glance, Draupadī's role appears to be exclusively that of victim; she was dragged into the assembly hall after the dice match by the victorious Kauravas, who taunted her and attempted to disrobe her. Such indignities were possible because the Pāṇḍavas had lost their freedom in the dice game and were thus reduced to the status of slaves. As the victim of the Kauravas' villainy, she provided motivation for the Pāṇḍavas, giving them ample reason for revenge against their evil cousins. Just as Śrī was the prize over which the gods and demons contended in the mythology of the *Brāhmaṇas*,[47] her epic counterpart Draupadī was central to the conflict between the Pāṇḍavas and Kauravas in the MBh. Yet Draupadī was neither passive nor patient in her suffering. She asked the assembly how Yudhiṣṭhira could stake her freedom on the last roll of the dice when he had already lost his own freedom on the prior roll, and by posing this dharma riddle, saved herself and the Pāṇḍavas from further contumely, at least on that occasion. Later, she forcefully urged the Pāṇḍavas to fight for their honor and inheritance, to avenge their enforced exile by killing the Kauravas.[48] Thus, she may well be said to have cooperated with Kṛṣṇa in the divine plan to defeat the

[45] See VI.26.8. = *BhG.* 4.8., where Kṛṣṇa describes his incarnation. See also III.187.26-30 and XII.337.29-36, Nārāyaṇa speaking.

[46] See, e.g., V.139.29-52 and Hiltebeitel's references to this theme in *Ritual*, especially pp. 292-96.

[47] As discussed in Hiltebeitel, *Ritual*, Chapter 7.

[48] Draupadī's most extensive discourses on this theme are III.13.41-113 and V.80.

demons on the battlefield; in fact, Draupadī did all she could to bring about hostilities with the Kauravas.

To what extent did Vyāsa's actions facilitate the outbreak of warfare among the Bhāratas, thus contributing to the effort to defeat the demons? The disastrous results produced by Vyāsa's interventions in the three crises discussed above, Vyāsa's "failures," may be reconsidered in light of the necessity of combatting the demons. First, Vyāsa's failure to father one qualified prince for the Bhāratas, his procreation of two flawed princes, led to rivalry for the throne. He left a legacy of confusion in the line of dynastic succession, creating the pre-conditions for war. Second, the failure of the Rājasūya rite which Vyāsa supervised resulted in the irreparable rupture between the Bhārata cousins. The exile of the Pāṇḍavas confirmed the inevitability of war. Third, the failure to reconcile the warriors resulted in the annihilation of both armies and even the unborn heirs of the Pāṇḍavas. Thus, Vyāsa's actions in these crises had the effect of facilitating the outbreak of war and the death of many warriors. Vyāsa, too, may be said to have cooperated with Kṛṣṇa in killing the incarnate demons in accordance with the plan of Brahmā.

A characteristic feature of the incarnations of the Vaiṣṇava triad, the three Kṛṣṇas, according to Hiltebeitel, is their "propensity to mediate" oppositions.[49] In rituals, games, and other situations in which two parties are opposed, one or more of the three Kṛṣṇas usually mediates between the two sides. A detailed examination of Vyāsa's role in mediating various oppositions reveals both similarity to and difference from Kṛṣṇa's role.

The MBh portrays Vyāsa as a brahmin who is deeply involved in the conflict between his grandsons, the Bhārata warriors. Indeed, the frequency with which he mediates conflicts between belligerent warriors is striking. As the father of Pāṇḍu and Dhṛtarāṣṭra, the grandfather of the Pāṇḍavas and Kauravas, Vyāsa was the respected patriarch of the Bhārata family, and was welcome in both camps. He is an epic character not only uniquely suited to the role of mediator, but one who had many opportunities to mediate between the two sides of the Bhārata family. Before the final rupture, Vyāsa tried to prevent his descendants from contending against one another, and kept the Pāṇḍavas out of danger.[50]

---

[49] Hiltebeitel, *Ritual*, p. 69. He refers specifically to Draupadī saving the Pāṇḍavas from the Kauravas at the dice match, Kṛṣṇa's peace embassy to the Kauravas on behalf of the Pāṇḍavas, and Vyāsa's intervention between Arjuna and Aśvatthāman.

[50] When the Pāṇḍavas were being oppressed, Vyāsa assisted them in eluding the Kauravas, escorting them to Ekacakrā to live in disguise (I.144), foreshadowing their exile. He may also have aided their escape from the firetrap in Vāraṇāvata; see II.69.12 and chapter 2, section (4).

He tried to resolve the inheritance dispute by installing Yudhiṣṭhira as emperor (*samrāj*) through the Rājasūya rite. This would have ended the rivalry and established the proper hierarchy within the Bhārata family by recognizing the sovereignty of the Pāṇḍavas, but Vyāsa's mediation was opposed by Duryodhana and his clique among the Kauravas, and the attempt failed. When the Pāṇḍavas were forced into exile, Vyāsa assisted them through threatening situations[51] and counselled restraint on the part of the Kauravas to avoid warfare.[52]

Even after the battle was joined at Kurukṣetra, Vyāsa tried to mediate the conflict. He spoke to the Kaurava warrior Aśvatthāman about the gods, telling him that his opponents Arjuna and Kṛṣṇa were the divine seers Nara and Nārāyaṇa incarnate (VII.172). He then told Aśvatthāman that in his previous lives he had been a devotee of Śiva, and that in this life he had been born of Śiva. Immediately thereafter, Vyāsa lectured Arjuna about Śiva (VII.172). When these two warriors later met on the battlefield for their final duel, Vyāsa intervened as a mediator in their conflict (X.14-16). In so doing, Vyāsa was mediating between Śiva and Nārāyaṇa as they were represented on earth, Aśvatthāman being born from, devoted to, and eventually possessed by Śiva, while Arjuna was the companion of Kṛṣṇa, Nārāyaṇa's incarnation. In the end, Vyāsa reconciled all the war's victors and victims by summoning the deceased warriors from their various heavens for one night of reunion with their families, friends, and enemies (XV.35-43). Vyāsa reconciled to one another all the principal participants in the epic story.

In mediating between the Pāṇḍavas and Kauravas in these various ways, Vyāsa was mediating between two groups which had not only personal and political differences, but perhaps religious differences as well. The epic seems to be suggesting that the Pāṇḍavas are aligned with the Vaiṣṇava religious tradition and the Kauravas with the Śaiva tradition. Of course, the Pāṇḍavas had Kṛṣṇa as their ally and kinsman, and from time to time they recognized his divinity and his identity with Nārāyaṇa.[53] In contrast, the Kauravas not only decisively rejected Kṛṣṇa, but show some evidence of being Śiva worshipers. Certainly some of the Kauravas' allies, including Jarāsaṃdha,[54] Śiśupāla,[55] and Aśvat-

---

[51] Stopping a Kaurava raid (III.8.21-III.11) and telling the Pāṇḍavas how to obtain divine weapons (III.37.20-III.38).

[52] III.9-10; V.65-68; VI.2-4.

[53] E.g., the Pāṇḍavas circumambulated Kṛṣṇa reverently on his arrival (II.22.55): Yudhiṣṭhira knew from Vyāsa that Arjuna and Kṛṣṇa were the eternal Nara and Nārāyaṇa (III.84.4); see also the revelations of Kṛṣṇa's divinity to Arjuna in the *Bhagavad-Gītā* (VI.32.13 = *BhG.* 10.13 and VI.33. = *BhG.* 11), and in the *Anugītā* (XIV.16-96).

[54] Jarāsaṃdha was born thanks to a demoness, who prophesied that he would behold

thāman,[56] were devotees of Śiva. Regarding the Kauravas themselves, the incident in which the demons disclosed to Duryodhana his purpose is especially revealing (III.239-40). Duryodhana, ashamed at having his life saved by the hated Pāṇḍavas, had resolved to fast to death, but when the demons learned of his intent they performed a sacrifical rite to summon him to their nether world. They addressed the Kaurava leader, "Long ago with our *tapas* we obtained you from Maheśvara (Śiva) ... Your body is imbued with both the Lord and the Goddess; you are divine, not human!" (III.240.5-10). They told him that demons had taken human form to help him, and that other demons would take possession of Bhīṣma, Droṇa, Kṛpa, and the others (III.240.11). "Go, hero, have no other purpose whatever; you are always our means, as the Pāṇḍavas are of the gods."[57] This passage reveals that the leader of the Kauravas was born as a result of the asceticism of the demons, as a boon from Śiva. Thus, the Kauravas not only did not worship Kṛṣṇa or Nārāyaṇa, they had Śiva worshipers among their principal allies and were led by Duryodhana, who was born as a boon from Śiva, while the Pāṇḍavas had Kṛṣṇa as their principal ally and received instruction in the worship of Nārāyaṇa. Vyāsa's mediation between these two groups, therefore, suggests mediation between opposing religious traditions.

Another conflict between epic characters which Vyāsa mediated did not involve the belligerent Kauravas. The marriage of the Pāṇḍavas to Draupadī was opposed by her father until Vyāsa revealed the divine sanction for the wedding and the divine identities of the principals.[58] Vyāsa's role in this episode was to reveal the subtle dharma within an action that seemingly was not in accord with dharma, showing that the dharma transcends the rules of the law books. In revealing the reasons for this extraordinary union, Vyāsa mediated a dispute regarding the

---

Rudra Śiva with his own eyes (II.16-17). Later, he wanted to sacrifice a group of captured kings to Śiva, as if they were beasts, which indicates his devotion to Śiva.

[55] Śiśupāla was born with three eyes and four arms, like Śiva, and is said to be an incarnation of the demon Hiraṇyakaśipu, the quintessential enemy of Vaiṣṇavism. See Dumézil's elucidation of Śiśupāla's affinity with Śiva in *Stakes*, Chapter 2.

[56] Aśvatthāman was born from and devoted to Śiva (VII.172), and possessed by Śiva in battle (X.7.65 and X.17.6).

[57] gaccha vīra na te buddhiranyā kāryā kathaṃcana /
tvamasmākaṃ gatir nityaṃ devatānāṃ ca pāṇḍavāḥ //
Another reading of III.240.24 could be "you are our own means ..." construing *nityaṃ* as "own."

[58] See I.188-89 on Vyāsa's role in the wedding, and I.189.29-30 on Nārāyaṇa and Śiva ordaining it. Śiva's curse and boon resulted in the polyandric marriage, which is disruptive of the social order and dharma, but the marriage is sanctioned by Nārāyaṇa in heaven and Kṛṣṇa on earth, who thus protect and restore the social order and dharma. On the complementary roles of these deities in the wedding, see Hiltebeitel, *Ritual*, pp. 84-85, and Biardeau, "Brāhmaṇes et potiers," pp. 38-39.

dharma between the Pāṇḍavas and the Pāñcālas, who became not only relatives by that marriage Vyāsa arranged and presided at, but political and military allies as well. Moreover, by uniting the goddess Śrī, now in her human form of Draupadī, with Indra, now replicated five times over as the Pāṇḍavas, Vyāsa had also mediated between the gods themselves, though in their human forms.

Vyāsa also mediated between the gods and mankind in the MBh. He acted as an intermediary between the gods and the Pāṇḍavas by telling the men how to secure weapons from the gods (III.37.20-III.38). Vyāsa told Yudhiṣṭhira to send Arjuna to the gods to ask for their aid, and gave him a powerful spell to teach Arjuna. Throughout the epic, Vyāsa revealed to people on earth various aspects of the divine plan, including the incarnation of all the gods for the purpose of defeating the demons on earth.[59] His teachings served to inform humanity of the divinely ordained dharma so that they might act in accord with it. As the supervisory priest at the Vedic rites of Rājasūya and Aśvamedha, Vyāsa was the intermediary for the men who sought the beneficence of the gods through sacrificial rituals. As a priest, his activities maintained the symbiotic relationship between humanity and the gods, with Vyāsa mediating between heaven and earth.

There is yet another sense in which Vyāsa's activities in the epic may be seen as mediation, namely, in the transmission of knowledge from one age to the next. Vyāsa altered the form of the *Veda* by dividing it into four texts when he transmitted it to the *Kaliyuga*. He is also credited with transmitting other knowledge, including the MBh itself, the tale of the Bhārata war which had terminated the prior age of *Dvāparayuga*. Vyāsa's mediation in the transmission of knowledge takes on great significance in view of the fact that humanity's capabilities were decreasing in *Kaliyuga*, since he was aiding humanity's attempt to know and conform to the divinely ordained dharma in the most difficult of times. Thus, Vyāsa is depicted in the epic as uniquely mediating in the transmission of knowledge within Hindu civilization.[60]

Kṛṣṇa Dvaipāyana Vyāsa may well be said to have a "propensity to mediate" oppositions in the MBh, perhaps to an even greater extent than the other two Kṛṣṇas. Vyāsa is less partisan than the other two Kṛṣṇas, who are supporters of the Pāṇḍavas throughout the epic. Vyāsa is more

---

[59] In addition to the marriage episode, see XI.8; XII.337; and XV.39.

[60] Another text, the *Sāmavidhāna Brāhmaṇa* (3.9.8) lists its line of teachers, with Vyāsa seemingly placed between the gods and men in the list. The list is Prajāpati, Bṛhaspati, Nārada, Viṣvaksena (a name for Nārāyaṇa Viṣṇu), then Vyāsa Pārāśarya, who taught Jaimini, etc. Thus, in this text's line of transmission, Vyāsa is apparently listed between the gods and men.

nearly neutral in the struggle between his grandsons, the Pāṇḍavas and Kauravas. Not only is he engaged in mediation between the Pāṇḍavas and Kauravas, but also between humanity and the gods, between *Dvāpara* and *Kali yugas*, and even between Nārāyaṇa and Śiva as they were represented on earth. Vyāsa's "in-betweenness" is so characteristic that even his name reflects his liminality: because he was born on an island in mid-river, he was called Dvaipāyana. So, although the three Kṛṣṇas may be said to cooperate in matters of dharma in the epic and to mediate oppositions, Vyāsa seems to be cast in the role of mediator more often than these other incarnations associated with Nārāyaṇa.

The MBh explicitly states that the role of Nārāyaṇa is the restoration of dharma and the destruction of the demons.[61] Somewhat less explicitly stated is the role of the other major divine actor in the epic, Śiva. These two deities have often been characterized as "the Pervader" and "the Outsider" respectively.[62] In the MBh in particular they are depicted in this way; Nārāyaṇa is usually central to the epic's action in the form of Kṛṣṇa, and Śiva is usually absent.[63] The roles of these two gods are complementary, Śiva's actions being generally the more disruptive and destructive, while Nārāyaṇa's actions are the more restorative and recreative, the two roles being regarded as interrelated and equally necessary.[64] From the *Vedas* through the *Purāṇas*, the characters of these two gods have remained remarkably consistent; Viṣṇu (Nārāyaṇa) defeats the demons, while Rudra (Śiva) does not come into conflict with the demons.[65] Śiva is not demonic, but performs the necessary role of destroyer of the world periodically, and the demons serve his purpose in this regard. Hence, Duryodhana is depicted as Śiva's creation and as the agent of the demons because he will be the means of destroying the armies of the Pāṇḍavas and Kauravas (III.239-40). At key moments, Nārāyaṇa's incarnation Kṛṣṇa absents himself from the epic narrative,

---

[61] Nārāyaṇa himself states his purpose in becoming incarnate in III.187.26-30 and XII.337.29-36.

[62] Jan Gonda, *Viṣṇuism and Śivaism* (London: Athlone Press, 1970), passim; see the index's citations "pervader" and "outsider." See also Dumézil, *Mythe et épopée*, 2:86, and Hiltebeitel, *Ritual*, chapter 14.

[63] As Hiltebeitel expresses their complementarity (see *Ritual*, p. 356), the gods are led by Nārāyaṇa's incarnation Kṛṣṇa, who stands "at their head, or at their 'center,' while Śiva remains typically remote until the moment when he must, after all, get his share and do his work."

[64] Biardeau, "Brāhmaṇes et potiers," pp. 38-39, and Hiltebeitel, *Ritual*, pp. 83-85, 332-34, and 355-56.

[65] Dumézil, *Stakes*, pp. 83-85, characterizes Viṣṇu as the god of civilized order and Śiva as the god of the uncivilized, the wild. On Kṛṣṇa in the MBh, see Hiltebeitel, *Ritual*; on Śiva in the MBh, see Jacques Scheuer, *Śiva dans le Mahābhārata* (Paris: Presses Universitaires de France, 1982).

allowing the forces of disruption, presided over by Śiva, to be ascendant.[66] The roles which these two.deities fulfill in the life of the universe as a whole are enacted by their earthly representatives in the MBh.

The brahmin Vyāsa and the warrior Kṛṣṇa are complementary to one another in ways which are similar to Śiva's complementarity with Nārāyaṇa. Like Śiva, Vyāsa is something of an "outsider" whose occasional dramatic interventions often have disruptive, even destructive, results. One need only recall Vyāsa's interventions in the three crises discussed above and the destructive, eventually fatal, outcomes of them. In addition, Vyāsa helped bring into the world the demonic horde of Kauravas by giving Gāndhārī the boon that she would bear 100 sons, and then acting as midwife at the delivery of the monstrous brood. By so doing, he introduced into the world of the epic a chaotic, anti-dharmic element. Moreover, Vyāsa's ascetic practices directed toward obtaining a boon from Śiva, as well as his praise of Śiva, all suggest some affinity for Śiva on the part of Vyāsa.[67] Certainly Vyāsa is never said to be Śiva's son or incarnation, nor is Vyāsa ever possessed by Śiva, as Aśvatthāman is. Nevertheless, the epic poets were aware of certain similarities between the two ascetics: "Vyāsa, surrounded by those five fine pupils at that spot in the Himālayas, resembled the Lord of Beings (Śiva) with his creatures." (XII.337.12). To reiterate, Vyāsa is by no means depicted in the MBh as Śiva's earthly representative,[68] but the cooperation between, and the complementarity of, Vyāsa and Kṛṣṇa in the MBh are in some ways comparable to the cooperation between and complementarity of Śiva and Nārāyaṇa.

The MBh depicts Vyāsa as an incarnation of Nārāyaṇa. As indicated in this chapter, however, there are suprisingly few passages in which this is said explicitly; in fact, the critical edition has only two such passages. Both of these are found in the *Nārāyaṇīya* section of the *Śānti Parvan*, which is generally regarded as one of the last sections to be incorporated into

---

[66] The crucial scenes from which Kṛṣṇa absents himself are the attempted disrobing of Draupadī and the slaughter of the sleeping warriors after the battle; see the comments by Hiltebeitel in *Ritual*, pp. 86-101, 312-16, and 332-35.

[67] On Vyāsa's asceticism, see XII.310. He encouraged Yudhiṣṭhira to chant the names of Śiva as he had done to obtain a son (XIII.18). See also Vyāsa's praise of Śiva and the recitation of the god's names and deeds in VII.172-73.

Alf Hiltebeitel has made very interesting observations on Arjuna's affinities with Śiva in recent articles; see his "Śiva, the Goddess, and the Disguises of the Pāṇḍavas and Draupadī, *HR* 20 (1980):147-74, and "The Two Kṛṣṇas on One Chariot," *HR* 24 (1984):1-26.

[68] A Śaiva *Purāṇa*, the *Liṅga* (Bombay: Veṅkaṭeśvara Press, 1906), 1.24.124 ff., identifies Vyāsa as Nārāyaṇa incarnate, but since Nārāyaṇa was considered only a form of the supreme deity Śiva, Vyāsa is said to be an *aṃśa* of Śiva! This passage, from a text composed some centuries after the MBh, is quite unusual, however.

the MBh.[69] Certainly the Hindu tradition, in the centuries after the epic's composition, has been both explicit and consistent in identifying Vyāsa as an incarnation of Nārāyaṇa.[70] Scholars who have commented on Vyāsa have also consistently interpreted him as an incarnation of Nārāyaṇa. However, that the MBh depicts Vyāsa as an incarnation of Nārāyaṇa consistently and exclusively should not be assumed on the basis of the unanimity of the *Purāṇas*. A great weight of interpretation has been made dependent on a very few citations in the MBh.

If, in fact, the idea that Vyāsa was, like Kṛṣṇa, an incarnation of Nārāyaṇa found expression in the epic only very late in the text's history, one might well wonder whether Vyāsa could be interpreted differently. As the next chapter demonstrates, there are many correspondences between Vyāsa and another deity, Brahmā, correspondences which are meaningful, appropriate and structurally integral to the epic narrative, and which are probably also earlier than the depiction of Vyāsa as Nārāyaṇa's incarnation.

---

[69] Anne-Marie Esnoul dates the *Nārāyaṇīya* in the third century A.D., describing it as among the most recent sections of the MBh, certainly composed after the *Bhagavad-Gītā*, and as contemporaneous with the *Harivaṃśa*; see her *Nārāyaṇīya Parvan du Mahābhārata* (Paris: UNESCO, 1979), p. 3. E. W. Hopkins, in *Epic Mythology*, p. 216, commented on this section that "by the end of the pseudo-epic, even Vyāsa Kṛṣṇa was ... an emanation of Nārāyaṇa ... But this is the last word of the Bhāgavatas and not early epic."

[70] *Viṣṇu Purāṇa* (Bombay: Veṅkaṭeśvara Press, 1910), 3.3-4., repeats the lines of MBh XII.334.9. See also the *Kūrma Purāṇa*, 1.51.48-50; 1.52; *Bhāgavata Purāṇa*, 1.3.21; 2.7.36; 6.8.19; *Garuḍa Purāṇa* (Bombay: Veṅkaṭeśvara Press, 1906), 1.1.29; 3.15.22 ff.; *Devībhāgavata Purāṇa* (Bombay: Veṅkaṭeśvara Press, 1918), 1.3.18-21.

CHAPTER FOUR

VYĀSA AS BRAHMĀ ON EARTH

While Vyāsa is certainly depicted in the MBh as Nārāyaṇa, or his *aṃśa*, on earth, the epic also portrays Vyāsa as corresponding in many ways to Brahmā. The fact that there are very few explicit citations in which Vyāsa is Nārāyaṇa's earthly representative, and that these are found in a comparatively recent section of the epic, suggests that there may be more to be said about the epic's depiction of Vyāsa. The various ways in which Vyāsa mediates between oppositions (between the Pāṇḍavas and Kauravas, between humanity and the gods, etc.), and the associations of Vyāsa with Nārāyaṇa and Kṛṣṇa, do not necessarily mean that Vyāsa can be seen only as an *aṃśa* of Nārāyaṇa; these actions would also be appropriate for a figure who symbolically represents Brahmā. A brief description of Brahmā in the MBh is followed by a detailed comparison of Brahmā and Vyāsa, which is based on three important characteristics they share: (1) each is a brahmin who symbolically represents brahminical orthodoxy; (2) each creates and disseminates *Veda*; and (3) each is called *pitāmaha*, "grandfather," because each is the progenitor of a family that splits into two factions which fight for sovereignty; Vyāsa is the *pitāmaha* of the Pāṇḍavas and Kauravas who fight a war often compared to the eternal war between the offspring of Brahmā, the gods and demons.

Brahmā appears in the MBh as the deity who created the world, as in the following typical verse (XII.121.55):

> Brahmā Prajāpati the Grandfather was of old the creator of all the worlds with their gods and *asuras* and *rakṣasas* and men and snakes; indeed, he is the maker of creatures.

Several Vedic gods have been seen as antecedents to Brahmā, including the gods' brahmin priest Bṛhaspati and the creator god Prajāpati.[1] How-

---

[1] On Bṛhaspati as an antecedent to Brahmā, see A. A. Macdonnell, *Vedic Mythology* (Strassburg: K. J. Trübner, 1897), pp. 101-4; Jan Gonda, *Die Religionen Indiens*, 2 vols. (Stuttgart: Kohlhammer, 1960), 1:73; and Greg Bailey, *The Mythology of Brahmā* (Delhi: Oxford University Press, 1983), pp. 76-82.

On Prajāpati as an antecedent, see Wendy O'Flaherty, *Hindu Myths* (Harmondsworth: Penguin Books, 1975), pp. 25-55, and her *Origins*, passim; Bailey, *The Mythology of Brahmā*, pp. 63-76; and the important recent work by Jan Gonda, including "The Popular Prajāpati," HR 22 (1982):129-49, and *Prajāpati's Rise to Higher Rank* (Leiden: E. J. Brill, 1986).

ever, in the MBh, Brahmā and Prajāpati are simply two names for the same deity.[2] Brahmā both creates the cosmos and preserves cosmic order in the epic. A creator who is by no means otiose, "no drowsy god sitting apart from his creation,"[3] Brahmā intervenes frequently in the activities of gods, demons, and men. For example, when the gods go to him asking for help in crises such as their recurrent battles with the demons, Brahmā typically responds with a plan for them. When an ascetic, whether a man, god, or demon, pleases Brahmā, the god grants the ascetic any boon he chooses on the condition that he discontinue his asceticism, but the consequences of the boon usually necessitate further interventions by Brahmā. This sketch of Brahmā's role in epic mythology is elaborated upon in the following analysis of specific correspondences between Brahmā and Vyāsa.

The first point of comparison between Brahmā and Vyāsa is their similar relationship to *brahman* and the brahmin class. Both are symbolic representations of *brahman* and brahmin values of the most orthodox/orthoprax type. Not only do both figures represent the brahmin in general, but in the context of Vedic ritual, both Vyāsa and Brahmā represent a specific priestly role, that of the *brahman* priest. An analysis of Brahmā's origin and meaning will lead us to a comparison with Vyāsa as the MBh depicts him.

The origin of the conception of the god Brahmā has been the subject of long scholarly debate. Uncertainty regarding the earliest citation of Brahmā is due in part to the fact that several similar and related words are difficult to differentiate. Brahmā is the conventional transliteration of the masculine noun *brahman* when it is used to refer to the god. However, the same word *brahman* may also be used to refer to a particular type of priest in Vedic rituals. Another word, the grammatically neuter noun *brahman*, has a range of meanings including "power inherent in ritual utterance and act; Vedic erudition; underlying source of existence,"[4] and the brahmin class as a whole. Moreover, the difficulty of differentiating these words is increased by the fact that in certain declensional cases the forms for neuter and masculine *brahman* coincide.[5] Brief references in some late Vedic texts, however, provide evidence that

---

[2] See, e.g., I.1.30 and I.32. Kurukṣetra is said to be the site of the *vedī* of Brahmā/Pitāmaha in III.81.177-78, and of Prajāpati in III.129.22. See also E. W. Hopkins, *Epic Mythology*, pp. 189-202.

[3] Hopkins, *Epic Mythology*, p. 193.

[4] van Buitenen, *MBh*, 1:436-37.

[5] E.g., *brahman* in the dative singular, for either the neuter or masculine, is *brahmaṇe*. The system of accentuation employed in early Vedic texts, which can help to distinguish neuter and masculine forms at times, was not used in late Vedic texts, nor in subsequent literature such as the MBh.

Brahmā was known at that time as a distinct deity comparable to the other *devas*.[6] The textual evidence indicates use of the neuter *brahman* throughout the Vedic texts, early and late, and of the masculine *brahman* as well, but only in the *Atharva Veda* and late Vedic texts is it clear that *brahman* at times refers to the god Brahmā. The assumption has usually been that the personal conception of *brahman* as a god was derived from the impersonal neuter *brahman*,[7] yet in the absence of definite evidence, it will remain an assumption.[8] Whether or not the impersonal neuter *brahman* was prior to the god Brahmā, they are two different representations of the same concept. Brahmā is the visible image of *brahman*, as Paul Mus expressed it.[9] Brahmā epitomizes *brahman* as a deity, while the brahmin epitomizes *brahman* among mankind. Both Brahmā and the brahmin possess *brahman* and are embodiments of *brahman*.

Brahmā is the brahmin among the gods; more specifically, he is a ritually active brahmin who adheres to *pravṛtti* values. According to Biardeau, Brahmā

> ... is always the god of *pravṛtti*, of activity directed toward outward endeavors (particularly sacrificial acts), as opposed to the *yogin* and to those forms of divinity which are devoted to *nivṛtti*, to the cessation of all activity due to *Sāṃkhyayoga*.[10]

Two *Śānti Parvan* sermons attributed to Vyāsa emphasize the connection between Brahmā and *pravṛtti*. In XII.327, Vyāsa says that the gods, led by Brahmā, performed sacrifices to Nārāyaṇa, who was pleased by this and spoke to them. Nārāyaṇa decreed that these gods, and the men who performed similar sacrifices according to Vedic injunctions, would receive the rewards appropriate to this religion of *pravṛtti*, i.e., heaven followed by rebirth.[11] On the other hand, *Sāṃkhyayogins* who followed the

---

[6] See references to *brahman* (masculine) which seem clearly to mean Brahmā in *Atharva Veda*, 5 vols. (Hoshiarpur: Vishveshvaranand Vedic Research Institute; 1960-64), 11.10.2 and 30; 19.22.21 and 19.23.30; see references to *pitāmaha* in 15.6.9 and 15.7.2; see *caturmukho brahmā* in Sāyaṇa's commentary on 19.9.12. See also *Śatapatha Brāhmaṇa*, 10.1.3.8; *Sāmavidhāna Brāhmaṇa*, 1.1-3; *Gopatha Brāhmaṇa*, 1.1.16; *Śaṅkhāyana Āraṇyaka* (or *Kauṣītaki Āraṇyaka*), ed. and trans. A.B. Keith (London: Royal Asiatic Society, 1908), 15; the following *Upaniṣads* are all published in S. Radhakrishnan's *The Principal Upaniṣads*: *Bṛhadāraṇyaka*, 4.4.4; *Chāndogya*, 3.10; 3.11.4; 8.15; *Aitareya*, 3.3; *Śvetāśvatara*, 5.6; 6.18; *Kauṣītakibrāhmaṇa*, 1.5; *Muṇḍaka*, 1.1.1.

[7] See p. 85 of Rudolph Roth, "Brahma und die Brāhmanen," *ZDMG* 1 (1847):66-86; Hopkins, *Epic Mythology*, p. 189; and p. 126, note 1, of Paul Thieme, "Bráhman," *ZDMG* 102 (1952):91-129.

[8] As Jan Gonda comments in *Notes on Brahman* (Utrecht: J. L. Beyers, 1950), p. 62.

[9] Paul Mus, *Barabuḍur*, 2 vols. (Hanoi: Imprimerie d'Extrême-Orient, 1935), 1:237.

[10] Biardeau, "Études" (1969):80, my translation.

[11] phalamāvṛttilakṣaṇam / XII.327.52.

religion of *nivṛtti* would attain *mokṣa* (XII.327.61-76). This passage contrasts the religion of *pravṛtti*, characterized by Vedic sacrifice and presided over by Brahmā, with the religion of *nivṛtti*, which leads to *mokṣa* and is presided over by Nārāyaṇa.

The second sermon attributed to Vyāsa (XII.336) makes a very similar point by emphasizing Nārāyaṇa-*bhakti*. Those persons who are devoted to Nārāyaṇa have the quality of purity (*sattvaguṇa*) and will attain *mokṣa* through Nārāyaṇa's grace (XII.336.61-70). But those whose natures are composed of *rajas* (passion) and/or *tamas* (darkness) and follow the path of *pravṛtti*, Nārāyaṇa does not look upon kindly (XII.336.71). "Brahmā the Grandfather of the World watches over that human who is completely overwhelmed by *rajas* and *tamas*" (XII.336.72). Again in this passage, Brahmā presides over the path of *pravṛtti* with its sacrificial activity leading to the temporary reward of heaven and the inevitable rebirth, with which is contrasted devotion to Nārāyaṇa which is said to lead to *mokṣa* and the permanent end of rebirth.

As these passages reveal, Brahmā is representative of the *pravṛtti* mode of religion as opposed to *nivṛtti*, and dharma as opposed to *mokṣa*. So strongly is Brahmā identified with the round of rebirth (*saṃsāra*) rather than release from rebirth (*mokṣa*) that the duration of the world's existence is conceived as coinciding with the life of Brahmā. The end of a day in the life of Brahmā is the end of the world, its reabsorption (*pralaya*) preparatory to its recreation in the next day of Brahmā.[12]

Vyāsa is also identified strongly with *pravṛtti* and dharma rather than *nivṛtti* and *mokṣa*. Vyāsa did not seek to attain *mokṣa*; in fact, the attainment of *mokṣa* by his son Śuka troubled Vyāsa. Overcome with grief at the loss of his son, and with shame for his own loss of equanimity, Vyāsa was consoled by Śiva, but he neither received *mokṣa* as a boon from Śiva, nor did he attempt to attain *mokṣa* through his own efforts (XII.320). As Nārāyaṇa said of Vyāsa at his creation, although he would be yoked to *tapas*, and though his son would be free from passion (*rāga*), Vyāsa himself would not be (XII.337.43-46). Vyāsa's reason for being was the dissemination of the *Vedas* in each creation, which necessitated his repeated rebirth.[13] Since Vyāsa was not a *saṃnyāsin* striving for *mokṣa*, he could be summoned to father children for the Bhārata dynasty, serve as priest for the Pāṇḍavas' royal rituals, and be the guru for the entire Bhārata family. Vyāsa's activities in the epic reveal a consistent concern for dharma, and epitomize *pravṛtti* values.

---

[12] E.g., III.186.16-24.

[13] This theme from XII.337 is elaborated upon in the *Purāṇas*, in which the Vyāsa of each *manvantara* is named; see, e.g., *Viṣṇu*, 3.3; *Kūrma* 1.52; *Liṅga* 1.7; 1.24; and *Vāyu Purāṇa* (Bombay: Veṅkaṭeśvara Press, 1895), 1.23.109 ff.

While both Vyāsa and Brahmā represent ideals of brahminical orthodoxy, an even more specific correspondence can be adduced in the context of sacrificial ritual: both perform the role of *brahman* priest. Vyāsa is the *brahman* at Yudhiṣṭhira's Rājasūya, presiding over that ritual which ended so disastrously for the Pāṇḍavas. Brahmā is also depicted as a *brahman* priest at various sacrifices. For example, a myth in which Soma is installed as king features Brahmā as *brahman* priest,[14] and a version of the myth of Dakṣa's sacrifice has Brahmā as *brahman* priest.[15] Since in Sanskrit one word refers to both Brahmā and the *brahman* priest, he is a particularly appropriate choice for that role. Moreover, the ritual role of the *brahman* priest is functionally congruent with the role of Brahmā in Hindu mythology. The priest sits off to the side, observing the ritual, but in the event that something goes wrong, this master of the four *Vedas* would intervene decisively to set it right. In Hindu mythology, the *Veda* master Brahmā is equally aloof, yet observant, and intervenes when needed or asked to do so. Given the linguistic and functional link between the two, it is not unreasonable to suggest that the *brahman* priest is, in addition to Prajāpati, Tvaṣṭṛ, Bṛhaspati, and Puruṣa, another Vedic antecedent of the figure Brahmā. In any case, Brahmā and Vyāsa are both depicted as aloof, detached brahmins who occasionally and dramatically intervene in the action. Thus, it is quite appropriate that both are at times cast in the role of the *brahman* priest.

Vyāsa and Brahmā are symbolic representations of the same brahminical ideals. Both are depicted as brahmins who adhere to *pravṛtti* values. It comes as no surprise, therefore, to find both of them presiding at weddings; Brahmā at Śiva's[16] and Vyāsa at the Pāṇḍavas' wedding (I.189). Both figures represent the dharma-oriented brahmin, Brahmā among the gods and Vyāsa among mankind.

As brahmins, Vyāsa and Brahmā embody and epitomize *brahman*, but the similarity between the two figures is particularly clear with regard to *brahman* in the form of speech, i.e., the *Vedas*. Just as Brahmā created the world, according to the MBh, he also created the *Vedas*; indeed, for each new creation, Brahmā recreates the *Vedas*. Brahmā is said to have created the *Vedas* and their ancillary texts, the sacrifices, etc. (XII.327.30-32). In another passage (XII.181.1-5), Brahmā Prajāpati creates the *Veda* and then the world. First he created some brahmins, then various principles (*satya*, *dharma*, tapas), and the eternal *Veda*. Only then did Brahmā create

---

[14] *Vāyu Purāṇa*, 2.28.1-47.

[15] *Śiva Purāṇa* (Bombay: Veṅkaṭeśvara Press, 1906), 2:2.27. See the end of this chapter for discussion of Brahmā's role in MBh versions of this myth.

[16] *Śiva Purāṇa*, 2.2.20.32.

the gods and demons, mankind, and the world. For the most part, Brahmā is the source of the *Vedas* in the epic.

Brahmā is often described as having four faces, one turned in each direction, symbolic of his omniscience. Brahmā's four faces are associated with the four *Vedas*; he is described as "the One of the four *Vedas*, the four forms, the four faces (or mouths)."[17] The four-faced Brahmā created the four *Vedas* as well as the world (XII.335.18-25). Brahmā's creation of the four *Vedas* at the beginning of each world-cycle is often described in the *Purāṇas*,[18] where each mouth produces one *Veda, Ṛg Veda* from the eastern mouth, etc. The myth of Brahmā's creation of the four *Vedas* is a continuation of the mythology of his Vedic antecedents. In late Vedic texts, Prajāpati is often credited with creation of the three *Vedas* as well as the world.[19] That only three *Vedas* were created indicates that the *Atharva Veda* had not been accepted as part of the Vedic collection by those composing these texts. The first chapter of the *dharmaśāstra* of Manu includes verses similar to these late Vedic citations, but in *Manu* the creation of the triple *Veda* is attributed to Puruṣa Brahmā,[20] indicating the identification with Brahmā of the mythology about the *Vedas*. The only statement within these three *Vedas* on the divine creation of the whole *Veda* is in the *Puruṣa-sūkta*, wherein the *Vedas* were created by the sacrifice of *Puruṣa*.

> From that sacrifice in which everything was offered, the verses and chants were born, from it the meters were born, and from it the formulas were born.[21]

Puruṣa, described in this hymn's first verse as having 1,000 heads and 1,000 eyes, is a precursor of the later figure Brahmā, whose four heads symbolize the same idea of omniscience. Prajāpati and Puruṣa of the late Vedic period subsequently came to be identified with Brahmā, and much of their mythology also came to be associated with Brahmā, particularly the theme of *Veda*-creation.[22]

---

[17] III.194.12. Brahmā is again *caturmukha* at III.275.17. Cf. *caturvaktra*, "who has four mouths" (XII.330.56).

[18] *Kūrma Purāṇa*, 1.7.55 ff; *Viṣṇu Purāṇa*, 1.5.52 ff; *Bhāgavata Purāṇa*, 3.12.34-37; *Matsya Purāṇa* (Poona: Ānandāśrama Press, 1907), 1.28 ff; 3.1-6; *Mārkaṇḍeya Purāṇa* (Bombay: Veṅkaṭeśvara Press, 1910), 48.31 ff; 102.1-7.

[19] *Śatapatha Brāhmaṇa* 11.5.8; 6.1.1.8-10, where he is called Puruṣa Prajāpati; *Aitareya Brāhmaṇa*, ed. K. S. Āgāśe, 2 vols. (Poona: Ānandāśrama Press, 1896), 5.32-34; *Chāndogya Upaniṣad*, 4.17.

[20] *Manu*, 1.11; 1.21-23; cf. 2.76-77.

[21] tásmād yajñā́t sarvahúta ŕ̥caḥ sā́māni jajñire /
chándāṃsi jajñire tásmād yájus tásmād ajāyata //
Ṛg Veda 10.90.9. "Meters" (*chándāṃsi*) refers to the *gāyatrī* and other metric patterns, while *ŕ̥caḥ* is the *Ṛg Veda, sā́māni* the *Sāma Veda,* and *yájus* the *Yajur Veda.*

[22] Brahmā is the source of the four caste groups in the MBh (XII.73.3-8), just as is Puruṣa in *Ṛg Veda* 10.90.

Brahmā is also the guardian of the *Veda*, ever interested in disseminating it among men. At the end of the world-cycle when the *Vedas* disappear, the seers regain the *Vedas* through the assistance of Svayaṃbhū Brahmā (XII.203.17). In another passage (XII.335.18-67), Brahmā was interrupted in the act of creation, and the *Vedas* were stolen from him by two demons. Brahmā appealed to Nārāyaṇa for aid, asking how his otherwise excellent creation could possibly function without the *Vedas*. He devotedly praised Nārāyaṇa, who recovered the *Vedas* for Brahmā, thus allowing creation to proceed. Since the world could not function without the *Veda*, Brahmā must keep the *Veda* intact and in the possession of the brahmins to preserve the world. Thus, in the MBh, the four-faced Brahmā is often depicted as having created the *Veda* and as being its guardian and disseminator among mankind.

In the epic, Vyāsa performs among humans the role that Brahmā performs in mythology. Kṛṣṇa Dvaipāyana's name Vyāsa was given him for his deed of dividing the *Veda*.

> Recognizing that in each successive age the dharma loses one foot, and that mankind's life and power correspond to the age, and wanting to show his grace to the *brahman* and brahmins, he divided the *Vedas*, and is therefore remembered as "Vyāsa."[23]

As another epic passage says of Vyāsa, "The famous sage learned the *Vedas* with their ancillary texts, as well as the histories ... He was the greatest of the scholars of the *Veda*, and divided the one *Veda* into four" (I.54.3-5). Vyāsa then transmitted these texts to the rest of mankind through his brahmin pupils.[24] In view of the imminent onset of *Kaliyuga*, Vyāsa rearranged the *Veda* to make it easier for mortals to learn and retain the text. Thus, at the beginning of the *yuga*, Vyāsa disseminated among mankind the four *Vedas* which he had arranged, an obvious parallel to the myth of Brahmā creating the four *Vedas* at the beginning of creation, one *Veda* from each of his heads.

In a further parallel to the mythology of Brahmā, Vyāsa also creates *Veda*, namely, the "fifth *Veda*," the MBh. The epic says that Vyāsa "taught the *Vedas* and the MBh as the fifth *Veda*."[25] In its opening chapter, the epic describes itself as "... the Collection of Vyāsa the wonder-worker, a dharmic collection that removes the danger of evil and is combined with the four *Vedas*" (I.1.19). The MBh is "the *Veda* of Kṛṣṇa,"[26] i.e., Kṛṣṇa Dvaipāyana Vyāsa's *Veda*; "in this work, Kṛṣṇa

---

[23] I.57.72-73; cf. I.1.52 and I.99.14.

[24] See, e.g., I.57.74-75 and XII.314-15.

[25] I.57.74; cf. XII.327.18.

[26] *kārṣṇaṃ vedam* / I.1.205 and I.56.17; cf. notes to XVIII.5.52.

Dvaipāyana has uttered a holy *Upaniṣad*" (I.1.191). The epic not only associates itself with the *Vedas*, but also presents itself as their equal in efficacy, saying that the MBh is "a supreme means of purification equal to the *Vedas*" (I.56.15). At times the MBh even insists upon its superiority: "A brahmin who knows the four *Vedas* with their ancillary texts and *Upaniṣads*, but who does not know this epic, has no learning at all" (I.2.235). A similar attitude lies behind the following tale (I.1.208-9), which is revealing despite its false etymology:

> Once the divine *ṛṣis* gathered and on a balance they placed the four *Vedas* in one scale and the *Bhārata* in the other scale, and both in size and weight it was the greater. Therefore, because of its size (*mahat*) and its weight (*bhāra*) it is called the *Mahābhārata*; he who knows this etymology is freed from all sins.

The MBh is Vyāsa's *Veda*, and he is often said to be the *ṛṣi* who revealed it to humanity.[27] As the epic's creator, Vyāsa is the source of this "fifth *Veda*," newly created for the new age, and he is depicted in it supervising the dissemination of this new *Veda* through his students.

The idea that there was a fifth *Veda* is not unique to the MBh. The *Chāndogya Upaniṣad* suggests that the *itihāsa-purāṇa* literature was the fifth *Veda*,[28] but does not refer to Vyāsa as the composer of it. Similarly, the *Arthaśāstra* says that there are five *Vedas*, of which the fifth is *itihāsaveda*.[29] The *Nāṭyaśāstra* refers to itself as the fifth *Veda*, created by Brahmā.[30] Generally, these fifth *Vedas* are regarded as creations of Brahmā or Vyāsa.

The similarity which Brahmā and Vyāsa have in their relationships to the *Vedas* is reflected in certain continuities in the myths about the *Vedas* which are associated with each of them. For example, there is a very old myth in which humanity and the *Vedas* were threatened with destruction but were saved from the flood by the timely intervention of a deity in the form of a huge fish (*matsya*). This myth is found in the MBh with Brahmā as the fish (III.185). Manu and the seven seers, representing humanity and the *Vedas*, were saved by the warning and assistance of *matsya*, who then revealed himself to be Brahmā. While Vyāsa is certainly never depicted as a fish, there are several ways in which the *matsya* theme, which the epic identifies with Brahmā, recurs in the story of Vyāsa. Brahmā cursed a celestial nymph to become a fish; doing so, she then

---

[27] As in I.2.95-231. See also Chapter 2, section (1) on Vyāsa as a *ṛṣi*.

[28] *Chāndogya Upaniṣad*, 7.1, 7.2, and 7.7 all list the three *Vedas, Atharvan* as the fourth, and *itihāsa-purāṇa* as the fifth, implying that it is the fifth *Veda*.

[29] *Arthaśāstra*, 1.3.1-2.

[30] *Nāṭyaśāstra*, ed. Manomohan Ghosh, 2 vols. (Calcutta: Manisha Granthalaya, 1967), 1.4-20.

gave birth miraculously to a boy and a girl.[31] The girl was known as Matsyagandhā because of her fishy odor, but when she grew up she met a sage named Parāśara who took away her odor and gave her a son, Kṛṣṇa Dvaipāyana Vyāsa. Vyāsa was conceived and born from this *matsya*-woman in the middle of the Yamunā River, and he eventually preserved the *Vedas* through the destructive period of transition to the new age. Incidentally, the boy, Matsyagandhā's brother, became Virāṭa, ruler of the Matsya kingdom, the capital of which was named Upaplavya ("to be flooded"), again recalling the myth of the flood and the divine fish. A second epic myth involving the *Vedas* associates Vyāsa with Brahmā. Immediately after creating Brahmā, Nārāyaṇa created from his speech a seer named Sārasvata who would later divide the *Vedas* and become known as Vyāsa (XII.337). Sārasvata means "son of Sarasvatī," a goddess who is the mind-born daughter and wife of Brahmā in the *Purāṇas*.[32] In calling Vyāsa "Sārasvata," the epic is associating Vyāsa with Brahmā. In fact, in this same chapter, Vyāsa is called "the sixth great seer from Grandfather" and a descendant of Vasiṣṭha "the mind-born son of the Grandfather," both of which references depict Vyāsa as a descendant of Brahmā. Clearly, the epic poets felt that it was appropriate to associate Vyāsa with Brahmā in various ways and to emphasize correlations between the two figures.

Vyāsa and Brahmā both epitomize the function of guru. Brahmā is often described as the Guru of the World (*lokaguru*) for having created the *Vedas* and other texts.[33] In the MBh, Vyāsa is the foremost guru, both for brahmins and for Bhārata warriors.[34] Both are depicted as omniscient, Brahmā with his four heads and Vyāsa with his divine eye both having unrestricted vision.[35] These two figures are credited with the creation and dissemination of much of the sacred literature of the Hindu tradition. Vyāsa's role as guru for most of the major characters in the epic parallels Brahmā's role as Guru of the World.

The third major motif of Brahmā's mythology with which the epic story of Vyāsa corresponds is the role of grandfather. In the MBh, Brahmā is the Grandfather of the World (*lokapitāmaha*), the Grandfather

---

[31] See chapter 2 for a translation of this story from I.57.

[32] The MBh also knows another brahmin named Sārasvata. He survived a terrible famine only by eating fish (*matsya* again) from the Sarasvatī River, and having become the last surviving master of the *Veda*, taught again the lost *Vedas*; see IX.50 and III.83.43-51. This Sārasvata and Vyāsa are paired as the two masters of the *Veda* in one verse (1.42) of the *Buddhacarita*.

[33] As in III.186.6; III.194.11; XII.327.46; *Ādi Parvan* Appendix I, No. 1, Line 4. He is the Guru of the Gods as well, as in I.1.30.

[34] See Chapter 2, section (4) for details.

[35] See Chapter 2, sections (1) and (3) for details.

of both the gods and demons who are eternally contending with each other. Vyāsa is also a grandfather, his royal sons having produced the Pāṇḍavas and Kauravas who contend for sovereignty throughout the epic. Brahmā and Vyāsa have structurally parallel relationships with their contentious grandsons. Thus, it is both appropriate and meaningful that the appellation *pitāmaha* is shared by these two grandfathers, the one divine, the other human.

The war between the gods and demons is a frequent topic of Vedic literature; indeed, from the *Vedas* on, it has been the central myth of Indian civilization.[36] As such, it has appeared in many different forms through the millenia, the one constant in the many renditions of the myth being the opposition of the two groups to each other. The gods and demons have similar powers and origins; they are "consubstantial"[37] and "consanguine."[38] Despite their brotherhood, they are constantly in conflict.

In the *Brāhmaṇa* literature, Brahmā's Vedic antecedent Prajāpati is the progenitor of the gods and demons. Many of the tellings of the myth set the scene with a statement such as the following: "The gods and demons, both born of Prajāpati, once contended for sovereignty," with each version then developing differently from that typical starting point.[39] The *Upaniṣads* also refer to the conflict between Prajāpati's offspring, the gods and demons.[40] In the Vedic literature generally, and in the *Brāhmaṇas* particularly, the gods win their battles with the demons by means of the sacrifice, and win possession of the sacrifice, because Prajāpati gives them knowledge.

In the MBh and *Purāṇas*, as has been indicated above, Prajāpati had evolved into Brahmā Prajāpati. Since asceticism had, to some extent, begun to replace the Vedic sacrifice as the focus of religious interest in India, the myth of the struggle between the gods and demons, as told there, reflects this shift. The MBh and *Purāṇas* often depict the gods and demons combatting each other by means of *tapas*, the gods winning because eventually Brahmā limits the *tapas* of the demons. Typically,

---

[36] Jan Gonda, *Aspects of Early Viṣṇuism*, 2d ed. (Delhi: Motilal Banarsidass, 1969), p. 162.

[37] Ananda Coomaraswamy, "Angels and Titans, an Essay on Vedic Ontology," *JAOS* 55 (1935):373-419.

[38] O'Flaherty, *Evil*, pp. 57-62; the entire chapter concerns gods, demons, and men in Indian myths.

[39] From a single text, the *Śatapatha Brāhmaṇa*, six such tales, beginning with the verse cited, may be compared: 1.2.4.1; 1.2.5.1; 1.5.3.2; 1.7.2.22; 2.4.3.2; 5.1.1.1.

[40] See, e.g., *Bṛhadāraṇyaka Upaniṣad*, 1.3, and *Chāndogya Upaniṣad*, 1.2. Such verses have traditionally been interpreted as referring to a struggle within an individual, the "gods" representing such sense-organs as are illuminated by sacred teachings, while the "demons" represent those inclined toward sensuality.

Brahmā persuades the demons to desist from asceticism for a boon which, although it seems good, has a loophole allowing the gods to win. Thus, in the epic and Purāṇic myths of the war between the gods and demons, Brahmā's role is a direct development from Prajāpati's role in Vedic texts.

The war between the gods and demons is certainly the central myth of the MBh. Very often the struggle between the Pāṇḍavas and Kauravas for sovereignty over the Bhārata kingdom is compared to the war between the gods and demons.[41] In fact, the Bhārata war is repeatedly referred to as a "sacrifice of battle" (e.g., V.139), an extended metaphor relating the Bhārata war to the myth of the war between the gods and demons. Thus, the site of the Bhārata war, Kurukṣetra, is considered Brahmā's *vedī*, the sacrificial altar.[42] The Pāṇḍavas are said to be sons of gods, or gods incarnate, while the Kauravas are said to be demons incarnate.[43] Divine or demonic identities have been specified for many of the epic characters, indicating that the epic poets were conscious of correspondences and continuities between their characters and certain divine or demonic beings, and emphasized this in their text. For example, Vyāsa is depicted advising Yudhiṣṭhira after the war, telling him the divine precedent which exonerates him, and showing the epic's audience the continuity between the divine and human beings.

> ... There was of old a battle between the gods and demons—the demons were the elder brothers, and the gods the younger. Among those desiring prosperity there arose a great battle that was 32,000 years long. Then the gods, making the earth an ocean of blood, killed the demons and seized the three heavens ... If by killing one the rest of the family may be saved, or by killing a family the nation may be saved, that course of action is no transgression. For dharma sometimes has the form of *adharma*, O king, and *adharma* the form of dharma—that is known by the wise. Therefore, Pāṇḍava, fear not. You are learned; you have followed the way travelled by the gods previously, O Bhārata.[44]

Vyāsa could not be more clear than this in stating that the Pāṇḍavas are conforming to the dharma established by the gods.

Recent interpretations of the MBh have centered on the meaning of the incarnation theme. Stig Wikander has shown that the five Pāṇḍava brothers, who are said to be the sons of deities in the epic, also represent symbolically, through their hierarchical arrangement, the ideal of the

---

[41] E.g., III.92 and VI.20.5.

[42] III.81.177-78 and III.129.22.

[43] See I.57.76-I.61; XI.8; XV.39. Most of XI.8 is translated in the Appendix. See also the discussions below and in Chapter 3.

[44] XII.34.13-21.

properly ordered society: Yudhiṣṭhira represents the brahmin class, Bhīma and Arjuna the *kṣatriya*, and the twins the *vaiśya*.[45] George Dumézil has promulgated and expanded upon Wikander's original insight, describing the incarnations as "transpositions" of the Vedic gods into epic characters.[46] Alf Hiltebeitel, while agreeing with Dumézil's view that the MBh contains material transposed from myth, has objected to his use of the term "transposition" to describe the process of epic composition because the word conveys an overly mechanical sense.[47] In his view, the epic poets perceived "connections" or "correspondences" between two dynamic, evolving traditions, the epic they were composing and the Hindu heritage of mythology. Accordingly, they composed the MBh emphasizing the continuities they had perceived. These seers also perceived correspondences between the epic and Vedic rituals, and made them part of the epic as well. The epic poets' perceptions of correspondences between epic characters and Vedic gods have resulted in the identification of almost every major character with a figure from earlier mythology.

Strikingly absent from the list of Vedic deties whose "transpositions" appear in the epic, however, is Prajāpati, certainly one of the major deities of the later Vedic period. No son or incarnation of Prajāpati appears in any of the MBh's lists of the *aṃśas* who descended to the earth. Nor has any scholar suggested any such correspondence between an epic character and Prajāpati. The same may also be said regarding Prajāpati's later counterpart Brahmā. As will be demonstrated below, however, Vyāsa is the epic character having the greatest degree of correspondence with Brahmā Prajāpati, and should therefore be regarded as that deity's "transposition" in the MBh.

The correspondence between the divine Brahmā and the *ṛṣi* Vyāsa is particularly clear with regard to the use of the appellation *pitāmaha* (grandfather) to refer to both of them, and with regard to the role each has as the grandfather of the family. The epic's evidence on these two grandfathers will be presented, first Brahmā and then Vyāsa. A specific

---

[45] See Stig Wikander, "Pāṇḍava-sagan och Mahābhāratas mytiska förutsättningar."

[46] See Georges Dumézil, *Mythe et épopée*, vols. 1 and 2. The most problematic figures in the Wikander-Dumézil interpretation are Pāṇḍu (= Varuṇa's transposition), Dhṛtarāṣṭra (= Bhaga), and Yudhiṣṭhira (= Mitra). The problem with the latter is that the Vedic antecedent for Dharma is not clearly Mitra. As for the former two transpositions, there is little evidence on Pāṇḍu, and Dhṛtarāṣṭra = Bhaga is based primarily on their mutual blindness. Gösta Johnsen maintained that Dhṛtarāṣṭra = Varuṇa; see his "Varuṇa and Dhṛtarāṣṭra," *Indo-Iranian Journal* 9 (1965-66):245-65. Dumézil responds in *Mythe et épopée*, 1:170-75.

[47] Hiltebeitel, *Ritual*, pp. 358-60 especially.

correspondence between Brahmā's role in a myth and Vyāsa's role in an epic event will then be cited.

The MBh contains a summary of the *Rāmāyaṇa* story (III.257-76), in which many of the salient themes of Brahmā's mythology are evident. A synopsis of part of it will serve to introduce this section on Grandfather Brahmā. Once, five demon brothers resolved to perform asceticism, and with their feats of *tapas* pleased Brahmā, who came to them with the offer of a boon for the cessation of their asceticism (III.259.15-40). Rāvaṇa chose never to be defeated by any kind of being, but because he thought so little of humans, he omitted them from his request. Brahmā granted him this boon, and the demon became irresistible. The gods sought refuge with Brahmā, asking to be saved from this invincible demon (III.260). Grandfather Brahmā told the gods that Viṣṇu had descended to earth taking human form to subdue the demon, and that they should all send down to earth portions of themselves to assist him. As a result of Brahmā's plan, eventually the demon, whose grandfather (*pitāmaha*) was Prajāpati Svayaṃbhū (III.258.11), was defeated. This myth shows Brahmā as the grandfather of both the gods and demons, deflecting the demons from their threatening course of action by granting a boon, but by means of his knowledge assisting the gods to circumvent that boon.

The preceding myth is obviously parallel to the MBh's myth of Brahmā's plan to defeat the demons. Earth, overrun by demons, approached Brahmā, who already knew her request. He instructed the gods to send portions of themselves to Earth (I.58-59). Another version of this myth depicts Earth saying to the gods, "What shall be done for me has been promised by you all previously in Brahmā's abode. Let it be done quickly!"[48] Both versions emphasize Brahmā's role as refuge for the oppressed, as the god to whom one appeals for a boon, and as the formulator of the divine plan by which Earth is delivered from demonic oppression.

Another myth which is part of the corpus on the struggle between the gods and demons is the story of the churning for the Elixir of Immortality (*amṛta*). It has a marked similarity to the myths cited above, and also features Brahmā in a similar role. One version of this often-told myth is in the epic's first book (I.15-17). The gods and demons churned the ocean to produce the Elixir, but without success. The gods then spoke to Brahmā, the granter of boons, who had remained seated, and asked for aid (I.16.27-30). Brahmā asked Nārāyaṇa to give them strength, and they then succeeded in producing the Elixir. The demons tried to take it all for themselves and the gods battled them, routing the demons and

[48] XI.8; see the translation in the Appendix.

winning the Elixir of Immortality (I.17). Again, Brahmā is depicted as the foremost boon-giver, seated to the side of the action, to whom the gods go for assistance.

In these epic myths, Brahmā often gives boons to demons. The story of Dhundhu is typical (III.193-95). Dhundhu the demon performed great *tapas*, standing on one foot, so emaciated that he was held together only by his veins. Brahmā was pleased by his *tapas* and gave him a boon. The demon, like Rāvaṇa, chose to be invincible to all kinds of beings, but he neglected to mention man. Grandfather granted his request, and Dhundhu soon made himself a nuisance. The gods found a man capable of the task, reinforced him with Nārāyaṇa's *tejas*, and he killed Dhundhu with his Brahmā-weapon. In this case as in so many others, Brahmā's boon has the effect of rendering the demon vulnerable. Brahmā also grants boons to non-demons, as he did to Śeṣa for his awesome *tapas* (I.32). Brahmā's boon-granting is such a well developed pattern that it was used as a plot device in the epic. For example, Brahmā gave Jarāsaṃdha the boon that he would not be killed by Kṛṣṇa (II.20.33-34), so that task had to be performed by Bhīma. Because of his propensity for giving boons, Brahmā is kept busy preserving the world from the consequences of his actions.

Any reference to Brahmā in the MBh, even the briefest, is likely to employ the word *pitāmaha*, which emphasizes his role as world-creator and benevolent preserver. The epic introduces him to the audience with the following line: "From it (the Cosmic Egg) was born the Grandfather, the Sole Lord Prajāpati, known as Brahmā, Guru of the Gods," etc.[49] One chapter (I.32), in twenty-five verses, refers to him as *pitāmaha* five times, Prajāpati twice, and Brahmā once. The name *pitāmaha* is identified so strongly with Brahmā that this chapter uses it exclusively several times before using any other name for him, but there is no doubt to whom *pitāmaha* refers.[50] A variant of this epithet is *lokapitāmaha*, Grandfather of the World, which occurs frequently.[51] Other related variants include *sarvalokapitāmaha*, Grandfather of All the Worlds,[52] and *sarvabhūtapitāmaha*, Grandfather of All Creatures.[53] Use of *pitāmaha* to refer to Brahmā would remind the epic's audience of his role as progenitor of both gods and demons, as well as mankind. In accord with his benevolent supervisory function, Brahmā formulates the plan to restore the dharma

---

[49] yasmāt pitāmaho jajñe prabhur ekaḥ prajāpatiḥ /
brahmā suraguruḥ sthāṇur manuḥ kaḥ parameṣṭhyatha // I.1.30.

[50] See also I.6.5; I.7.23; II.11.5 and 31 and 46; III.275.17; XII.337.4 and 47-49.

[51] E.g., I.6.7; II.11.13 and 37; XII.327.30.

[52] I.6.5; III.193.20; XII.327.46.

[53] I.58.37; XII.200.13.

to its proper balance by means of the incarnation of the gods on earth to subdue the demons.

The MBh also uses the word *pitāmaha* in reference to Vyāsa, sometimes in ways suggestive of a correspondence with Pitāmaha Brahmā.[54] Vyāsa is, in fact, the grandfather of the Pāṇḍavas and Kauravas, having fathered Pāṇḍu and Dhṛtarāṣṭra to save the dynasty from the imminent disaster of having no heir to the throne (I.99-100). When he later advises the Pāṇḍavas, he is appropriately called their *pitāmaha.*[55] Yudhiṣṭhira addresses Vyāsa as *pitāmaha* in their discussions,[56] and the Pāṇḍavas are Vyāsa's grandsons.[57] Particularly suggestive of the divine Pitāmaha, progenitor of the gods and demons, are those references to Vyāsa as the grandfather of both the Pāṇḍavas and Kauravas.[58] Similarly, he is described as "the grandfather of the Bhāratas,"[59] or "grandfather of the Kurus."[60]

There is a second *pitāmaha* in the Bhārata family, though. Kauravas and Pāṇḍavas alike respectfully address Bhīṣma as "grandfather,"[61] and the fact that he is the Bhārata family patriarch is often cited.[62] This is not due to confusion or carelessness on the part of the epic poets. In fact, Vyāsa the brahmin and Bhīṣma the *kṣatriya* are in many ways mirror-images of each other, and were surely intended to be regarded as complementary figures. King Śaṃtanu's extramarital son Bhīṣma is paralleled by Vyāsa, the extramarital son of Śaṃtanu's wife Satyavatī. Bhīṣma was the son of the Gaṅgā River goddess in human form, while Vyāsa was "Dvaipāyana," not exactly the son of the Yamunā River but born on an island in the Yamunā of a woman who was herself Yamunā-born. These two river-born sons, one on either parent's side of the family, remained unmarried but were vigilant guardians of their family's fortunes. Bhīṣma won the hands of two women to be the wives of his younger half-brother, but when they were left widowed and childless, a family member was needed to produce an heir. Because Bhīṣma had vowed celibacy, Vyāsa was summoned to substitute for Bhīṣma. Upon

[54] Another epic character, Bhīṣma, is also called *pitāmaha* at times; see below for discussion of his relationship to Vyāsa.

[55] I.54.2; I.144.5; I.157.16.

[56] E.g., XII.33.2-3 and 12.

[57] *pautrān* / III.245.11.

[58] E.g., VI.4.13.

[59] E.g., VI.2.2 and X.14.12.

[60] *kurūṇāṃ prapitāmahaḥ* / VI.2.15. Literally, "great-grandfather of the Kurus," but since he would be the great-grandfather of the sons of the Pāṇḍavas and Kauravas (Abhimanyu et al.), this is not inaccurate. This chapter, VI.2, is using "Bhāratas" and "Kurus" synonymously.

[61] V.23.8; XIII.152-54.

[62] VI.14.3; XII.38.6.

the birth of the Bhārata princes, Vyāsa disappeared, returning only occasionally, while Bhīṣma remained at court, substituting for Vyāsa in the role of father. Bhīṣma, the omnipresent family man, is a celibate ascetic in a social setting, while Vyāsa, though a father, is anything but a family man, and is an ascetic of a more solitary inclination. Both Vyāsa and Bhīṣma are called the father of Dhṛtarāṣṭra,[63] and both are called "Grandfather" by Yudhiṣṭhira (III.30.45-46). The fact that the Bhārata family has these parallel patriarchs cannot be accidental. The composers of the MBh delighted in genealogy, and intentionally structured the epic this way. The complementarity of this pair of *pitāmahas* is meaningful, and deserves further consideration. Bhīṣma's "several similarities" to Brahmā have been briefly noted,[64] but Vyāsa's more significant correspondence to Brahmā has gone unnoticed. Greg Bailey has observed that Bhīṣma and Brahmā share the appellation *pitāmaha*, are impartial (*madhyastha*) in the conflicts between the Pāṇḍavas/gods and the Kauravas/demons, and that both "are great teachers of dharma." This insight certainly reveals deeper meaning in the relationship between Bhīṣma and the Bhāratas, particularly the impassioned plea of Vidura, third son of Vyāsa at the Bhārata court, to his "father" Bhīṣma.

> After creating Dhṛtarāṣṭra and me, O brilliant sir, like a painter creates a painting, do not destroy us now, as Prajāpati, creating creatures, then destroys them.[65]

But Bhīṣma's correspondence with Brahmā Prajāpati is not as strong as this simile and Bailey's note might indicate. For the epic poets, Bhīṣma was an incarnation of Dyaus Pitṛ,[66] not Brahmā; just as these two deities are somewhat similar, so also are Bhīṣma and Vyāsa. With regard to Vyāsa, he too is a great exponent and teacher of dharma; he is the grandfather of the Bhāratas, and hence is called *pitāmaha*. Like Bhīṣma, Vyāsa too has declared that the Pāṇḍavas and Kauravas are "equal before me."[67] Vyāsa and Bhīṣma are similar in these respects, and, to some extent, both are similar to Brahmā; Vyāsa corresponds much more closely, however.

Vyāsa's relations with the Pāṇḍavas and Kauravas demonstrate particularly well his correspondence to Pitāmaha Brahmā. The Pāṇḍavas and Kauravas had developed considerable personal animosity for each other through a lifetime of insults and injuries. Their rivalry was political

---

[63] Compare VI.3.44 and VI.16.7 with VI.17.7.

[64] Bailey, *The Mythology of Brahmā*, p. 123, note 40.

[65] V.146.22.

[66] I.93 tells how Dyaus came to be born as Bhīṣma. Dyaus Pitṛ is cognate with Greek Zeus and Latin Jupiter.

[67] samāste caiva me sarve yūyāṃ ... / I 144.9.

as well as personal; both sets of cousins thought that the legitimate right to rule the kingdom was theirs. When both sides chose a military solution to their conflict, Bhīṣma took up arms and fought for the Kauravas because they had been his support for a dozen years. He even bemoaned his dependence on Kaurava wealth, as did Droṇa, Kṛpa, and Śalya (VI.41.30-83), but this does not alter the fact that Bhīṣma and the others fought against dharma. So much for Bhīṣma's impartiality. Vyāsa, though, remained neutral and counselled peace repeatedly, even advocating reconciliation after hostilities erupted. In this regard as well, Vyāsa corresponds to Brahmā more closely than does Bhīṣma.

Vyāsa gave boons to both the Pāṇḍavas and Kauravas in the epic, and in so doing, parallels Brahmā's granting of boons to gods and demons alike. Vyāsa is the Pitāmaha Prajāpati of the Bhāratas, procreating Pāṇḍu and Dhṛtarāṣṭra, creating, even delivering, the Kauravas, and performing the role of guru of all the Bhāratas. Vyāsa's boon to Queen Gāndhārī that she would have 100 sons resulted in the birth of the demonic Kauravas (I.107), a birth that required Vyāsa's further assistance in midwifery. This belligerent horde was Vyāsa's creation, inevitably reminding one of Prajāpati Brahmā's creation of the demons. In light of Vyāsa's correspondence to Brahmā, perhaps his supervision of the disastrous Rājasūya rite could be construed as a boon to the Kauravas; certainly it had the effect of strengthening them against their rivals, at least temporarily. Vyāsa, impartial in this family feud, made clear the meaning of his neutrality in these words:

> Both yourselves and they are equal before me, certainly, but relations love those who are young and suffering. Consequently, my love for you is stronger now, and because of that love I want to help you. Listen: this nearby town is pleasant and healthy; stay here in disguise awaiting my return.[68]

His boons to the Pāṇḍavas helped them in their struggle against their cousins. Like Brahmā's boons to the demons, Vyāsa's boon of 100 sons to the Kauravas necessitated his further intervention on the side of dharma, aiding the Pāṇḍavas until they could overcome the demonic Kauravas. His advice to them is analogous to the knowledge Prajāpati gives the gods that helps them defeat the demons. Vyāsa is kept busy aiding the Pāṇḍavas in ways such as the following: he guarded them from trouble when the Kauravas were strong and aggressive (I.144; II.69.12 perhaps; III.8.22-III.11); he arranged and presided at the Pāṇḍavas' wedding, which allied them with Drupada and the Pañcālas (I.157; I.187-89); he gave the Pāṇḍavas a secret *brahman*, a spell, to aid them in

[68] I.144.9-11.

acquiring weapons from the gods (III.37-38); his advice and teachings aided the Pāṇḍavas in attaining and retaining sovereignty. Vyāsa's generosity makes appropriate the epic descriptions of him as a "foremost granter of boons"[69] and "lord of boons,"[70] phrases which might well be used in describing Brahmā. The pattern of *pitāmaha* Vyāsa's boon-giving is similar to that of Pitāmaha Brahmā, particularly in that his boons to the Kauravas necessitate his helping the Pāṇḍavas overcome them.

The epithet *pitāmaha*, so strongly associated with Brahmā, when applied to Vyāsa must have evoked in the epic's audience some recognition of his correspondence to the divine Pitāmaha. The nature and function of Brahmā in mythology are strikingly similar to those of Vyāsa in the MBh. Both are brahmins who adhere to *pravṛtti* values, and for whom the dharma is fundamental. Both are *Veda* creators and disseminators, and each composed a fifth *Veda* for the benefit of all people in *Kaliyuga*. Both are gurus credited with omniscience. In Indian mythology, each of these *pitāmahas* creates a family which feuds and then requires the intervention of the grandfather.

The correspondence between the mythology of Brahmā and the epic story of Vyāsa is illuminated by examination of the *Sauptika Parvan*. Alf Hiltebeitel has shown the extensive correlation between the events of this part of the MBh's narrative and the myth of Dakṣa's sacrifice.[71] The epic's narrative is clearly based on this myth, a version of which is told at the end of the *Sauptika Parvan*. Its placement there serves to explain to the Pāṇḍavas, and to the epic's audience, the meaning of the events which have just occurred; the text provides the key to its own exegesis.

The narrative of this section of the epic is as follows. After the battle in which the Pāṇḍavas conquered the Kauravas, the victorious warriors went to sleep, Kṛṣṇa taking the five Pāṇḍava brothers to another place outside the camp. As they slept, their camp was invaded by Aśvatthāman, who massacred the sleeping warriors and left. The next morning, the Pāṇḍavas found and confronted Aśvatthāman, and a battle ensued into which the sages Nārada and Vyāsa intervened. Vyāsa negotiated a resolution of the conflict, but the price was high: all the Pāṇḍavas' offspring died, while Aśvatthāman was banished. Yudhiṣṭhira asked how it was possible for Aśvatthāman to slaughter all those great warriors, and Kṛṣṇa responded that Aśvatthāman, who had been born from Śiva (I.61.66), was devoted to Śiva (VII.172.81-87), and eventually was possessed by Śiva (X.7.65; X.17.6). Kṛṣṇa then revealed some of

---

[69] variṣṭho varado ... / I.57.75.
[70] varāṇāmīśvaro / VI.2.8.
[71] Hiltebeitel, *Ritual*, pp. 299-335 especially.

Śiva's great deeds, primarily his destruction of Dakṣa's sacrifice (X.18).

There are many versions of the myth of Dakṣa's sacrifice, from the *Atharva Veda* through the *Purāṇas*, including half a dozen versions in the MBh.[72] In general, the myth's pattern is as follows. Dakṣa and the gods gathered for a sacrifice, but Śiva was excluded and was angered. He attacked the sacrifice and disrupted it. Brahmā intervened, reconciling Śiva and the sacrificing gods by offering Śiva a share of the sacrifice.[73]

Hiltebeitel's comparison of the myth and the epic's *Sauptika* story reveals many correspondences, of which I will focus on only the comparison of the roles of Brahmā in the myth and Vyāsa in the epic. The intervention between the angry Śiva and the sacrificing gods by Brahmā is analogous to the intervention between Aśvatthāman (= Śiva) and the Pāṇḍavas (= gods) by Vyāsa and Nārada. Brahmā is often accompanied by *ṛṣis*; in the epic account, Nārada represents those seers who form Pitāmaha's retinue, while Vyāsa, at the moment of intervention, is identified only as the *pitāmaha* of the Bhāratas (X.14.12). They stop the hostilities with a joint request, but thereafter Vyāsa is in control, and only he speaks. Just as Brahmā resolves the dispute between Śiva and the gods, Vyāsa resolves the conflict between Aśvatthāman and the Pāṇḍavas; like Śiva, Aśvatthāman gets his share (he kills Dhṛṣṭadyumna) and is sent away.[74] Thus, Brahmā's role in most versions of this myth is paralleled by Vyāsa's role in the epic narrative of the *Sauptika Parvan*. The pattern in the myths is complemented by a very similar pattern in the epic story.

A myth such as this, however, does not exist in a vacuum; it derives some of its meaning and longevity from real sacrifices performed by real people. Passages in the *Brāhmaṇas* describe ritual offerings made to Rudra Śiva that are suggestive of this very myth; e.g., *Śatapatha Brāhmaṇa* 1.7.4. describes the *brahman* priest making the offering that placates Śiva. This

---

[72] O'Flaherty, *Hindu Myths*, pp. 324-25, lists fifty. See also Klaus Klostermaier's discussion of many versions of this myth, and his effort to link the myth with historical conflict between Vaiṣṇavas and Śaivas at Kanakhala, in "The Original Dakṣa Saga," *JSAL* 20 (1985):93-107.

[73] The *Sauptika* version of this myth is brief and primarily answers the question how Aśvatthāman could have done this, so it is focused on the identification of Aśvatthāman with Śiva. Brahmā is not mentioned; the gods manage to stop Śiva on their own. But the epic narrative utilizes more of the myth than simply what is told in *Sauptika*. Most versions of the myth, including the epic's versions, feature Brahmā prominently in the role of intercessor. Moreover, most also involve a confrontation between Śiva and Nārāyaṇa; in the epic narrative, this is represented by the duel between Aśvatthāman and Arjuna. The version told in XII.330 (= Roy, *MBh*, 10:167-70) corresponds more closely to the epic's narrative.

[74] There is an inversion here, the divine Śiva being blessed while the human Aśvatthāman in the epic is cursed; see Hiltebeitel, *Ritual*, pp. 330-31.

brahman priest does in the ritual what Brahmā does in the myth and what Vyāsa does in the epic story; each one confronts and pacifies the dangerous "Outsider" Śiva, gives him his share, and thereby keeps him away, where he belongs. This is an example of the congruity between the *brahman* priest, Brahmā, and Vyāsa, each in his own domain performing an act which corresponds to the acts of the other two.

Myths and rituals of the *Vedas* and *Brāhmaṇas* have shaped the epic in many ways: the Rājasūya ritual providing the structure of the *Sabhā Parvan*, the myth of Dakṣa's sacrifice providing the structure of the *Sauptika Parvan*, etc. Similarly, many of the epic characters reflect correspondences or continuities with figures of earlier mythology. Many of these epic characters have been recognized in the epic itself as sons of, or "portions" of, the deities to whom they correspond, leading Dumézil to call them "transpositions" of those earlier figures. The epic characters reincarnate important features of, and reenact the mythology of, the deities. Although the MBh never does explicitly state that Vyāsa is an incarnation of Brahmā or a portion of the god or his son,[75] it says in many subtle ways that Vyāsa corresponds to Brahmā.

The *Vāyu Purāṇa*, however, is more explicit in recognizing Vyāsa as an incarnation of Brahmā. This early *Purāṇa*, which is contemporaneous with the last phase of epic redaction,[76] contains the following brief passage on Vyāsa:

> pitṝṇāṃ duhitā yogā gandhakālīti viśrutā /
> **caturtho brahmaṇaścāṃśaḥ parāśarakulodvahaḥ** // 74
> vyasya tvekaṃ caturddhā tu vedaṃ dhīmān mahāmuniḥ /
> mahāyogaṃ mahātmānaṃ yo vyāsaṃ janayiṣyati // 75

This passage from the *Vāyu Purāṇa* (2.15.74-75) identifies Vyāsa as the perpetuator of the lineage of Parāśara, the divider of the *Veda* into four parts, and as a quarter-portion of Brahmā. Perhaps this is a reference to the quarter of Puruṣa which is said to be here below, while the other three-quarters remains immortal in heaven.[77] The unusual name given for Vyāsa's mother, Gandhakālī, occurs once in the MBh (I.90.51) and is a combination of two of her names, Gandhavatī and Kālī. Although this passage has certain grammatical problems which suggest emenda-

---

[75] XII.337.4 describes Vyāsa as "the sixth great *ṛṣi* from Pitāmaha," and XII.337.47-49 describe him as born in the family of Vasiṣṭha, who is "the mind-born son of Pitāmaha," both suggesting that Vyāsa is descended from Brahmā.

[76] *Purāṇa* material was gathered for centuries, so dating is somewhat arbitrary, but *Vāyu* is clearly an early one; O'Flaherty, *Hindu Myths*, p. 18, estimates that it was completed about A.D. 350.

[77] See *Ṛg Veda*, 10.90, the *Puruṣa sūkta*.

tion,[78] it is wholly in accord with the epic account of Vyāsa. Thus, while the recognition of Vyāsa as an *aṃśa* of Brahmā is not explicit in the MBh, it is explicit in the *Vāyu Purāṇa.*

While Brahmā's plan to defeat the demons by means of divine incarnations seems not to include the incarnation of Brahmā himself, not explicitly at least, the role that Brahmā would perform on earth is performed by Vyāsa in the MBh. As a brahmin who takes the role of *brahman* priest, as creator and disseminator of the *Veda*, as the *pitāmaha* of a warring family, Vyāsa reenacts on earth much of the deity's deeds in mythology. Just as Prajāpati in the *Brāhmaṇas* witnesses the struggle over the sacrifice between the gods and demons, and as Brahmā Prajāpati in the MBh and *Purāṇas* witnesses their struggle, Vyāsa in the MBh witnesses the struggle between the Pāṇḍavas and the Kauravas, their sacrifice of battle. In the MBh, Brahmā's functions, traits, and even epithets have been incarnated in the figure of Vyāsa.

---

[78] All editions of the *Vāyu Purāṇa* consulted (the Veṅkaṭeśvara and Ānandāśrama Press editions and that of Rajendralal Mitra) have the same reading. There is a variant reading of *yogā* as *yogād*, which is probably preferable. *Yo* should probably be emended to *yā*. Word order is the main problem with the passage as printed, however. Two sets of nominatives, one feminine and the other masculine, are available for the one finite verb in this passage. The second line of verse 74 and the first line of verse 75 are about Vyāsa exclusively and would constitute a verse if put together. Combining the first line of verse 74 with the second line of 75 would unite the feminine nominative with the verb and its object, and would yield the following meaning: "Gandhakālī will give birth to Vyāsa." These emendations would clarify this jumbled passage. The identification of Vyāsa as a quarter-*aṃśa* of Brahmā would be unaffected.

CHAPTER FIVE

OTHER PERSPECTIVES ON VYĀSA

The MBh depicts Kṛṣṇa Dvaipāyana Vyāsa as the foremost master of the Vedic texts, a priest for the important sacrifices, as well as the guru for *bhakti* practices and a great ascetic. Other sources, however, offer different perspectives, including popular traditions about Kṛṣṇa Dvaipāyana that are not found in the MBh and that may deepen our understanding of his significance in Hindu culture. Consideration of variant versions of a story found in the MBh, the *Jātaka* tales, the *Arthaśāstra*, and some Purāṇas sheds light both on the character of Vyāsa and on the evolution of the epic as well. Later in this chapter, a comparison of the Buddha and Vyāsa is suggested by certain correspondences between them. Finally, the play *The Mahabharata*, recently written by Jean-Claude Carrière and directed by Peter Brook, emphasizes in various ways the significance of Vyāsa and attributes to him control of the epic's plot. I will begin with consideration of variant versions of the annihilation of the Andhaka-Vṛṣṇi clan.

The *Mausala Parvan* (Book XVI) of the MBh narrates the destruction of Kṛṣṇa Vāsudeva's kin, the Andhaka-Vṛṣṇi or Yādava clan, a summary of which follows.[1] One day, thirty-six years after the Bhārata war had ended, some young males of the clan approached three brahmin sages, Viśvāmita, Kaṇva, and Nārada, having dressed one of the young warriors as a pregnant woman. The Vṛṣṇis asked the brahmins if they knew for certain what this "woman" would bring forth. The sages in anger replied that "she" would give birth to an iron club that would exterminate the Vṛṣṇis and Andhakas, the only exceptions being Baladeva, who would cast off his body and enter the ocean, and Vāsudeva, who would be wounded by a hunter and die. After pronouncing this curse, the brahmins departed. Just as they had said, the boy brought forth an iron club, which the Vṛṣṇis ground into powder and threw into the ocean. Kṛṣṇa Vāsudeva realized that the time had come for him to act and decided to bring about the destruction of his kinsmen; he commanded that they make a pilgrimage to the ocean. Upon their arrival at the beach they began to celebrate, drinking the wine they had with them, and giving to monkeys the food they had intended to give to

[1] This paragraph summarizes MBh. XVI.2-4.

brahmins. The Vṛṣṇis fell to quarreling among themselves, recalling old grudges from the war, and demeaning one another for departing from the warriors' code of chivalry. Fatal blows were struck, and Kṛṣṇa Vāsudeva himself entered the fray, plucking a handful of *eraka* grass that turned into an iron club with which he killed many Vṛṣṇis. After this bloody fulfillment of the brahmins' curse, both Baladeva and Vāsudeva died as had been foretold. This account of the annihilation of the Andhaka-Vṛṣṇi clan as told in the MBh involves Vyāsa only after the event; he is depicted advising Arjuna that, with the death of Kṛṣṇa Vāsudeva, the time had come for the Pāṇḍava brothers to retire from ruling the kingdom and depart on the final journey (XVI.9).

A different version of this story is presented, however, by the *Jātaka* tales of the Pāli Buddhist canon. The Buddhist form of this tale corresponds with the Hindu epic in many particulars, but differs in certain respects, most strikingly in the larger role of Kṛṣṇa Dvaipāyana, or as he is known in the Pāli language, Kaṅha Dīpāyana.[2] He appears in three *Jātakas*, two of which have to do with the death of the Vṛṣṇi clan.

The *Ghata Jātaka* tells the story of Vāsudeva, his brother Baladeva, and their eight other brothers, the Andhaka-Veṅhu brothers,[3] who seized the city of Dvaravatī and killed its king, Kaṃsa. In so doing, they were aided by the brahmin Kaṅha Dīpāyana, who told them the strategem that would win the city. Later, some sons of the Andhaka-Veṅhus played a practical joke on Kaṅha Dīpāyana, dressing up one of the boys as a pregnant woman and asking the sage when "she" would deliver. Dīpāyana perceived that the time had come for the death of the Andhaka-Veṅhus, and of himself as well. He told them that the boy would bring forth a knot of *khadira* wood which would destroy Vāsudeva's lineage within a week. The boys called Dīpāyana a false ascetic and killed him. The clan's elders, finding out what had happened, watched over the boy who, as predicted, brought forth a knot of wood. It was burned and the ashes were scattered in the river, but gathered together downstream and an *eraka* plant grew from the clump of ashes. One day, with the clan assembled at the riverbank, playful wrestling turned into a quarrel. One of the Andhaka-Veṅhus picked a branch from the *eraka* plant growing

---

[2] See *Ghata Jātaka*, tale number 454, and *Saṃkicca Jātaka*, tale number 530, in *The Jātaka*, ed. V. Fausbøll, 6 vols. (London: Trübner & Co., 1877-90); translated in *The Jātaka*, trans. E. B. Cowell, 6 vols., (Cambridge: Cambridge University Press, 1895-1907). Alf Hiltebeitel discusses *Ghata Jātaka*'s account in *Ritual*, pp. 64-68.

[3] The text's *Andhakaveṅhuyo* is clearly intended as a reference to the Andhaka-Vṛṣṇis. Veṅhuyo is a reading that has troubled copyists, and manuscripts now offer various other readings. Veṅhu would be Pāli for Viṣṇu, while Veṅhi would be Vṛṣṇi. Perhaps the presence in the tale of Viṣṇu's incarnation Kṛṣṇa led to this alteration in the word.

there, and it became a club. Others picked portions of the plant, all of which became clubs, and the Andhaka-Veṅhus fought to the death, the only warriors to survive the carnage being Vāsudeva and Baladeva. The *Jātaka* tale goes on to describe the death of Baladeva at the hands of a demon and of Vāsudeva at the hands of a hunter.

The *Saṃkicca Jātaka* tale makes reference to the same story in a single verse: "Assailing the *ṛṣi* Kaṅha Dīpāyana, the Andhaka-Veṅhus, killing one another with clubs, attained the realm of Yama."[4] This very brief reference to the story told at length above apparently was sufficient to remind the audience of a well known incident.

The *Arthaśāstra* of Kauṭilya also refers briefly to the same incident, and in a very similar fashion. In illustration of the point that a king who fails to control his senses and desires will soon perish, examples are cited of such reprehensible conduct and its consequences. Rāvaṇa and Duryodhana are among the examples not to be emulated, and the series ends with this verse: "Vātāpi (perished) when he passionately assailed Agastya, as did the clan of the Vṛṣṇis when they passionately assailed Dvaipāyana.[5] Again, this brief reference sufficed to remind the audience of a story already well known to them.

Elements of the epic's version of this story suggest that it is later than the *Ghata Jātaka* tale. The iron club of the MBh tale seems an element unlikely to have been in the earliest versions of this story. Moreover, the iron club does not fit comfortably with the other elements of the story; ground to powder and thrown in the ocean, it does not reappear, while Kṛṣṇa kills the Vṛṣṇis with a different iron club. Thus, in the epic account the curse of the brahmins does not exactly come true, since the iron club brought forth by the boy is not the lethal instrument. The *Ghata Jātaka* tale is a simpler and more coherent version of the story.

Comparison of these different versions of the story is also aided by consideration of their likely chronology, though of course dating Indian texts is usually problematic. The *Arthaśāstra* is widely regarded as having been composed about 300 B.C.[6] The *Jātaka* tales are the product of a long oral tradition, but were included in some form in the Pāli Canon when it was committed to writing about 80 B.C.[7] Both these texts were composed in

---

[4] Verse 97 of tale number 530; See Fausbøll, *The Jātaka*, 5:267.

[5] *Arthaśāstra* 1.6.10: *harṣādvātāpiragastyamatyāsādayan vṛṣṇisaṃghaśca dvaipāyanamiti* // The verb *vinanāśa* is understood from verse 5. *Harṣād* is translated by Kangle as "foolishly," but "passionately" is both more appropriate to this context and closer to the usual meaning of *harṣād*.

[6] The traditional association of the text with the foundation of the Maurya dynasty about 300 B.C. is not supported by Trautmann, who concludes (p. 184) that the text was composed about 150 A.D.; See Thomas Trautmann, *Kauṭilya and the Arthaśāstra* (Leiden: E. J. Brill, 1971).

[7] As discussed in Winternitz, *A History of Indian Literature*, 2:113-56.

the last few centuries before the common era, and both present a version of the death of the Vṛṣṇis in which Dvaipāyana is responsible for their demise. The MBh itself, while certainly existing in oral form in the last few centuries before the common era, probably was not written in a form similar to the text we now have until the first few centuries A.D.[8] Apparently these texts reached a form very much like the form in which we now know them in the following order: *Arthaśāsta* first, *Jātakas* and MBh afterwards.

Extending forward in time the comparison of variant versions of this tale, one finds that the *Purāṇas* treat the death of the Vṛṣṇis in a variety of ways. Those devoted to Śiva such as the *Liṅga* and *Śiva Purāṇas* do not present versions of this story at all, presumably because Kṛṣṇa Vāsudeva and his kin are of little interest to their composers. None of the *Purāṇas* consulted attributes to Dvaipāyana the fatal curse, as did the *Jātakas* and *Arthaśāstra* in an earlier era. I have seen three different Purāṇic versions of the annihilation of Kṛṣṇa's clan:

(1) the fatal curse is attributed to an unnamed brahmin;
(2) the curse is attributed to the brahmin Durvāsas; and
(3) the curse is attributed to the brahmins Viśvāmitra, Kaṇva, and Nārada, more or less as in the MBh.

Purāṇic versions most similar to the MBh account include the *Viṣṇu, Brahmā*, and *Bhāgavata Purāṇas*. All these renditions of the story emphasize the control Kṛṣṇa exercised over these events; the curse of the brahmins is the means Kṛṣṇa used in his role as *avatāra* to eliminate his kinsmen, thereby lightening earth's burden, a motif found in the epic but given even more emphasis in these *Purāṇas*. *Viṣṇu* and *Brahmā Purāṇas* attribute the curse to the brahmins Viśvāmitra, Kaṇva and Nārada, and follow the epic very closely regarding the details of this episode.[9] The *Bhāgavata*, however, while paralleling the epic in most respects, gives a long list of brahmins who were insulted by and who cursed the Yādavas, Andhakas, and Vṛṣṇis, as follows: Viśvāmitra, Asita, Kaṇva, Durvāsas, Bhṛgu, Aṅgiras, Kāśyapa, Vāmadeva, Atri, Vasiṣṭha, Nārada, and others.[10] This is a list of all the most important brahmin sages of Vedic and Purāṇic literature except Kṛṣṇa Dvaipāyana, who is conspicuous by his absence from this list.

The MBh and the *Purāṇas* that closely correspond to it feature as the agents of the lethal curse brahmins who are very strikingly out of place. Viśvāmitra and Kaṇva, as well as most of the others from the *Bhāgavata*'s

---

[8] See Chapter 1 for discussion of dating the MBh.
[9] See *Viṣṇu P.*, 5.37., and *Brahmā P.*, 101.
[10] *Bhāgavata P.*, 11.1.12-13.

long list, are Vedic *ṛṣis* whose presence in the MBh is surprising in view of the fact that they have nothing else at all to do with the epic's main story about the Pāṇḍavas and Kṛṣṇa. Even Nārada's presence in this incident is surprising, though for a different reason. He is a celestial brahmin who occasionally appears in the epic story, but who in this episode is very much out of character; becoming angry, cursing the Vṛṣṇis, indeed taking dramatic action of any kind, is surprising for Nārada.[11] These brahmins, then, seem very much miscast in their role as the cursers of the Vṛṣṇis.

The other Purāṇic versions may be best understood as different kinds of transformation of the earlier version of this story which featured Dvaipāyana. The version in which one unnamed brahmin curses the Vṛṣṇis may be seen as continuing the *Arthaśāstra* and *Jātakas* tradition, though without specifying the brahmin responsible.[12] The version in which Durvāsas is named as the brahmin who cursed the Vṛṣṇis to their death is a form of the story seen in only one of the *Purāṇas* consulted.[13] Durvāsas is, of course, the archetypal irascible sage of Indian literature, and as such he is by no means out of character in this incident. He makes several appearances in the epic as well, and is more appropriate in this episode than would be a Vedic *ṛṣi*.

It seems evident that the earlier version of the story of the death of the Vṛṣṇi clan, as found in the *Jātakas* and *Arthaśāstra*, has been transformed in the MBh, and in the *Purāṇas* in a variety of ways. With regard to the epic context for this story, it was necessary that Kṛṣṇa Dvaipāyana survive this incident so that he could participate in the events of the epic's last two books, and later compose the MBh. While this is not something about which the *Jātakas* or even the *Arthaśāstra* would be concerned, it would be vital to the epic's composers. Moreover, replacing Dvaipāyana with the trio of brahmins we find in the epic would have the effect of absolving Dvaipāyana of responsibility for this inauspicious event. This would have been appealing to the epic's composers because of the fact that within the developing Hindu tradition, Kṛṣṇa Dvaipāyana occupied an important and unique position. As Vyāsa, the transmitter of the Vedic heritage to a later era, composer of the epic and Purāṇic material,

---

[11] Nārada usually appears only to reveal something about the gods or dharma. His most important appearances in the epic are at the beginning of Book II, where he urges the Pāṇḍavas to perform the Rājasūya, and in Book X, where he intervenes with Vyāsa between the converging missiles. As discussed above, however, clearly Vyāsa is the more important of the two, taking a significant role in the action while Nārada is silent in the background.

[12] *Devībhāgavata P.*, 4.25.60-62, and 4.20.42; *Brahmavaivarta P.*, 4.132.88.

[13] *Varāha P.*, 149.10-23.

he came to represent the authority and authenticity of virtually the whole of Hindu sacred literature. For him to be a figure of such symbolic significance, to fulfill this role for the Hindu tradition, required a version of the story different from what we see in the *Jātakas*.

The correlation between Vyāsa and Brahmā which this study has demonstrated can be extended by a comparison with the Buddha. Paul Mus has compared the Buddha with Brahmā, and shown various ways in which the depiction of the Buddha in Mahāyāna Buddhism developed similarly to the depiction of Brahmā in Brāhmanism or early Hinduism. As Mus comments,[14] Brahmā, the visible image of the *brahman*, is on his lotus and the world is a reflection of himself; he is at the center and top of the developed system. This ontology of position is replicated by Buddhism's installation of the Buddha on his lotus and the multiplication of his reflections into many Buddhas, so that he became as omnipresent as the *brahman*. Mus draws a parallel between the verbal body of the Buddha, his *dharmakāya*, and the verbal body of Brahmā, namely, the *Veda*, the *brahman*.[15] Just as the brahmin has a personal rapport with *brahman*/Brahmā, and is described as *brahmadāyāda*, so too the Buddhist *bhikṣu* has a personal rapport with the Buddha's body of dharma, and is described as *dhammadāyāda*; they are sons of the *brahman* or dharma.[16] One even finds the epithets associated with Brahmā, such as *lokapitā* and *svayaṃbhū*, applied to the Buddha.[17] Mus saw Buddhism as patterned on Brāhmanism in many ways, and the Buddhist system as conserving Brahmā and absorbing Brāhmanism.[18] In view of the correlation that this study has shown between Brahmā and Vyāsa, Mus's comparison of the Buddha and Brahmā leads naturally to a comparison of the Buddha and Vyāsa.

The Buddha and Vyāsa are associated in the *Kaṅha Dīpāyana Jātaka* tale,[19] which may be summarized as follows. Two men, Maṇḍavya and Kaṅha Dīpāyana, renounced their wealth and went to the Himālayas for an ascetic life, which they followed for fifty years without attaining the goal of concentration (*dhyāna*). After a story about Maṇḍavya in which Kaṅha Dīpāyana was marginally involved, the main story begins. Kaṅha Dīpāyana was at the home of a householder when the family's son was

---

[14] Paul Mus, *Barabuḍur*, 1:237.

[15] Ibid., 1:254.

[16] Ibid., 1:259. Mus also cites the terms *brahmanimmita* and *dhammanimmita*, by which he apparently means *nimitta*, "caused by."

[17] Ibid., 1:257-58.

[18] Ibid., 1:292.

[19] Fausbøll, *The Jātaka*, tale number 444.

bitten by a snake. The householder asked the sage to cure the boy by performing an Act of Truth, to which he agreed. Dīpāyana declared that he had lived for a week as an ascetic (*brahmacārin*), his mind serene, but since then had lived the ascetic life for fifty years unwillingly; by the power of this truth, he commanded, may the poison be overcome and the boy live. But only a portion of the poison came out; the Act of Truth was only a partial success. Kaṅha Dīpāyana said to the boy's father, "I have used my power; now use yours." The boy's father said that he had given to all comers without stint, but had done so these many years unwillingly; by the power of this truth, he commanded, may the poison be overcome and the boy live. His Act of Truth also was only a partial success, and he turned to his wife, asking her to use her power. She declared that she, in her indifference, saw her husband and the serpent that bit her son as indistinguishable; by the power of this truth, she commanded, may the poison be overcome and the boy live. Immediately the boy revived. His father asked the sage why he had lived as a *brahmacārin* unwillingly when those who renounce are serene and controlled. Kaṅha Dīpāyana answered that to renounce and then return would cause him to be called an idiot or a fool, and to avoid this he remained an ascetic, though unwillingly. The husband revealed that he had given gifts to all, though unwillingly, because it was the ancestral way of life which he was following as best he could, and the wife revealed that she had never thought of leaving her husband with whom she lived unwillingly because that simply was not done. Her husband forgave her and asked her to love him, while the sage told the householder to give liberally and with faith, and the householder told the sage to walk the path of *brahmacarya* with a tranquil mind and cultivate *dhyāna*. Afterwards, the wife loved her husband, he gave gifts with faith, and the sage, ridding himself of his unwillingness, cultivated *dhyāna* and became intent on the world of Brahmā. The Buddha then revealed to his audience the identities of the story's characters, saying that in a former life he himself had been Kaṅha Dīpāyana.

In this *Jātaka* tale, the future Buddha, the Bodhisattva, has identified himself as Kṛṣṇa Dvaipāyana, the unwilling ascetic who followed the rules but did not have a purpose to his asceticism beyond avoiding the embarrassment of returning to the society he had renounced. The Buddhists are here criticizing Hindu asceticism along the same lines as van Buitenen did, namely, that it is largely lacking in any purpose other than the accumulation of ascetic power for oneself.[20] In this story, which is quite unknown to the MBh or to the Hindu tradition, Dvaipāyana

[20] See the discussion in Chapter 2, section (3) on Vyāsa as an ascetic.

learned from the householder that his asceticism fulfilled the householders as well through their donations, and this helped him to rid himself of his attitude of unwillingness. The unsuccessful ascetic became successful through his interaction with the householder and his wife, found a purpose for his asceticism, and rededicated himself to it. The lesson learned and the progress made in that life as Kṛṣṇa Dvaipāyana helped the Bodhisattva to become the Buddha in a later life. The figure who, in the *Jātaka* tale, was simultaneously the Buddha-to-be and Kṛṣṇa Dvaipāyana thus became intent on attaining *Brahmaloka.*

Vyāsa and the Buddha are also in mythology associated with Brahmā in the same way. Brahmā appears before both sages to encourage them to promulgate their teachings. In the MBh, Brahmā is depicted appearing before Vyāsa to help him put the MBh into written form as a more effective means of transmitting his tale of the Bhārata war and the teachings it included.[21] In a strikingly similar scene, Brahmā is depicted in Buddhist literature appearing before the Buddha to convince him to teach what he had learned about the means of attaining *nirvāṇa.*[22] Brahmā helped both sages spread the dharma. Thus, Vyāsa and the Buddha occupy similar positions within the Hindu and Buddhist traditions respectively, as the sages who formulated the dharma of each tradition.

The play by Carrière and Brook, *The Mahabharata*, is based on the Sanskrit text and traditional art forms in which epic characters and events are depicted: "Theyyems, Muddiattu, Yakshagana, Chaau, Jatra ...".[23] Indeed, the playwright and director experienced the epic in many media. They read translations of the MBh and short plays by Rabindranath Tagore, they listened for five years to Professor Philippe Lavastine tell stories from the MBh, then went to India: "We gathered all kinds of images and impressions—images of dance, film, marionette theater, village celebrations and plays."[24] The result of their research is the remarkable drama which portrays the epic story of the Bhārata war in three parts: "The Game of Dice," "Exile in the Forest," and "The War."

Noteworthy in the play is the prominence of Vyāsa and an emphasis on his control over the events depicted. The play opens on a scene in

---

[21] See the translation of this passage in the Appendix, and the discussion of it in Chapter 1.

[22] See the discussion and references in Chapter 1.

[23] Brook, "Foreword," in Carrière, *The MBh*, p. xv.

[24] Carrière, "Introduction," *The MBh*, p. vii.

which Vyāsa meets Ganesha and engages his services as scribe for the epic poem he has composed. Carrière[25] observes:

> It became obvious that we needed the storyteller/author, Vyasa, even though the characters he creates sometimes escape him (he is both their author and their father), and even though Ganesha and later Krishna dispute the reality of his inventions.

As Vyāsa begins his narration of the tale of the Bhāratas, Ganesha interrupts him to ask, "These children you've just created, you're going to lead them to the slaughter?"[26] During the Pāṇḍavas' forest exile, Draupadī vents her frustration on the sage: "Vyasa, have you condemned us to stay all the time in the same place? To watch our life ebb away in this forest?"[27] Just prior to the war, Gāndhārī is is moved to ask, "Who is going to die? Who will be your victims?"[28] As the war reaches its climax, the wounded Bhīma exclaims, "Vyasa, I'm finished. If you're still in charge, why are you forcing us to die?"[29] Vyāsa's presence is felt throughout the drama, and he often comes on stage to narrate, or explain, or intervene in the action.

Even Krishna is another character in the story Vyāsa creates; as Vyāsa says, Krishna is "going to play, as always, the leading role."[30] And, of course, he does so, but Krishna is powerful and mysterious, and once asks the unanswered question, "Vyasa, which of us has invented the other?"[31] Less playfully, Krishna asks, "You who are narrating me, haven't you already traced out my path?" to which Vyāsa replies, "No path is traced completely, as well you know. You are in life and you live."[32] As his death nears, Krishna asks, "What role have you in store for me now?"; Vyāsa answers, "You know well."[33] In this drama, Vyāsa too is a powerful and mysterious figure. He moves in and out of the action, creating his poetic history of the Bhāratas—creating the Bhāratas themselves! Though there is no identification of Vyāsa as Viṣṇu or Brahmā on earth, the drama depicts Kṛṣṇa and Vyāsa apparently cooperating in a common cause, never in conflict.

---

26 Ibid., p. x..
26 Ibid., p. 15.
27 Ibid., p. 92.
28 Ibid., p. 156.
29 Ibid., p. 211.
30 Ibid., p. 40.
31 Ibid., p. 107.
32 Ibid., p. 108.
33 Ibid., p. 230.

These perspectives on Vyāsa, both ancient and modern, highlight aspects of his nature. The attribution to Vyāsa, in literature other than the MBh, of the annihilation of the Vṛṣṇi clan may also reveal something about the evolution of the epic itself. Correspondences between the Buddha and Vyāsa, and the identification of him as a prior incarnation of the Buddha-to-be, emphasize Vyāsa's significance within the Hindu religious tradition. The drama, a distillation of so many forms of the MBh, depicts the cooperation between Vyāsa and Kṛṣṇa, and features frequent appearances by Vyāsa as the tale's author.

CHAPTER SIX

CONCLUSIONS

A scene much beloved by many who know the MBh features Vyāsa, on Brahmā's recommendation, calling upon Gaṇeśa to be his scribe for the writing of the great epic poem narrating the tale of the Bhāratas. It is the captivating and charming first scene of the drama by Carrière and Brook,[1] and is found at the beginning of some manuscripts of the MBh, though the Critical Edition has deemed it a comparatively recent interpolation. For all its charm and humor, this scene is significant for the way it augments the status and authority of the MBh. It is to this theme that I shall return in concluding my interpretation of Kṛṣṇa Dvaipāyana Vyāsa.

In the MBh, an effort is being made to define the proper role of the brahmin in Hindu society. The classical Vedic paradigm of the brahmin was that he be a master of the orally transmitted text of the *Veda* and of the rituals associated with it. The Vedic paradigm was being modified by the addition of other practices to the brahmin's repertoire, namely *tapas* (including *yoga*) and religious devotion (*bhakti*), and Vyāsa reflects this change. He is depicted as a great ascetic and a guru for *bhakti* practices as well as the foremost priest and master of the *Veda*; his activities encompass the full range of activities traditionally deemed appropriate for a brahmin.

Analysis of Vyāsa's actions in the epic reveals his central role in three crises, the outcomes of which were disastrous for his kinsmen, the Bhārata dynasty. While it is possible that ancient Indo-European mythological patterns may have influenced the structure of Vyāsa's career, a more directly relevant influence is the complex of ideas centering on the *avatāra* and his function of restoring dharma. Later Hindu tradition has interpreted Vyāsa as an incarnation of Nārāyaṇa Viṣṇu, assisting Kṛṣṇa Vāsudeva to defeat the demons who are overburdening the earth. In fact, however, the MBh refers to Vyāsa as an incarnation of Nārāyaṇa very rarely—in only two chapters. Yet the epic seems to invite us to see them as related in some way: they share the name Kṛṣṇa and a dark hue, they cooperate in matters of dharma and are never in conflict, and they are the two characters who always perceive the course

---

[1] Carrière, *The MBh*, pp. 1-23.

of dharma, however subtle. They are complementary figures, working toward the same end.

This does not mean, however, that one is confined to the interpretation of Vyāsa as an incarnation of Nārāyaṇa. This study documents extensive correspondences between Vyāsa and Brahmā, suggesting that the epic poets are evoking Brahmā through the figure of Vyāsa, and are encouraging us to see Vyāsa as the earthly counterpart of Brahmā. Both figures are depicted as brahmins who adhere to *pravṛtti* values, the this-worldly practices which fulfill one's obligations to dharma. Both are ritually active brahmins who are particularly well suited to the role of *brahman* priest. They correspond also in their relationship to the *Veda*. Brahmā is depicted as having created the *Veda* just prior to his creation of the world, Vedic verses issuing from each of his four faces. Vyāsa is depicted in the MBh as having divided the one *Veda* into four texts just prior to the beginning of Kaliyuga, the new era.

The most compelling correspondence between them is centered on their shared epithet *pitāmaha*, "grandfather." Brahmā is the grandfather of the gods and demons who are eternally contending against each other. Vyāsa is the grandfather of the Pāṇḍavas and Kauravas who contend against each other for sovereignty over the Bhārata realm. The two figures have structurally parallel relationships with their offspring. The epic depicts the gods and demons transposed into the Pāṇḍavas and Kauravas respectively, the Pāṇḍavas as sons of gods and the Kauravas as demons incarnate. This transposition is completed by Vyāsa in the role of *pitāmaha* of the Bhāratas.

Vyāsa thus reenacts much of the mythology of Brahmā, just as other epic characters reenact the mythology of the deities of whom they are sons or *aṃśas*, or by whom they are possessed in the case of Aśvatthāman. Vyāsa does not reenact the mythology of Nārāyaṇa; in fact, the two citations to him as Nārāyaṇa's incarnation are shown to be very late in being incorporated into the MBh. While the epic does not state explicitly that Vyāsa is Brahmā's son or *aṃśa* or *avatāra*, the correspondences between them are many. The epic's depiction of Vyāsa as the earthly counterpart to Brahmā, its subtle evocation of Brahmā in the figure of Vyāsa, adds meaning to the description of Vyāsa as the MBh's composer and *ṛṣi* of the fifth *Veda*. The attribution of the epic text to Vyāsa, and the depiction of him as if he were the *aṃśa* or *avatāra* of Brahmā, serves to augment the status and authority of the MBh as a religious text.

To return to the scene in which Brahmā and Gaṇeśa assist Vyāsa in the writing of his composition, the association of both deities with this effort is quite meaningful. Gaṇeśa, the god invoked by Indians at the beginning of so many enterprises, makes his appearance at the beginning of the enormous epic. As the remover of obstacles, his assistance in transforming the poem from oral to written text, and in comprehending its teachings, is most appropriate. Moreover, Gaṇeśa's presence is auspicious and serves to balance the inauspicious elements to be encountered later in this text—the humiliation and exile of the Pāṇḍavas and Draupadī, the war in which respected elders, teachers, and noble warriors died and the Bhārata family nearly annihilated itself, even killing the unborn generation still in the womb, and finally the death of the *avatāra* Kṛṣṇa himself. These events, so distressing to the epic's audience, and the reticence and trepidation induced by the vastness of the MBh, were to some extent ameliorated by the auspicious association with Gaṇeśa. Brahmā's appearance with Vyāsa, his praise of both Vyāsa and the MBh, are even more significant. Vyāsa described his poem as comprehensive, conveying to its audience knowledge both sacred and profane, and he desired that it be put in writing. Brahmā, knowing his desire, appeared before Vyāsa and gave his approval of the poem, then suggested Gaṇeśa as scribe. As we have seen, Brahmā here performs a role he performs often, including in Buddhist literature and the *Rāmāyaṇa*; he is often associated with the creation and dissemination of knowledge. In the creation and dissemination of the MBh, Vyāsa is functioning as would Brahmā. This scene is the explicit commendation and blessing of Vyāsa's efforts by Brahmā. As James Fitzgerald observes,[2] Brahmā's endorsement of the MBh "incorporated an important new audience into the imagination of the text," namely, women and *śūdras*. C. Mackenzie Brown[3] makes the same point:

> The story as a whole strongly suggests that one of the primary reasons for the commitment to writing is to benefit all people. While paying its respects to the high Vedic tradition, the epic makes clear that, unlike the Vedas, it is not the exclusive prerogative of the priestly class.

More than this, however, Brahmā's appearance augments the status and authority of the MBh and its composer Vyāsa.

The epic's depiction of Vyāsa in ways which evoke Brahmā adds meaning to the MBh's description of itself as the fifth *Veda*. For the MBh and much of the Hindu tradition, the *Veda* is the Revelation, created by Brahmā as he created the world and its creatures. Vyāsa emulates Brahmā by creating and disseminating the fifth *Veda*, the new knowledge for the world's latter days. As the author and revealer of this *Veda*, Vyāsa

---

[2] Fitzgerald, "India's Fifth Veda," pp. 136-37.

[3] C. Mackenzie Brown, p. 76 of "Purāṇa as Scripture: From Sound to Image of the Holy Word in the Hindu Tradition," *HR* 26 (1986):68-86.

is the symbol of the authority and authenticity of the MBh as a religious text. But for other Hindus, the *Veda* was not authenticated by its creator, Brahmā, for to have an author, any author, would be to limit the *Veda* and make it subject to error. For the philosophers of the Pūrva-Mīmāṃsā school, the *Veda* is authorless, eternal truths, and therefore not subject to error or any limitation on its authority.[4] The MBh, however, takes a different approach to establishing the authority of the text, and the *Purāṇas* follow the epic's lead in this regard. For them, authorship is attributed to Vyāsa, whose presence at the beginning of the textual tradition guarantees their value. As Michel Foucalt has commented,[5] having one or more texts attributed to a particular author has "a classificatory function" and "indicates the status of this discourse" within its society. Certainly this is true of Vyāsa and the MBh. Moreover, Foucault describes an author who stands at the head of a long tradition to which many others also contribute as a "transdiscursive" author,[6] a term appropriate to Vyāsa as the *ṛṣi* of the epic and Purāṇic collections, the *ṛṣi* for Kaliyuga. The anonymous epic poets augmented the status and authority of the MBh by attributing authorship of the text to Vyāsa and through Vyāsa evoking the presiding deity of creation and knowledge, Brahmā.

If this important purpose was one reason that Vyāsa was identified with Brahmā, why does the MBh not more explicitly express their identity? It is possible that the MBh once did have more explicit identifications of Vyāsa with Brahmā, but these were lost or removed for some reason. This, however, is quite unlikely; almost everything that was introduced into the manuscript tradition is still there. If the identification of Vyāsa with Brahmā was never more explicit than we now find it, could this be because it was already sufficiently clear to the audience? The epithet *pitāmaha*, so strongly associated with Brahmā, when applied to Vyāsa in the context of the Bhārata war must have evoked in the epic's audience some recognition of their relatedness. Many people probably would not have seen the correspondences between them, however, and apparently their correspondence has in fact been forgotten. Only the

---

[4] The key text of this tradition is the *Pūrva-Mīmāṃsā Sūtras* of Jaimini, circa 200 B.C. (Interestingly, the author has the name of one of the five pupils of Vyāsa). See the article by Francis X. Clooney, "Why the Veda has No Author: Language as Ritual in Early Mīmāṃsā and Post-Modern Theology," *JAAR* 55 (1987): 659-84, for an excellent analysis of the Mīmāṃsā position, the post-Mīmāṃsā Vedānta position, and a discussion of similar themes in contemporary theology.

[5] Michel Foucault, "What is an Author?" in *Textual Strategies: Perspectives in Post-Structuralist Criticism*, edited by Josué V. Harari (Ithaca: Cornell University Press, 1979), pp. 147-48.

[6] Ibid., p. 153; Foucault cites as examples Homer, Aristotle, and the Church Fathers, *inter alia*.

identification of Kṛṣṇa with Nārāyaṇa, and of his companion Arjuna with Nara, is repeated frequently in the text. Probably the other divine/human correspondences were once less explicitly stated than we now find them in the MBh, the text developing in the direction of greater specificity on this theme. Certainly this development can be seen with regard to the *Rāmāyaṇa*'s depiction of Rāma.[7] The MBh's lists of *aṃśas* may well be comparatively late in the history of the text, "transpositions" of the deities into epic characters having been more subtly expressed in earlier stages of the MBh's composition.

Vyāsa's identification with Brahmā in the MBh may not be expressed more explicitly, moreover, as a result of historical change during the period of the epic's composition. From the time of the composition of the epic to its last redaction,[8] the religious significance of Brahmā had declined. Whereas Brahmā had been worshiped extensively in the centuries before the Christian era, worship of Brahmā apparently became less and less widespread in the first few centuries A.D.[9] At the same time, devotion to Nārāyaṇa and Śiva was increasing.[10] By the time of the last redaction of the MBh, Brahmā was no longer as prominent as he had been earlier, and Nārāyaṇa was much more important to the epic's redactors. The *Nārāyaṇīya* section of the *Śānti Parvan*, in which Vyāsa is said to be Nārāyaṇa incarnate, is apparently a product of the last phase of epic redaction. Thus, it seems clear that worship of Brahmā declined as worship of Nārāyaṇa increased. The epic's poets may not have more explicitly expressed Vyāsa's identification with Brahmā, and instead incorporated references to Vyāsa as an incarnation of Nārāyaṇa, because over the course of several centuries the relative importance of the two deities had changed.

The epic has two distinct attitudes toward Vyāsa as its *ṛṣi* and composer. While the epic poets want Vyāsa to be seen as the *ṛṣi* of the fifth

---

[7] As argued, e.g., by Herman Jacobi in *The Rāmāyaṇa* (Baroda: Oriental Institute, 1960), trans. by S. N. Ghosal from the 1895 German edition.

[8] Generally regarded as taking place from 400 B.C. to 400 A.D.; see Chapter 1.

[9] See G. M. Bailey, "Notes on the Worship of Brahmā in Ancient India," *Annali del Instituto Orientali di Napoli* 29 (1979):149-70. He concludes that "it seems likely that Brahmā was worshipped over most parts of Northern India from about four hundred BC to about four hundred AD." (p. 170). In a series of articles based on W. Kirfel's *Das Purāṇa Pañcalakṣaṇa* (Bonn: K. Schröder, 1927), Paul Hacker has shown the important position of Brahmā in Hindu cosmology and argues for the existence of a Brahmā cult in the first few centuries B.C. which then declined, lasting only until about the fifth century A.D. See Hacker's "The Sānkhyization of the Emanation Doctrine Shown in a Critical Analysis of Texts," *WZKSO* 5 (1961):75-112, especially p. 112. See also "Purānen und Geschichte des Hinduismus," *Oriental Literaturzeitung* 55 (1960):341-50, and "Zur Geschichte und Beurteilung des Hinduismus," *Oriental Literaturzeitung* 59 (1964):232-35.

[10] See Jan Gonda, *Viṣṇuism and Śivaism*, Chapter 2.

Veda, he is also much more than simply the revealer of divinely created eternal truths, as was the Vedic *ṛṣi*; Vyāsa is also the creator of the text, its author. The Vedic *ṛṣi*, like the Indian artist in general, was not regarded as the creator of the product of his artistry, but as the means by which the eternal forms were made manifest. In relation to the text, Vyāsa has a dual role; he is depicted as both the creator and revealer of the MBh, hence he corresponds to Brahmā and to the *ṛṣi* as well.

The MBh depicts Vyāsa in some passages as Brahmā's earthly counterpart, and in other passages as a portion of Nārāyaṇa. In this regard as well, Vyāsa's is a dual role in the epic; he follows the path of *pravṛtti*, over which Brahmā presides, yet often reveals aspects of the *nivṛtti* path, over which Nārāyaṇa presides. The fact that Vyāsa can have this dual role in the MBh suggests that we see him as both Brahmā's earthly counterpart and Nārāyaṇa's *aṃśa*. After all, Brahmā is depicted in the MBh as being born on a lotus emerging from the recumbent Nārāyaṇa's navel (e.g., XII.337), so that Brahmā himself is, for Vaiṣṇavas, a portion of Nārāyaṇa. The Matsya incarnation, which the MBh identifies with Brahmā (III.185), also became identified with Nārāyaṇa eventually. In much the same way as, and for the same reasons that, Brahmā came to be seen as a portion of Nārāyaṇa, Vyāsa apparently also did. Hence, in the MBh, Vyāsa is said to be Nārāyaṇa's *aṃśa* occasionally, yet is depicted reenacting the mythology of Brahmā, taking on Brahmā's epithets and performing the role Brahmā would perform on earth. Grandfather Brahmā is transposed into human form as Vyāsa in the MBh.

APPENDIX

1. Brahmā and Gaṇeśa help Vyāsa write down the MBh.

(From *Ādi Parvan* 1.55-87 of Nīlakaṇṭha's text; see also the Critical Edition's vol. I, Appendix I, passage no. 1.)

(Sauti said): The wise son of Parāśara, the brahmin seer of strict vows, Lord Dvaipāyana, having created this greatest of tales, considered how to teach it to his students. Knowing the thought of the seer Dvaipāyana, the Lord Brahmā, Guru of the World, came there to gratify the seer and to benefit all humanity. He (Vyāsa), surrounded by groups of all the sages, was surprised to see him, and stood with palms joined, bowed, and offered him a seat. After circumambulating Hiraṇyagarbha (Brahmā) who was seated there, Vyāsa stood nearby. Summoned by Brahmā Parameṣṭhin, Kṛṣṇa (Vyāsa) sat near by, joyful and smiling brightly. The splendorous one said to Brahmā Parameṣṭhin, "O Lord, I have created this highly venerated poem in which I have proclaimed the profundity of the *Veda* and other topics, O Brahmā; the ritual activity of the *Vedas* with their *Upaniṣads* and ancillary texts; what was created and brought forth of the *Purāṇas* and history (*itihāsa*); past, present, and future, that three-fold entity called Time; the determination of old age, death, fear, illness, being and non-being, and the characteristics of the modes of life and various dharmas, and the rule of the four castes and of all the *Purāṇas*; of asceticism, and of celibacy (*brahmacarya*); the measure of the earth, moon, and sun, planets, stars, and asterisms, as well as the ages; the *Ṛg*, *Yajur*, and *Sāman* verses, knowledge of the Supreme Spirit, logic, orthoepy, medicine, charity, and Pāśupata philosophy; birth, both divine and human for particular purposes; a description of holy pilgrimage sites, and countries and rivers and mountains and forests and oceans, celestial cities, sacred precepts, the art of war, various languages, social groups, and the manner of the people's livelihood, as well as the all-pervading Spirit. All that is represented, but of this no writer at all can be found on earth."

Brahmā said, "Because of your outstanding asceticism and your promulgation of profound knowledge, I consider you even better than the foremost sages. I know that since your birth you have truthfully given voice to the *brahman*. You have called this a poem, and therefore a poem it shall be. No poets are equal to the excellence of this poem, just as the other three modes of life are not equal to the excellence of the householder. O sage, think of Gaṇeśa for the writing of this poem." Saying that to him, Brahmā went to his own abode.

Then Satyavatī's son Vyāsa thought of Gaṇeśa. In the very moment he was thought of, Gaṇeśa the Lord of Obstacles, gratifying those who think of him devotedly, came to Vyāsa. When he had been received with honor and was seated, Vyasa said, "O faultless Gaṇanayaka, be the scribe of this *Bhārata* which I have composed in my mind, and will now recite."

Hearing that, the Lord of Obstacles replied, "If my pen does not for a moment stop writing, then surely I shall be the scribe." Vyāsa said to that deity, "Do not write anything that you do not understand." Assenting to that, Gaṇeśa did indeed become the scribe. Then the sage, for the sake of diversion, mysteriously wove knots into the composition, but in so doing, the sage Dvaipāyana recited it according to the agreement.

I (Sauti) know 8,800 verses, as does Śuka, and perhaps also Saṃjaya. Even today, O sage, no one is able to penetrate that closely woven mass of verses because of the profundity of their hidden meaning. Even the omniscient Gaṇeśa would ponder for a moment, and all the while Vyāsa created many more verses.

While everyone wallowed in the darkness and blindness of ignorance, something made their eyes open up, (as if touched) by pens filled with the collyrium of knowledge; humanity's darkness has been dispelled by the sun of *The Bhārata*, with its discourses both extensive and brief about Dharma, Profit, Pleasure, and Emancipation. The full moon of the *Purāṇas* with moonbeams of *śruti* caused this blossoming of the lotuses of human minds.[1] The world's inner chamber is fully and properly illuminated by the lamp of *itihāsa*, which destroys the darkness of delusion.

2. Vyāsa reveals the divine plan to Dhṛtarāṣṭra. (XI.8.11-48)

Having heard this speech, Lord Kṛṣṇa Dvaipāyana said to his son, who was tormented by grief for his sons, these words: "O Dhṛtarāṣṭra, of mighty arms, heed what I say to you. You have learning, you are intelligent, and you are skilled in Dharma and Profit (*artha*). There is nothing unknown to you that could be known, O scorcher of foes. Certainly you know the impermanence of mortals. When the world of living beings is unstable, and when the world is not eternal, when life has its end in death, O Bhārata, why do you grieve? This feud was born before your very eyes, O Indra of kings, brought about by Time, with your son as the cause. While the slaughter of the Kurus surely had to be, O King, why do you grieve for those heroes, who have gone to the highest place? The great-spirited Vidura knew this, and he made every effort toward peace, O strong-armed man. The path made by Fate cannot be controlled by any creature, even if he strives for a long time; this is my counsel.

I heard directly what was to be done by the gods. I will tell you about it so that tranquility may be yours. Once upon a time, overcoming fatigue, I went quickly to the Hall of Indra, and there I saw the assembled heaven-dwellers and all the divine seers with Nārada at their head. And there, O King, I saw Earth, who had come to the gods' presence for a particular purpose. Earth, having approached the assembled gods, then said: 'What shall be done for me has been promised by you all previously in Brahmā's abode, O Eminent Ones. Let it be arranged quickly!' Having heard her words, Viṣṇu, to whom humanity makes obeisance, smilingly said to Earth in the assembly of gods these words: 'The eldest of Dhṛtarāṣṭra's sons is named Duryodhana. He shall do what will be done for you. Obtaining him as king, your aim will be accomplished. For his sake, kings who come to Kurukṣetra as warriors will kill one another with hard weapons. Then, O Goddess, your burden will be eliminated in battle. Go quickly to your place and support humanity, O beautiful lady!'

Your son, O King, was a portion of Kali, born in the womb of Gāndhārī for

---

[1] Verse 86 of Nīlakaṇṭha's text requires emendation to complete the metaphor. For this translation, his *nṛbuddhikauravānāṃ* is read as *nṛbuddhikumudānām*, a reading supported by the critical edition's *Ādi Parvan* Appendix I, No. 1, lines 44-45.

Ancient Indian literature was classified in two categories, *śruti* ("what was heard", the Vedic Revelation, divine in origin) and *smṛti* ("what was remembered", later Tradition, purely human in origin). The *Mahābhārata* is often described as an *itihāsa*, and therefore *smṛti*, but at times describes itself as "the fifth Veda", as indicated in Chapter 1 of this study.

the purpose of destroying humanity. He was impatient, fickle, angry, and hard to deal with; as a consequence of Fate, brothers like him were born. Śakuni was his maternal uncle and Karṇa his best friend. Kings were born on earth along with him for the purpose of destruction. Nārada truly knew this matter, O strong-armed man. Your sons have died through their own fault, O King. Do not grieve for them, King, for there is no reason to grieve. The Pāṇḍavas are not at all guilty, Bhārata; your sons were evil-natured, and by them this earth was caused injury. Bless you. At the Rājasūya in the assembly of Yudhiṣṭhira this was made known truly by Nārada: 'The Pāṇḍavas and Kauravas, meeting each other, will not survive, O Kaunteya. Do what is proper.' Hearing Nārada's words on that occasion, the Pāṇḍavas were aggrieved. What has been told you is an eternal mystery of the gods: how there may be compassion in your life, O Lord, and love for the sons of Pāṇḍu, and the elimination of your grief, knowing that this act was done by Fate.

I heard this matter formerly, O strong-armed man. It was related to King Dharma at the best of sacrifices, the Rājasūya. When I explained this mystery, the son of Dharma attempted reconciliation with the Kauravas but Fate was too strong, for the law of Death is not to be superseded by any means or by any creature mobile or immobile, O King. You are devoted to proper actions and have the best of intellects, O Bhārata, and know what is the way and what is not the way for confused creatures. But, burning with grief, you are stupefied from time to time. If he knew this, O King, Yudhiṣṭhira would abandon his very life. He is a man who is always compassionate even to animals; how, O King, will he not be compassionate towards you? Because of my directive, and from compassion toward the Pāṇḍavas, and because it should not be abandoned, bear your life, Bhārata. Of your living thus, there will be fame in the world, and great would be the dharma, my dear son, and for a long time your ascetic merit (*tapas*) would last. Always extinguish the burning fire of grief with the water of wisdom, O King."

And having heard that speech of Vyāsa whose energy is unlimited, and pondering it a while, Dhṛtarāṣṭra spoke: "I am controlled by the great net of grief, O best of the twice-born. I am not aware of myself and am confused from time to time. But hearing your words about what has been ordained by Fate, I will bear my life and will try not to grieve."

Hearing Dhṛtarāṣṭra's words, Vyāsa the son of Satyavatī then vanished, O King.

3. Vyāsa reveals that he is Nārāyaṇa's incarnation. (XII.337.)

Janamejaya said: "Sāṃkhya, Yoga, Pañcarātra, and Vedāraṇyaka are the systems of knowledge that exist in the world, O brahmin seer. Are these the same or different, O sage? I ask that you speak freely about the application (of them).

Vaiśaṃpāyana said: "Obeisance to the great seer born in the midst of an island from Parāśara and Gandhavatī, to the dispeller of darkness who has great intelligence and a superior spirit; to Dvaipāyana the great repository of *Veda*, who is, they say, the sixth great seer from Grandfather, and who is endowed with great power from the seer, an only son born a portion of Nārāyaṇa. In the beginning, the mighty Nārāyaṇa of great energy created him as his son, Vyāsa the great-spirited who is unborn and ancient, that great repository of *brahman*."

Janamejaya said: "O best of the twice-born, earlier you said that the son of Vasiṣṭha was Śakti, and the son of Śakti was Parāśara, and the son of Parāśara was Kṛṣṇa Dvaipāyana the ascetic. Now you say that he is the son of Nārāyaṇa. Was that birth a previous life of Vyāsa whose energy is unlimited? O most intelligent man, tell me about his birth from Nārāyaṇa."

Vaiśaṃpāyana said: "Wanting to know the meaning of the *Vedas*, my guru, the lawful, the treasury of austerities, devoted to knowledge, lived at a place in the Himālayas. When the sage was tired from his austerities of creating the *Bhārata* tale, we were reverently attentive. Sumantu and Jaimini and Paila of rigorous vows, and I was the fourth pupil, and Śuka born of Vyāsa himself, surrounded by those five pupils at that spot in the Himālayas, Vyāsa resembled the Lord of Beings with his creatures. As he was reciting the *Vedas* with their ancillary texts and the meanings of the *Bhārata* in full, together we approached him whose mind was concentrated and controlled. Then at an interval we asked that best of the twice-born about the meanings of the *Vedas* and the *Bhārata*, and about his birth from Nārāyaṇa. First he spoke on the meanings of the *Vedas* and the *Bhārata*, then that knower of principles began to speak of his birth from Nārāyaṇa.

"Listen you all to this fine story about an eminent seer, about his birth at the time of creation, O inspired seers. It is known to me from asceticism. In the seventh creation, that of the Lotus-Born, the great yogi Nārāyaṇa, transcending good and evil, created from his navel Brahmā as his son, and immediately spoke to him: 'You are born from my navel as a Lord, Creator of Creatures. Create various creatures with and without intellect.' Thus addressed, he thought and was confused, and turned away. Bowing to the boon-giving god Lord Hari, he said, 'O Lord God, what power is mine to create beings? I bow down. Let it be yours. I am not wise, O God; ordain what is to be done now.'

Thus addressed, the Lord then disappeared, and the Lord of the gods, the best of the intelligent, summoned Intellect (*buddhi*). Then before Lord Hari stood Intellect in her own form, and by means of yoga he effortlessly enjoined her. The immutable Lord, the intelligent God, said to her who was powerful and good, and established in sovereignty by yoga. 'For the success of the goal of creating the worlds, enter Brahmā.' Then as the Lord wished, she quickly entered him. And when he saw him (Brahmā) united again with Intellect, Hari said again to him, 'Create diverse creatures.' And having said that the Lord disappeared from there and went immediately to his own place, known as Deva. And having attained his natural state, he concentrated his mind completely. 'Hordes of *daityas* and *dānavas* and *gandharvas* and *rakṣas* are being born; indeed, the rich earth is undergoing austerities, overburdened with them. Numerous and strong are the *daityas* and *dānavas* and *rākṣasas* on the earth. They will be yoked to asceticism and they will receive fine boons. The troops of gods and the seers rich in asceticism will be harassed; thus it is proper that I remove this burden by means of various births upon the earth from time to time. By restraining the wicked and favoring the good, I will support the good rich earth, she who is undergoing austerities. She is, indeed, supported by me as a snake abiding in the nether region. Supported by me, she will support the whole of creation, mobile and immobile. Thus, having come into existence, I will accomplish the salvation of earth.' Reflecting thus, the Lord by whom Madhu was slain created many forms for the purpose of becoming manifest. Boar and Man-Lion and Dwarf and Man—by means of these are to be struck down the gods' enemies who have become unruly.

Then, moreover, the Creator of the World emitted sound (*sarasvatī*), making to resound the word "*bho*!", and there arose Sārasvata. Born the son of speech and named Apāntaratamas, he was powerful, knew past, present, and future, spoke the truth, and was faithful to his vows. To him, who had bowed his head, he who is the first among the gods and is immutable said, 'O best of the intelligent, in the transmission of the *Veda*, the *śruti* is to be done by you. Therefore, do as ordained by me, O sage.' Then by him the *Vedas* were divided in the time of Manu the Self-Born. Lord Hari was pleased by that, by his act and by his well-performed asceticism and by his observances and self-control. 'In each of the periods of Manu, O son, you are to be active in the world this way. You will be immutable and unassailable forever, O brahmin. When Tiṣya (*Kaliyuga*) has arrived, Bhāratas named Kuru will be great-spirited kings spread over the earth. Among offspring of them who are descended from you there will be a split in the family resulting in their killing one another, except for you, O best of the twice-born. In that time, you, being endowed with asceticism, will divide the *Vedas* severally, and in that black age you will be black colored. You will be the author of various laws and systems of knowledge, you will be yoked to austerities, yet you will not become free from passion. Your son will become one whose passion has departed—a superior spirit—by the grace of Maheśvara (Śiva). This speech will not be false. Vasiṣṭha, who is, they say, the mind-born son of the Grandfather and yoked to the supreme intellect—the foremost, the treasury of austerities whose splendor surpasses the sun's—in the family descended from him there will be a son, a great seer named Parāśara of mighty power. That repository of *Veda*, that foremost of men, a great ascetic, the abode of austerities, he will be your father, and you will be the son of a young virgin from that seer; you will be born from that girl belonging to her father. All uncertainty about the meaning of past, present, and future removed, endowed with asceticism because of your meditation on me, you will see thousands of cycles of ages which have elapsed earlier, and all those things will be explained by me. And you will see again (in the future) many thousands of cycles of ages and me, birthless and deathless, O sage, in the world, discus in hand. My speech will not be false, O sage. And in that period of Manu, Śani the son of Sūrya will be the great Manu, and you will be superior to the group of seven seers by my grace, O my calf, have no doubt.'

Having thus spoken to the seer Apāntaratamas Sārasvata, the Lord said, 'Accomplish it.'

I am Apāntaratamas, he who was born of Hari, by the grace of Harimedhas the God. And again I was born as the famous son in the family of Vasiṣṭha. That description is of my prior birth as a portion of Nārāyaṇa because of Nārāyaṇa's grace. I became heated by asceticism of the utmost severity at one time, O best of the intelligent, with the highest meditative union. From my love of the devotees, I have told everything about which you all ask me, O sons, about my prior birth and about the subsequent one.

Vaiśampāyana said: "Narrated to you as requested, O King, is the prior birth of our guru Vyāsa of unstained mind. Listen again: Sāṃkhya, Yoga, Pañcarātra, *Vedas*, and Pāśupata, O royal sage, you must know that these systems of knowledge are various doctrines. The spokesman of Sāṃkhya is Kapila the superior seer, it is said; the primeval Hiraṇyagarbha and none other is the master of Yoga. And it is said that Apāntaratamas is the teacher of *Vedas*; some here call that seer Prācīnagarbha. The Lord of Umā, Lord of Creatures, Śrīkaṇṭha the son of Brahmā, Śiva the undistracted proclaims the Pāśupata system of knowledge. Bhagavān himself is the master of the whole of Pañcarātra. And, O best of kings, in all systems of knowledge it is seen that Lord Nārāyaṇa is the basis for the knowledge from inherited tradition as well as the knowledge from direct experience, and the creatures who are in darkness do not know him as such, O King. The wise call him the author of teachings; the teachers say, "The seer Nārāyaṇa is the basis; there is no other.' Hari lives eternally within all those who are free from doubt. Mādhava does not live in those who have doubts because of their power of disputation. But those who are intent on observances, who know the Pañcarātra, O King, those who have become single-mindedly devoted, enter Hari. Sāṃkhya and Yoga are both eternal, O King, as are all the *Vedas* in their entirety; by all the seers together is said, 'Nārāyaṇa is this whole ancient universe.' One should know that he does whatever action, good or evil, is done in all the worlds—in heaven, in the atmosphere, on earth, and even in the waters—from that seer it comes into being.

SELECTED BIBLIOGRAPHY

Texts and Translations

The Bhagavadgītā in the Mahābhārata. Edited and translated by J. A. B. van Buitenen. Chicago: The University of Chicago Press, 1981.

The Mahābhārata, 3 vols. Edited and translated by J. A. B. van Buitenen. Chicago: The University of Chicago Press, 1973-78.

The Mahabharata, 12 vols., 3d ed. Translated by K. M. Ganguli and published by P. C. Roy. New Delhi: Munshiram Manoharlal, 1972-75.

The Mahābhārata, 19 vols. Edited by V. S. Sukthankar et al. Poona: B.O.R.I., 1933-59.

Mahābhārata, 6 vols. Edited by Krishna Shastri Gurjar, with the commentary of Nīlakaṇṭha. Bombay: Jagadīśvara Printers, 1888-90.

Studies

Bailey, Greg. The Mythology of Brahmā. Delhi: Oxford University Press, 1983.

——. "Notes on the Worship of Brahmā in Ancient India." *Annali del Instituto Orientale di Napoli* 29 (1979): 149-70.

Bhandarkar, R. G. "Consideration of the Date of the Mahābhārata." *JBBRAS* 10 (1871-72): 81-91.

Biardeau, Madeleine. "Brāhmaṇes et potiers." *EPHE Annuaire* 79 (1971-72):31-55.

——. Clefs pour la pensée Hindoue. Paris: Seghers, 1972.

——. "Conference de Madeleine Biardeau." *EPHE Annuaire* 77 (1969-70):168-73.

——. "Études de mythologie hindoue." *BEFEO* 54 (1968): 19-54. *BEFEO* 55 (1969):59-105. *BEFEO* 58 (1971):17-89. *BEFEO* 63 (1976):111-262. *BEFEO* 65 (1978):87-238.

——. Histoire de poteaux: Variations védiques autour de la Déesse. In Press.

——. "The Salvation of the King in the *Mahābhārata.*" *Contributions to Indian Sociology*, n.s. 15 (1981):75-97.

——. "Some More Considerations About Textual Criticism." *Purāṇa* 10.2 (July 1968):115-23.

——. "The Story of Arjuna Kārtavīrya Without Reconstruction." *Purāṇa* 12.2 (July 1970):286-302.

Bodewitz, H. W. "The Fourth Priest (The *Brahmán*) in Vedic Ritual." In Selected Studies on Ritual in the Indian Religions. Leiden: E. J. Brill, 1983. Pp. 33-68.

Brown, C. Mackenzie. "Purāṇa as Scripture: From Sound to Image of the Holy Word in the Hindu Tradition." *HR* 26 (1986):68-86.

Bühler, Georg, and Kirste, J. "Indian Studies II: Contributions to the History of the Mahābhārata." *Sitzungsberichte der philosophisch-historischen Classe der kaiserlichen Akademie der Wissenschaften* 127, no. 12 (1892):1-58.

Carrière, Jean-Claude. The Mahabharata: A Play Based Upon the Indian Classic Epic. Translated by Peter Brook. New York: Harper & Row, 1987.

Chatterji, Suniti Kumar. "Kṛṣṇa Dvaipāyana Vyāsa and Kṛṣṇa Vāsudeva." In Sasibhusan Dasgupta Commemoration Volume. Edited by R. K. Dasgupta and Sisir Kumardas. Calcutta: New Age Publishers, 1968. Pp. 13-38.

Clooney, Francis X. "Why the Veda Has No Author: Language as Ritual in Early Mīmāṃsā and Post-Modern Theology." *JAAR* 55.4 (1987):659-84.

Dahlmann, Joseph. Genesis des Mahābhārata. Berlin: Verlag F. L. Dames, 1899.

——. Das Mahābhārata als Epos und Rechtsbuch. Berlin: Verlag F. L. Dames, 1895.

De Jong, J. W. "Recent Russian Publications on the Mahābhārata." *Adyar Library Bulletin* 39 (1975):1-42.

Dumézil, Georges. The Destiny of a King. Translated by Alf Hiltebeitel. Chicago: The University of Chicago Press, 1973.
——. The Destiny of the Warrior. Translated by Alf Hiltebeitel. Chicago: The University of Chicago Press, 1970.
——. Mythe et épopée, 3 vols. Paris: Editions Gallimard, 1968-73.
——. The Stakes of the Warrior. Translated by David Weeks. Berkeley: University of California Press, 1983.
Esnoul, Anne-Marie. Nārāyaṇīya Parvan du Mahābhārata. Paris: UNESCO, 1979.
Fitzgerald, James, "The Great Epic of India as Religious Rhetoric: A Fresh Look at the *Mahābhārata*." *JAAR* 51.4 (1983):611-30.
——. "India's Fifth Veda: The *Mahābhārata*'s Presentation of Itself." *JSAL* 20 (1985):125-40.
Foucault, Michel. "What Is An Author?" In Textual Strategies: Perspectives in Post-Structuralist Criticism. Edited by Josué V. Harari. Ithaca: Cornell University Press, 1979.
Gehrts, Heino. Mahābhārata: Das Geschehen und Seine Bedeutung. Bonn: H. Grundmann, 1975.
Gitomer, David. "Rākṣasa Bhīma." In Essays on the *Mahābhārata*. Edited by Arvind Sharma. Leiden: E. J. Brill, in press.
Goldman, Robert P. Gods, Priests, and Warriors: The Bhṛgus of the *Mahābhārata*. New York: Columbia University Press, 1977.
Gonda, Jan. Notes on Brahman. Utrecht: J. L. Beyers, 1950.
——. "The Popular Prajāpati." *HR* 22 (1982):129-49.
——. Prajāpati's Rise to Higher Rank. Leiden: E. J. Brill, 1986.
——. "Reflections on *sarva-* in Vedic Texts." *Indian Linguistics* 16 (1955):53-71. Reprinted in Jan Gonda. Selected Studies, 4 vols. Leiden: E. J. Brill, 1975. 2:495-513.
——. Triads in the Veda. Amsterdam: North-Holland, 1976.
——. "The Vedic Gods Aṃśa and Bhaga." In Monumentum H. S. Nyberg. Leiden: E. J. Brill, 1975. Pp. 291-310.
——. The Vision of the Vedic Poets. The Hague: Mouton & Co., 1963.
——. Viṣṇuism and Śivaism. London: Athlone Press, 1970.
Hacker, Paul. "Zur Entwicklung der Avatāralehre." *WZKSO* 4 (1960):47-70.
——. "Zur Geschichte und Beurteilung des Hinduismus." *Oriental Literaturzeitung* 59 (1964):232-35.
——. "Purānen und Geschichte des Hinduismus." *Oriental Literaturzeitung* 55 (1960):341-50.
——. "The Sānkhyization of the Emanation Doctrine Shown in a Critical Analysis of Texts." *WZKSO* 5 (1961):75-112.
Heesterman, Jan. The Ancient Indian Royal Consecration. The Hague: Mouton & Co., 1957.
Held, G. J. The Mahābhārata: An Ethnological Study. London: Kegan Paul, 1935.
Holtzmann, Adolf. Das Mahābhārata und Seine Theile, 4 vols. Kiel: C. F. Haesler, 1892-95.
Hiltebeitel, Alf. The Cult of Draupadī, vol. 1: Mythologies: From Gingee to Kurukṣetra. Chicago: The University of Chicago Press, 1988.
——. "Draupadī's Garments." *IIJ* 22 (1980):97-112.
——. "Epic Kṛṣṇa at Mathurā." In Mathura: A Cultural Heritage. Edited by Doris Srinivasan. New Delhi and Mathura: Munshiram Manoharlal, 1987.
——. "Kṛṣṇa and the Mahābhārata." *ABORI* 60 (1979):65-107.
——. The Ritual of Battle: Krishna in the Mahābhārata. Ithaca: Cornell University Press, 1976.
——. "Śiva, the Goddess, and the Disguises of the Pāṇḍavas and Draupadī." *HR* 20 (1980):147-74.
——. "The Two Kṛṣṇas on One Chariot: Upaniṣadic Imagery and Epic Mythology." *HR* 24 (1984):1-26.

———. "Two Kṛṣṇas, Three Kṛṣṇas, Four Kṛṣṇas, More Kṛṣṇas: Dark Interactions in the *Mahābhārata*." *JSAL* 20 (1985):71-77.

Hopkins, E. W. "The Bhārata and the Great Bhārata." *American Journal of Philology* 19 (1898):1-24.

———. Epic Mythology. Strassburg: K. J. Trübner, 1915.

———. Great Epic of India. New York: Scribner, 1901.

———. "Professed Quotations from Manu found in the Mahābhārata." *JAOS* 11 (1885):239-75.

———. "Yoga-Technique in the Great Epic." *JAOS* 22 (1901): 333-79.

Johnsen, Gösta. "Varuṇa and Dhṛtarāṣṭra." *IIJ* 9 (1965-66): 245-65.

Karve, Irawati. Yugānta: The End of an Epoch. Poona: Desmukh Prakashan, 1969.

Klostermaier, Klaus. "The Original Dakṣa Saga." *JSAL* 20 (1985):93-107.

Lal, B. B. "Excavation at Hāstinapura and other explorations in the Upper Gaṅgā and Sutlej basins, 1950-52." *Ancient India*, vols. 10-11 (1954-55).

Lévi, Sylvain. "Tato Jayam Udīrayet." In Commemorative Essays Presented to Sir R. G. Bhandarkar. Poona: B.O.R.I., 1917. Pp. 99-106.

Lüders, Heinrich. Review of the *Mahābhārata*'s critical edition. *Deutsche Literaturzeitung* 24 (1929):1138-46.

Mehta, Mahesh. "A Study of the Critical Edition—Part II." *Bhāratīya Vidyā* 32 (1972):1-74.

O'Flaherty, Wendy D. Review of recent publications on the *Mahābhārata*. *Religious Studies Review* 4.1 (1978):19-28.

Oldenberg, Hermann. Das Mahābhārata: Seine Entstehung, sein Inhalt, seine Form. Göttingen: Vandenhoeck & Ruprecht, 1922.

Péterfalvi, Jean-Michel, and Madeleine Biardeau. Le Mahābhārata, 2 vols. Paris: Flammarion, 1985-86.

Pisani, Vittore. "The Rise of the Mahābhārata." In A Volume of Eastern and Indian Studies. Edited by S. M. Katre and P. K. Gode. Bombay: Karnatak Publishers, 1939. Pp. 166-76.

Roth, Rudolph. "Brahma und die Brāhmanen." *ZDMG* 1 (1847): 66-86.

Scheuer, Jacques. Śiva dans le Mahābhārata. Paris: Presses Universitaires de France, 1982.

Smith, Mary Carroll. "The *Mahābhārata*'s Core." *JAOS* 95 (1975):479-82.

Sukthankar, V. S. "The Bhṛgus and the *Bhārata*: A Text-Historical Study." ABORI 18 (1936-37):1-76.

———. The Meaning of the Mahābhārata. Bombay: Asiatic Society of Bombay, 1957.

Thieme, Paul. "Brahman." *ZDMG* 102 (1952):91-129.

Trautmann, Thomas. Kauṭilya and the Arthaśāstra: A Statistical Investigation on the Authorship and Evolution of the Text. Leiden : E. J. Brill, 1971.

Trikha, Urmila Rani. The Concepts of Religion in the *Mahābhārata*. Delhi: Nag Publishers, 1980.

van Buitenen, J. A. B. "On the Structure of the Sabhāparvan of the Mahābhārata." In India Maior. Edited by J. Ensink and P. Gaeffke. Leiden: E.J. Brill, 1972. Pp. 68-84.

Winternitz, Moriz. Review of *Genesis des Mahābhārata* by Joseph Dahlmann. *WZKM* 14 (1900): 51-77.

Wikander, Stig. "Fran Bravalla till Kurukṣetra." *Arkhiv för Nordisk Filologi* 75 (1960): 183-93.

———. "Germanische und Indo-Iranische Eschatologie." *Kairos* 2 (1960): 83-88.

———. "Nakula et Sahadeva." *Orientalia Suecana* 6 (1957): 66-96.

———. "Pāṇḍava-sagan och Maha-bha-ratas mytiska forutsattningar." *Religion och Bibel* 6 (1947): 27-39. Translated into French by Georges Dumézil. In Jupiter Mars Quirinus IV. Paris: Presses Universitaires de France, 1948. Pp. 37-53.

GENERAL INDEX

INDEX OF AUTHORS

INDEX OF TEXT CITATIONS